THE
GARDEN BOOK
OF EUROPE

First published 1973 in Great Britain
by Elm Tree Books · Hamish Hamilton Limited
90 Great Russell Street London WC1

Copyright © D. G. & J. P. Hessayon
SBN 241 02386 6

Printed lithographically in Great Britain
by Ebenezer Baylis and Son Limited
The Trinity Press Worcester and London
Colour separation by
Fotolitomec · Milano/Laren (n.h.)

Vaux-le-Vicomte, France

THE GARDEN BOOK OF EUROPE

D. G. & J. P. Hessayon

Elm Tree Books · Hamish Hamilton Limited

Stourhead, England.

Contents

	Page
Introduction … … … … … …	7
A gardener's eye view of Europe … … …	8
The garden scene in BRITAIN … …	13
A picture guide to Flower Colours … …	48
A picture guide to Pelargoniums … … …	51
The garden scene in FRANCE … … …	53
A picture guide to Plants in the Home … …	61
A picture guide to Conifers … … …	71
The garden scene in GERMANY … …	73
A picture guide to Topiary … … …	80
A picture guide to Roses … … … …	83
The garden scene in ITALY … … …	93
A picture guide to Dahlias … … …	99
A picture guide to Bedding Plants … …	103
The garden scene in HOLLAND … …	109
A picture guide to Cacti … … … …	115
International Exhibitions … … … …	119
A picture guide to Climate … … …	120
The garden scene in SPAIN … … …	121
The garden scene in SCANDINAVIA …	125
A picture guide to Chrysanthemums … …	131
A picture guide to Begonias … … …	135
A picture guide to Concrete … … …	138
The garden scene in BELGIUM … …	141
The garden scene in SWITZERLAND …	145
A picture guide to Bulbs … … … …	148
The garden scene in the REST OF EUROPE	152
Acknowledgments … … … … …	160

Caserta, Italy

Introduction

"Britain has been the most important gardening nation in Europe since the time of the Romans." Wrong. For most of history we have been content to follow the French and Italian masters. It was the Dutch who dominated the early years of garden science.

"Ah, but we lead now." Even this statement is not strictly correct, as we lag behind many Continental countries in the use of indoor plants and outdoor allotments.

The one undeniable fact is that no other nation on Earth can match our British interest in and love of gardens and gardening. Others must come to us to learn about a nation's skill in using garden plants.

But we can learn too . . . about design, about the outdoor living room and so on. Yet you will search in vain for a book to tell you about the garden scene in Europe today. The pendulum has swung from the eighteenth century idea that Europe had everything to teach us to our modern notion that we have nothing left to learn.

This book is for all those who wish to look over the garden fence for the first time . . . at Europe's great gardens, the international flower shows, the facts and figures about gardening at home and abroad.

From all of this there will be much to learn and perhaps just a little to use. But we must pray that the national differences will stay and that the basic charm of the English garden will remain the envy of all. And we must hope that the idea of a standardised Eurogarden will never take root.

Ideas, people and products are now crossing national frontiers at an ever-increasing rate. We drive foreign cars, eat exotic foods and wear clothes from abroad. But in designing a garden we remain tradition-bound, and we know little or nothing of the styles in other countries.

Open an English cookery book. You could well find a recipe for French *potage parmentier* or German *sauerkraut*. Now open a garden book printed in English; choose the biggest one you can find. You will search in vain for a description of the French *potager* (vegetable garden) or German *paradiesgartlein*.

If you really wanted a gardener's eye view of Europe it would be necessary to travel right across the Continent, from the Arctic areas where a pear tree or bush rose is a southern exotic to the baked plains of southern Italy where ordinary lawn grass is a northern luxury.

This journey would be filled with many surprises, and one of the purposes of this book is to point these out to the armchair traveller. A small section of Britain grows more daffodils than you will find in the whole of Holland, but it is in Holland and not Britain that gardening ousts TV as the nation's most popular pastime.

According to the British they don't bother with gardens on the Continent...but in Germany there is twice the garden acreage found in Britain. The British don't like joining organisations . . . . yet there are far more horticultural societies and clubs than in any other country.

THE GARDENER'S EYE VIEW

Obviously the traveller in search of Europe's gardens must leave behind his preconceived notions. He cannot even be sure about the words *Europe* and *garden*. Europe is the western end of the great Eurasian land mass with the Atlantic Ocean as a major boundary. But its eastern boundary depends on which book you read. Modern practice is to regard Europe as the area west of the Soviet frontier; in this book and in most atlases it is regarded as double this size, extending through Russia to the Urals and Caucasus.

The clear definition of a garden is even more difficult. According to the Oxford English Dictionary it is "an enclosed piece of ground devoted to the cultivation of flowers, fruit or vegetables." This definition may be satisfactory for Britain but it is woefully inadequate for Europe. There are famous Spanish gardens devoted almost entirely to coloured tiles, archways and cool water. In Norway and Sweden there are gardens where only grass, silver birch and conifers grow. Bomarzo, one of the popular great gardens of Italy, consists of nothing but grotesque stone statues of animals and giants in an ordinary woodland setting.

The gardener's eye view across Europe will cover a myriad "enclosed pieces of ground", each of which is that indefinable something – a garden. Some of them will be showpieces, but the vast majority will be ordinary home gardens and a survey of the European gardening scene must deal with both these facets. Before starting out on this voyage of discovery, it is essential to understand the nature of the three basic types of garden.

The **formal** garden is the oldest, and its shape is controlled by simple geometry. Outlines of beds, borders, pools, paths and so on are straight lines or regular curves; planting is done with a ruler as well as a trowel. The **informal** garden is much more recent in Europe, although in China it was in vogue before the Christian era. In this style there are irregular shapes and an apparently random spacing of vegetation and ornaments. It can still be clearly artificial and it may require regular attention; the rock garden is a good example with its need for removal of surface litter, pruning of shrubby specimens and winter

protection of tender varieties. An informal garden which is left largely to nature after its creation is called a **wild** garden. Some woodland gardens with naturalised bulbs provide good examples.

Now we can begin to look at the home gardens across Europe. Moving down from the tundra and barren wastes the first gardens to appear are those of Scandinavia, and these are generally informal or wild. There is an attempt to ensure that the garden blends in with the landscape, with trees being more important than flowers. The Scandinavian love of the countryside and their love of active sports leave little time or inclination to have a time-consuming garden. The pattern changes as we move south into Germany. Fewer households have a garden and the average plot is smaller and more formal, with trees playing a less significant role. But our traveller from Scandinavia will detect at once a strong family likeness. The ornamental aspect remains the all-important one and the use of the garden as a play/dining area is even more highly developed. This is *the* key aspect of the German garden, with one in every two possessing a patio. Food crops are not often grown, and soft fruit is preferred to peas and potatoes.

The gardener's eye view changes dramatically once the French border is crossed. More than three quarters of the gardens grow some food – in the rural areas 50 per cent grow nothing else. It is strange for the English visitor to cross a mere 25 miles of water to find gardens where less than 40 per cent have lawns and more than 50 per cent have fruit trees.

It is not possible to generalise about the Benelux pocket between W. Germany and France. The Dutch garden is a hybrid between the British and German pattern – it is small, well-tended, time-consuming and filled with flowers as in England, but it is also designed for outdoor entertaining and play like the German garden. More than 70 per cent have a patio or terrace, and the reason most frequently given for tending the garden is to ensure that the house will look prosperous. Gardens are just as frequent in Belgium, but the style is quite different. The average size and the utilisation of the land is similar to the gardens of France rather than those of its partner in Benelux. The tiny third member – Luxembourg – has a proud gardening record; nearly 25 per cent of all the homes in the country belong to the national horticultural society – *La Ligue Luxembourgeoise du Coin de Terre et du Foyer.*

9

Turning south our travelling gardener reaches the Mediterranean lands of Italy, Spain and Portugal, and here the home garden scene is completely transformed. Only a small minority of homes possess a private garden, and this possession is usually associated with wealth. The Mediterranean garden is nearly always purely ornamental, and its culture is similar to that of a heated greenhouse in temperate climes. The winter warmth expands the range of plants which can be grown but the need for constant watering during summer makes their upkeep difficult.

Back north again to the mecca of home gardening – Britain. Here we find more households with private gardens than in any other major country of Europe:

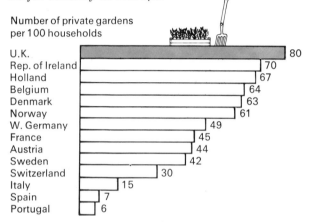

Number of private gardens
per 100 households

U.K.	80
Rep. of Ireland	70
Holland	67
Belgium	64
Denmark	63
Norway	61
W. Germany	49
France	45
Austria	44
Sweden	42
Switzerland	30
Italy	15
Spain	7
Portugal	6

Britain's fairly narrow lead in this table could not possibly account for her pre-eminence on the domestic scene. Nor could the size of her gardens – the average of 2,000 sq.ft. is less than half the French, German, Scandinavian or Belgian figure. The key factor is the approach of the British householder to his or her garden. This is land to be *worked*, and the satisfaction derived from producing fine blooms and early crops with one's own hands is often greater than that obtained from sitting back and enjoying the total picture.

This explains many things – the traditional dislike of stone and concrete which "robs" valuable land from the garden, the reticence to employ help even when finance is not the problem (40 per cent of Holland's richer homes employ a gardener; the corresponding figure for Britain is 6 per cent). About 750,000 Britons enter their flowers and vegetables at the local horticultural show each year, but Beautiful Garden competitions have never become popular.

Through Continental eyes the British devotion to gardens and gardening is not easy to understand. There appears to be no attempt to save time or labour – even the multitude of pocket handkerchief gardens have complex planting schemes, and the beloved herbaceous borders and bedding plants provide colour for the passerby and considerable work for the gardener. Lawns are, of course, a much-admired feature due to the kindness of the climate and the habit of close shaving at weekly intervals. Gardening in Britain is a husband-and-wife affair. In Germany, France and Belgium it is the man's responsibility, in Italy and Ireland it is woman's work.

On this pinnacle of admiration the British gardener tends to look no further than the coastline. But across the Channel there are several features which should be studied – not to copy perhaps, but to note because one or more could well provide tomorrow's New Look in the British garden scene.

First of all, our allotments have maintained their outdated masculine working-class image. As the law now stands these 400,000 plots must be used primarily for food production, and building on the allotment is strictly limited. In Holland, Germany and Scandinavia allotments have been transformed into Chalet Gardens, so that gardenless families can spend their weekends surrounded by lawns and flowers. The Second Home movement has taken root in several countries, such as France (owned by 11 per cent of all households) Scandinavia (19 per cent of households) and the U.S.S.R. These holiday homes have a garden, so a new dimension has been added which is unlikely to occur in Britain to any great extent.

Another feature of the Continental scene which may never reach Britain is the spring-to-autumn Garden Exhibition. These shows allow fine new parks to be created in the large towns, paid for by the entrance fees. For the gardener there are scores of informative exhibits and ideas and it is a day out for the whole family.

In a survey conducted at the 1972 International Horticultural Exhibition at Amsterdam it was found that the British visitors favoured the plant exhibits whereas the Continental visitors spent most of their time at the architectural exhibits – paving, walling, statuary, plant containers, garden lighting etc.

For the British gardener it is flowers, flowers all the way . . in beds and borders but not in plant tubs and window-boxes. It is strange that in the world's most knowledgeable flower-growing nation so little attention should be paid to growing plants in containers. The Continent leads the way here, as it does in indoor gardening.

After looking through the windows of houses and apartments on the Continent our travelling gardener, like any other tourist, will have gained the impression that more house plants are grown and many more cut flowers are purchased than in Britain. The 1971 statistics of the International Association of Horticultural Producers confirm this view:

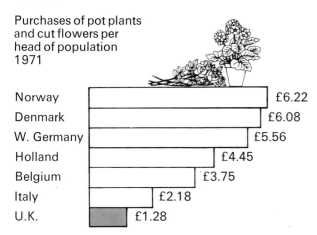

Purchases of pot plants and cut flowers per head of population 1971

Norway	£6.22
Denmark	£6.08
W. Germany	£5.56
Holland	£4.45
Belgium	£3.75
Italy	£2.18
U.K.	£1.28

Exact comparisons of international statistics are notoriously difficult, but the differences here are great enough to remove any doubts that Britain lags behind Scandinavia, W. Germany and the Benelux countries. Some of the reasons put forward to account for this are either wrong or only partly correct. It is often credited to heavy advertising expenditure, and it is true that both Holland and W. Germany do allocate large sums each year to promote the idea of plants and flowers in the home. But the Norwegian house-wife spends more than any of her counterparts, yet there is very little advertising activity in Norway. A more popular theory is that as there are fewer gardens on the Continent the house-holders have a greater need for flowers and plants indoors to satisfy the craving for greenery around them. This cannot be the whole story; the keen gardener in Britain has at least as many pot plants as the flat dweller, and Germans spend twice as much as the British on plants for the garden.

The simple basic truth is that our customs and living habits are different. The British use pot plants to add living touches to the furnishings of a room, a few pots here and there to add interest and colour. In Scandinavia, W. Germany and Benelux plants are used as *part* of the furnishing. Plants have a structural job to do – to clothe windows, cover walls, split up rooms and divide offices. The plant window illustrates the point. This structural adaptation of the ordinary window sill provides a mini-garden between the glass and the interior of the room, and enables indoor plants to be a major part of the interior decoration. In Britain such windows are very rare, but they are a feature of many houses in Holland and W. Germany.

The main reason for the differences in cut flower purchases is even easier to understand. In low-purchase countries, such as Britain and France, flowers are bought regularly for personal use by only 20 per cent of the population. The large majority of purchases are for special occasions – anniversaries, birthdays, bereave-ments, hospital visits, etc. The Interflora sales figures on page 12 show that *sending* flowers for these special occasions is extremely popular in Britain. In the high-purchase countries, such as W. Germany, Denmark and parts of Switzerland, there is the custom among the middle and upper-income groups of *taking* flowers when visiting friends or relatives. In these countries one finds a multitude of flower stalls, florists, station kiosks and flower-vending machines in the larger cities; in Britain the outlets are much more restricted:

Number of flower shops per 100,000 people

Copenhagen	79
W. Berlin	74
Oslo	38
Amsterdam	35
Brussels	33
Berne	26
London	14
Paris	11
Birmingham	10
Belfast	5
Glasgow	4

It is essential not to confuse the cut-flower purchasing habits of a country with its interest in flower arranging. Nowhere in Europe can claim greater support than Britain for this hobby, where most of the plant material is obtained from the garden and hedgerow. Our travelling gar-dener must now go back to the outdoor garden once again, taking with him the discovery that you must look at more than the annual sales figures if you want to learn of the skills and involvement of a country with its plants.

Within the closely woven fabric of European home gardens lie the sparkling sequins — the show gardens to which visitors come to enjoy the view. Such gardens may be state, university or municipality owned and the public admitted free or for a nominal charge; others are privately owned and an entrance fee is imposed. They take a variety of forms – the Public Park, Botanical Garden, Permanent Exhibition and the classical showpiece – the Grand Garden around *kasteel*, *château*, *villa*, *schloss*, *palazzo* or stately home. Britain has more grand gardens open to the public than any other European country, and millions come to admire them each year. Unfortunately the history of these gardens is often mistaken for the history of *gardening*, but between 1500 and 1800 the grand garden architects had little or no interest in flowers – for them it was views and vases, trees and terraces, pavilions and pools. The beloved garden flowers of today survived in cottage gardens, ordinary home gardens and especially in the backyards of the industrial workers from which the flower show and its judging standards were evolved.

Both home and grand gardens began from the same root – the open and cultivated area within the walls of the house. The *atrium* of Ancient Rome was followed by the *patios* within the early Spanish gardens and the *paradise* gardens within the monasteries throughout Europe.

In fifteenth century Florence the garden moved outside – green squares with fountains and pathways, marble seats and hidden arbours. The early Renaissance garden was a place for quiet meditation like its predecessor, the Mediaeval garden within the castle walls. In sixteenth century Rome the style changed – spectacular fountains, ornate terraces and elaborate staircases provided places for entertaining on a lavish scale. The grand Renaissance garden had arrived.

This style was dominant until the Frenchman, Le Nôtre, produced Vaux-le-Vicomte in 1660. For 100 years his rules guided Europe's garden makers. The long vista, the avenues, the rectangular canal and the elaborately-patterned beds outside the windows were now all-important. The formal *jardin français*, appeared in Britain, Italy, Spain, Germany, Russia and elsewhere.

By 1750 Britain had taken over as the garden designers of Europe, and her archpriests Brown, Repton and Kent ruled that there must be an informal look – hills, lakes, trees . . . no fences, flowers nor geometry. The English Landscape park was now the fashion for Europe, and remained so until the neo-Italianate revival and William Robinson's Wild garden concept, which insisted that plants should be introduced into the natural landscape and then left to their own devices. Rules, rules, rules . . . today's eclectic approach is much more sensible – this means that no set of rules is perfect, and features of several styles are blended to give a pleasing combination.

Gardens and gardening provide peace in an increasingly hostile, noisy and complex world. The garden is where the wounds are healed, as symbolised by the *Deutsch-Französischer Garten* at Säarbrucken – 125 acres of an old battlefield transformed into a garden which is jointly maintained by France and Germany. But even a tiny plot can help to restore inner peace. At the end of Voltaire's great classic *Candide* the secret of surviving the horrors and injustices of the world is revealed – *Il faut cultiver notre jardin* (We must cultivate our garden).

INTERNATIONAL GARDEN CENTRE ASSOCIATION

As described elsewhere in this book, the Garden Centre movement has expanded rapidly in the past 15 years and these outlets are becoming increasingly important in Europe as a source of plants, sundries, services and advice.

The idea of European co-operation began in Germany where the I.G.C.A. was formed. Its headquarters were moved to Switzerland and the structure of the organisation was changed in 1969. A quarterly magazine (*iga*) is published, member Garden Centres display the I.G.C.A. symbol at their premises, and Congresses are arranged in various countries at which the national groups can learn from each other.

Number of members

U.K.	115
Holland	60
W. Germany	50
Scandinavia	45
France/Belgium	30
Italy	25
Switzerland	20
Austria	3

FLEUROP – Interflora in Europe
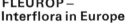

Interflora was founded in 1910 in the U.S.A. by a small group of florists. Now there are 45,000 florist members in 130 countries spanning the globe and dealing in their own currency, the *Fleurin*.

The sender contacts his or her nearest Interflora florist and arranges the price and type of flowers or plants for the floral gift. The address, delivery date and message are then transmitted to the Interflora florist nearest to the destination.

Members are carefully inspected and trained by Interflora, and test orders are regularly transmitted to test the system. Each member company pays a levy on its turnover.

In Europe more than 10 million orders are executed annually and the most popular flower is the rose.

Fleurop Turnover 1972

W. Germany	£11 million
U.K.	£ 7 million
France	£ 4¼ million
Sweden	£ 2½ million
Italy	£ 2 million
Holland	£ 1½ million
Norway	£ ½ million
Denmark	£ ½ million
Switzerland	£ ¼ million
Belgium	£ ¼ million

THE GARDEN SCENE
IN BRITAIN

NYMANS

A Nation of Gardeners

A photograph of Nymans appears on the previous page to introduce the Garden Scene in Britain. This is one of our Grand Gardens, there are about two thousand which open their gates for a day or two or throughout the year to visitors who come to pay their entrance fee and stare in admiration at another world.

Here are laid out the various styles of Britain's gardening history, varying from green landscapes with hardly a flower in sight to vast arrays of convoluted beds.

Yet there is an equally important face to the garden scene in this country—the 14½ million Home Gardens which range in size from a few square yards to many acres. These are open only to the owners and their friends, and nearly always it is the owner and his or her family who do the work.

Unfortunately home gardens are generally dismissed in a few paragraphs in the gardening history books. At best they are briefly referred to as inferior relatives of the grand garden. At worst they are abused as monotonous replicas of a standard pattern without originality or artistry.

In fact the home garden should be judged by different standards from the horticultural showpiece. It

has a different history, a different set of styles and a different purpose, as described on page 27-31.

It is the nature and number of home gardeners which makes the garden scene in Britain unique. Sixty per cent of the total adult population work in the garden. It is not money we spend (our annual purchases are only half the German figure), it is time ... 12 per cent of our total leisure time and that makes gardening the number one active hobby.

This desire to work with the land spills over, and nearly half a million gardeners own an allotment on which vegetables and fruit are grown. As yet the allotment holder is not permitted to turn his plot into a leisure garden, and so the allotment is becoming a smaller part of the garden scene each year.

This British characteristic of wanting to work as well as walk in the garden is coupled with a consuming interest in garden flowers (rather than garden design) and a strong competitive spirit. This results in that peculiar British institution, the local Flower Show, remaining as popular as ever. This is the big day for the thousands of horticultural societies, and an even bigger day for the exhibitors who take home their treasured prizes or certificates.

1. The Grand Garden
(page 15)

A garden which is occasionally or constantly open to visitors, who may or may not be known to the owner. The purpose of these visits is primarily to see the garden features and there is usually an admission charge.

2. The Home Garden
(page 27)

A garden which is not open to inspection by visitors other than those invited by the owner. Most or all of the work in the garden is generally carried out by the owner and family.

THE GARDEN SCENE IN BRITAIN

There are seven basic localities where garden plants and garden features can be seen in Britain. Most places fit neatly into one or other of these seven boxes but inevitably, with an infinitely variable subject such as gardening, there are some borderline cases.

3. The Allotment
(page 35)

A plot of land some distance from house of the tenant who rents it from local council or industrial organisati Vegetables, fruit and perhaps so flowers are raised for use by the fam

5. The Public Park
(page 41)

An area of open land owned by crown, state or city and to which public has access. Occasionally simila the grand garden or botanical gard but usually the plant displays are the prime purpose for the visit.

4. The Botanic Garden
(page 37)

A garden in which the prime purpose is the scientific study and collection of plants. Many are administered by a University and are extremely attractive as well as informative. Some are open to the public.

6. The Flower Show
(page 46)

A display of flowers, produce and/or equipment at which competitions are generally held. There are usually trade stands present. Horticultural exhibitions, which may be permanent, are classed in this group.

7. The Supplier
(page 47)

An organization which displays and offers for sale plants, seeds, ornaments, equipment and/or sundries to the general public. The plants may be pre-packed, in containers or growing in open soil.

1. The Grand Garden

❝ Keddlestone or Hagley should be reserved for the gardener to
show on a Sunday to travelling fools and starers ❞
Mrs.Thrale's Tour in Wales with Dr Johnson (1774)

'Sunday staring', once contemptuously dismissed by Dr Johnson, has now become a popular pastime and each year millions of visitors walk through the grand gardens of Britain.

The garden story began about two thousand years ago with the Roman invasion. Recent excavations at Fishbourne have revealed that the legions brought their gardens as well as their roads and laws; but these gardens were simple courtyards within the villas and with none of the grandeur of the magnificent hillside estates of Ancient Rome.

So at first gardens were *within* the house and not outside as today. This pattern continued for a thousand years, until the classical ideas of art and architecture which we call the Renaissance swept in from Italy at the beginning of the 16th century.

Before then we had our Mediaeval gardens, which throughout the whole of the troubled middle ages remained poor imitations of the elegant and flowery enclosures found in Italy and France. In Britain it was a time for fighting and not for flowers, and the small walled plots found in monastery and castle had two non-ornamental jobs to do. They provided herbs, fruit and a few vegetables and they provided a place to walk, sit and meditate away from the smells of indoor living.

Then came Henry VIII, with his revolutionary ideas on marriage, religion . . . and gardening. A garden was now a place to be adorned and admired, and the artificial hill he built with a quarter of a million bricks at Hampton Court was the foundation stone of the Grand Garden in Britain.

The king went on to build the fabulous Palace of Nonsuch (now vanished) based on the old Palace of Fontainbleau. The inspiration was Italian, the application was French and the lines were strictly geometrical. This was to be the formula for garden design for the next two hundred years – the patterned, fully-furnished, outdoor living room.

Tudor gardens were built by the new aristocracy, following Henry's lead. Trees were restricted to the park outside, and within the walls were the fountains, pools, statuary, wooden rails, terraces, mounts, mazes and knots (see page 18). Plants were incidental, and were used as an alternative to coloured stones to fill the spaces between the dwarf hedges in the knot garden.

In the Elizabethan age there were refugees with continental ideas, wealth and peace at home. On these three pillars were built the vast mansions. Many remain but their gardens are gone. The records tell us that we were beginning to add our own ingredient, one which has in recent centuries given Britain its horticultural reputation – a passionate interest in plants. So the Elizabethan gardens were basically large versions of the Tudor ones, but with fascinating new flowers from the "Indies, Americas, Taprobane, Canary Islands and all parts of the worlde".

The beginning of the 17th century saw James I on the throne and the start of the Jacobean age of gardening. This lasted for 50 years and was a time for pioneers. Lawson and Parkinson produced the first English gardening text-books and John Tradescant was the first in a long line of British plant hunters. But the great gardens of the day were created by French architects – de Caus and Salomon.

In this 1610–1660 period Britain at last joined the league of great gardening nations. We could not yet match the French designers nor the Dutch growers but the Continentals did come to admire the quantity and quality of our Jacobean gardens, and also a new feature. This henceforth was to arouse the envy of gardeners everywhere – the closely cut English lawn.

Then suddenly the spirit of Le Nôtre, brought back from France by Charles II when he was restored to the throne, took root in English soil. Now garden design was transformed – grand parterres in place of the simple knots, vast lakes and canals, broad avenues stretching to the horizon. The nurseries of London and Wise were perhaps the main driving force. Throughout the land they sold plants and designs for large and not-so-large gardens.

But though the French style took root, it never really flowered. Charles transformed his Royal Gardens, but they were pale shadows of Versailles. Our parterres were described as the meanest in Europe, and canals (so beloved by Le Nôtre) were never popular. Melbourne gives the best impression of *le jardin français* in England.

In 1689 William of Orange was crowned and once again Hampton Court received its coronation face-lift. But the Dutch style with its mobile statues, stone-filled parterres and tortured tree shapes never became an important part of the English scene.

The wind of change was now beginning to blow. The number of gardens had increased ten-fold in half a century but the styles were formal and we were

still second-rate copiers of foreign patterns. The first critics of all this artificiality were writers, like Addison, Steele and Pope. Then the garden designers Schwitzer and Bridgeman took the first faltering steps towards the informal garden. William Kent came back from Italy "leaped the fence and saw that all nature was a garden". He created Chiswick and Rousham, and the day of the Landscape garden had arrived.

There were no walls, no hedges – just a hidden ditch. So the whole landscape became part of the garden and the garden became a classical picture. 'Capability' Brown was followed by Humphry Repton as the leader of the movement. Hundreds of formal gardens, and even a village or two, were obliterated.

We were now the garden masters of Europe. *Le jardin anglais* appeared in many countries, yet by 1830 we had turned our backs on this 'classical picture' approach and the quite different Victorian age of gardening had begun. For many years this era has been criticized for its garish carpet bedding, fussy ornaments and lack of taste. But it did for the first time establish our present-day creed – that flowers are the most important part of the garden, to be tended, admired and placed in the forefront. The grand French style had used them as alternatives to stones for filling parterres. The Landscape style had banished them to a walled enclosure where they couldn't spoil the view. The Victorians, despite their faults, remembered that flowers make a garden.

This 'gardenesque' approach we owe to Loudon and his wife, whose ideas profoundly influenced the pattern of the small suburban garden. On the grand scale Barry and Nesfield worked in the formal Neo-Italian style with terraces, fountains, statuary and bedded-out parterres. Paxton set out to build similar designs on a gigantic scale – Chatsworth became one of the wonder gardens of Europe.

And so to the Modern Garden, as pioneered by two Victorians, the fiery William Robinson and the gentle Gertrude Jekyll. They believed in Loudon's approach to plants, but were opposed to the Victorian mixture of strict geometric design, carpet bedding and 'pastry-work gardening'.

Robinson believed in the wild garden – trees and shrubs from other countries planted in our natural landscape and then left to themselves. Many fine examples exist, especially in Scotland and Ireland; Caerhays is perhaps the best. But over the years the odd partnership evolved a less extreme style – the central lawn, herbaceous border, shrub border and rockery of our present-day suburban garden.

The grand gardens which have been created this century are of many types, but there are three common threads running through the most notable examples. At Nymans, Hidcote, Sissinghurst Castle and the rest there are areas where the plants dominate, areas where the architecture of the garden is dominant and the remaining areas where the vista is all-important. At last Design and Plant have learnt to live together. ∎

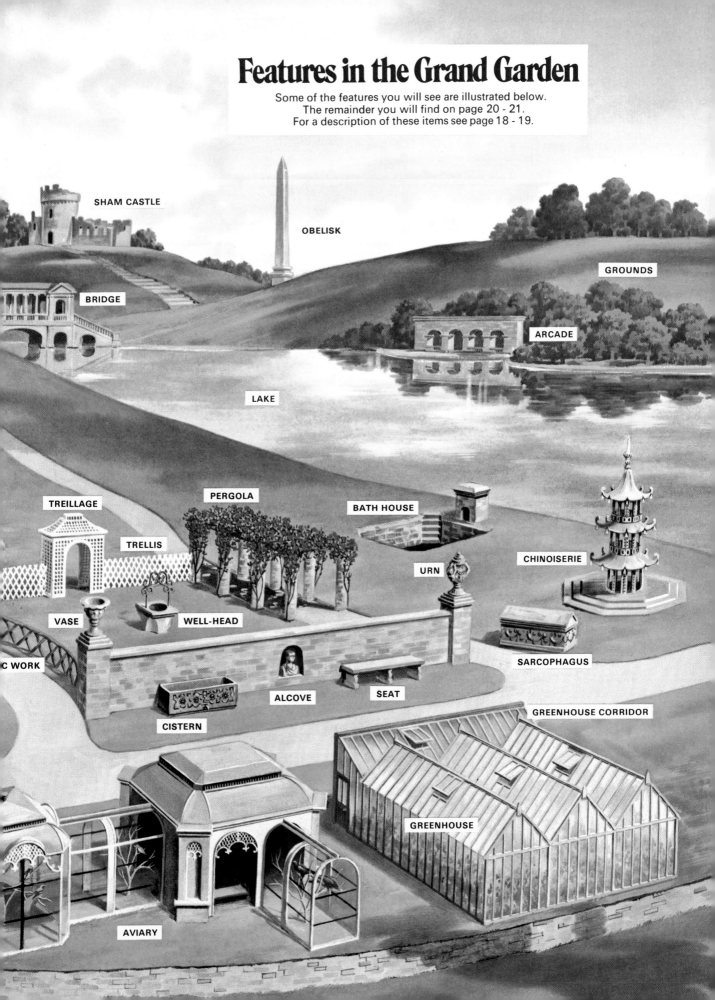

Features in the Grand Garden

Some of the features you will see are illustrated below.
The remainder you will find on page 20 - 21.
For a description of these items see page 18 - 19.

SHAM CASTLE

OBELISK

GROUNDS

BRIDGE

ARCADE

LAKE

TREILLAGE

PERGOLA

BATH HOUSE

CHINOISERIE

TRELLIS

URN

VASE

WELL-HEAD

SARCOPHAGUS

C WORK

ALCOVE

SEAT

GREENHOUSE CORRIDOR

CISTERN

GREENHOUSE

AVIARY

Features in the Grand Garden

for illustrations see
pages 16, 17, 20 and 21

ALCOVE A recess in a wall or gatepost, used to house statuary or a seat. When the use was to house a bee-hive, the alcove is called a **bee-bole**; example at Packwood.

ALLEY A broad path cut through trees, the branches of which may be trimmed. Like the avenue (described below) it is a feature of the French style.

ARBOUR The smallest and most ancient of garden houses, dating back to the middle ages. It is a shady retreat or bower, large enough for a seat, and often covered by climbing plants. The most famous arbour is the 'Birdcage' at Melbourne.

ARCADE A series of connected arches.

AVENUE A broad road lined on both sides with trees planted at regular intervals. The most popular trees for this purpose have been the elm, lime and horse chestnut.

AVIARY Ornamental bird houses are not common in our grand gardens. The best is at Waddesdon, and there are others at Sezincote and Dropmore.

BALUSTRADE An important feature in the formal garden, consisting of a row of balusters supporting a coping or parapet. See Elizabethan ones at Montecute, or Victorian examples at Cliveden and Harewood House.

BASON The receptacle which collects the water issuing from a fountain.

BATH HOUSE A small sunken pool with steps leading down into it and seats around the side. It was for cold-water bathing, not swimming. Good restoration at Wrest Park, less elaborate original at Packwood.

BELVEDERE A look-out tower commanding views of the surrounding countryside. Examples at Alton Towers and Rous Lench Court (Worcs.).

BOLLARDS Short posts set at regular intervals to prevent the entry of animals or vehicles into restricted areas. Common in public parks, rare in grand gardens.

BOSKET A block of closely-planted trees providing a dark background to the bright colours of the parterre (see below) in the foreground. Good example at Bramham Park.

BRIDGE A feature of many grand gardens, ranging from simple utility structures to the ornate early Landscape bridges at Wilton and Stowe.

CANAL The proper name for the long rectangular pool of the formal garden. Fine specimens at Chatsworth, Wrest Park, Buscot Park and Westbury Court.

CASCADE A series of man-made waterfalls; a great feature of Italian gardens. Britain's finest cascade is at Chatsworth, others at Bramham Park and Hever Castle.

CATTLE GRID A metal grating set in a driveway to prevent access by cattle.

CHINOISERIE Chinese-style buildings and ornaments, popular in the 18th century. The Pagoda at Kew is the most famous piece of *chinoiserie;* the Island Pagoda at Alton Towers perhaps the best. Many others – Wrest Park, Dropmore and Woburn Abbey.

CISTERN Made for purely utilitarian purposes – the collection of rainwater. Now used as an ornament or as a plant trough. Types displayed are usually made of lead and bear date of manufacture.

CLAIR-VOYÉE A wrought-iron screen set into a wall so as to extend the view. Hampton Court has a famous *clair-voyée.*

COLONNADE A classical feature, consisting of a row of columns. Can be seen at Iford Manor.

CONSERVATORY Like the greenhouse, a glass-covered structure for tender plants. Unlike the greenhouse it is sometimes accessible from the house and may be highly ornate, but the dividing line between the two is vague. Many fine Victorian examples – Syon Park, Chatsworth, Frogmore etc. The **palm house** is the largest type.

COURTYARD An enclosed garden with flower beds, lawn or paving. There are many noteworthy courtyards such as Nymans, Hardwick Hall and Barrington Court.

DOVECOT One of the oldest garden features. Many brick or stone-built pigeon houses or columbaria can still be seen. Good ones at Cotehele, Athelhampton, Rousham and Nymans.

EXEDRA A semi-circular expanse of turf usually bearing statuary and with a hedge and trees forming the curved boundary. Typical one at Chiswick.

FERNERY No longer popular now that the Victorian fern craze has passed. Ferns, rocks, tree stumps . . . can still be seen at Tatton Park.

FINIAL The ornament placed on top of a gatepost, roof, tower or column. The **ball** is popular and so is the **pineapple** which was introduced at the end of the 17th century.

FISH-POND Good examples at St. Paul's Waldenbury and Castle Ashby. Until the introduction of goldfish in the 18th century, the fish-pond was not an ornamental feature; it was for the raising of carp for the table.

FOLLY A general term for the many types of decorative but useless structures such as sham castles, sham bridges (there is one at Kenwood, London), pagodas, temples, pyramids, stone circles and so on.

FOUNTAIN Range from simple spouts to the 270 ft *jet d'eau* at Chatsworth. Elaborate designs can be seen at Ascott, Waddesdon and Holkham Hall.

GARDEN HOUSE A general term for structures designed for housing people rather than plants. The **arbour,** less than room size, is the simplest and the **pavilion** is the largest and most ornate. The **gazebo** is between these two extremes, as is the more recent **summer house.**

GATEHOUSE A building which houses the gates and through which the roadway passes. Early examples were fortified. Notable gatehouses at Lanhydrock, Oxford Botanic Gardens and Cranbourne Manor.

GAZEBO An early type of garden house. There are two storeys – the upper one serving as a viewing point and the lower one as a store. See the gazebos at Packwood, Montecute and Melford Hall.

GREENHOUSE A glass-covered structure for the raising and protection of tender plants (see conservatory). Originally the tile-roofed 'greenshouse' which protected evergreens during the winter. Glass roofing and proper heating did not appear until the 19th century.

GREENHOUSE CORRIDOR A glass-roofed walkway connecting several greenhouses. Prevents cold air from entering the houses when the doors are opened and also acts as a support for climbing exotic shrubs. A popular feature of botanic gardens.

GROTTO A cave-like structure (sometimes natural but usually artificial) often lined with shells, pebbles or bones. Can be seen at Stourhead, Hever Castle and Woburn Abbey.

GROUNDS A vague term covering the large estate where the word 'garden' is inappropriate. Called the **policies** in Scotland and the **demesne** in Ireland.

HA-HA A basic feature of the Landscape garden. It is a wide ditch separating the garden from the surrounding countryside. The view is not interrupted but animals are prevented from straying. Good examples at Blenheim and Charlecote.

HERBACEOUS BORDER Described under Home Gardens (page 28) but still a feature of many grand gardens – Wisley, Nymans, Hampton Court etc.

HERB GARDEN One of the earliest features, containing some of the plants on which gardening was founded. Good examples at Claverton Manor, Sissinghurst, Kew, Wisley and Hardwick Hall.

HERMIT CELL The strangest of all garden houses, in vogue during the 18th century. Simple wooden structure which housed a hermit on the estate. Few hermit cells survive.

ICE HOUSE Igloo-like building with an underground chamber for storing ice. Very few remain.

KNOT GARDEN Small and often rectangular beds bearing geometric patterns outlined in clipped hedges of box or other low-growing shrubs. The spaces between are filled with flowers or coloured stones. Reconstructions at New Place (Stratford-on-Avon), Hampton Court, Ludstone Hall and Elizabethan Gardens (Plymouth).

LAKE A feature of the informal garden. Many lakes were created during the Landscape period — Blenheim, Stourhead, Sheffield Park, Nostell Priory etc.

LAWN The close-cut lawn is not one of the ancient features of the garden. Until Jacobean times there was a 'flowery meadow'. Quality in grand gardens is sometimes indifferent — best examples are in college gardens and various public parks.

LODGE Gatekeeper's house situated at the entrance to the driveway. Fine lodges at Castle Howard, Keddleston, Blenheim and Nostell Priory.

MAUSOLEUM A large ornate tomb. Most famous one is at Castle Howard. Others at Bowood (Wilts.), Frogmore and West Wycombe.

MAZE One of the earliest garden features. The mazes at Somerleyton, Hatfield House, Hever Court and Hampton Court attract many visitors.

MOUNT A small artificial hill with an arbour or seat on top. A basic garden feature until 1650. Examples at Rockingham Castle and Packwood.

OBELISK Common feature in grand gardens, usually erected at the end of an avenue to commemorate an outstanding event.

ORANGERY Orange and lemon trees were the first tender evergreens to adorn British gardens. In winter they were housed in the Orangery, which became the most ornate of the early plant houses. Famous architects (such as Wren, Adam and Holland) designed them. Many examples — Kensington Palace, Kew, Blickling etc.

ORCHARD HOUSE Conservatory or greenhouse used for growing sub-tropical fruits such as figs, vines and peaches. Now quite rare, but still to be seen at Weston Hall and Luton Hoo.

PALISADE A line of deciduous trees with branches trimmed and interlaced.

PARTERRE A large, intricately patterned garden feature constructed close to the house. Derived from the knot garden, its hedge patterns are much larger in scale and there are other features such as topiary, statuary and fountains. The **parterre broderie** is the most complex form. The Victorians revived the parterre — see Blenheim. Modern reconstructions at Pitmedden and Kirby Hall.

PATTES D'OIE A 'goose foot' is the fan-wise spread of avenues or walks from a single point. A feature of the French style.

PAVILION The largest and most ornate of the garden houses. Derived from the Tudor **banqueting house**. Always architecturally designed, yet never approaching the mini-palaces of France. Good U.K. examples to be seen at Stowe, Badminton and Wrest Park.

PERGOLA An arched structure which supports climbing plants. Popular feature ever since the earliest days of gardening. Rambler roses are the usual covering.

PLEACHED ALLEY A tree-lined walk where the branches are arched over and interlaced. Can be seen at Hidcote, Bateman's and Sissinghurst.

PROSPECT An attractive view covering a large area, both wide and long (compare vista).

RIBBON BED Narrow band of bedding plants bordering the lawn. A feature of Victorian gardens.

RUSTIC WORK The use of sawn but unbarked branches for making seats, fences and garden houses. It was a Victorian fad. Walls of rustic summer houses were sometimes packed with moss to make **moss houses.**

SARCOPHAGUS A stone coffin. You can see sarcophagi at Chatsworth and Hever Castle.

SEAT Earliest seats were turf-covered; good example in Queen's Garden, Kew. Many materials have subsequently been used — wood, stone, iron, concrete and so on.

SHAM CASTLE A folly built in castellated form, sometimes as a ruin. Badminton and Hagley have examples. Sanderson Miller was the famous designer of these follies.

STATUARY Figures of many different types, periods and materials can be found. Cibber, van Nost, Scheemakers, Cheere and Rysbrack were the great names but the work of many sculptors, including Henry Moore, can be seen. Gardens famous for their statuary are Chiswick, Rousham, Hever Castle, Iford Manor, Wilton House and Anglesey Abbey.

STEPS There is nothing to rival the great Continental staircases. Some of our best work is Victorian, as at Shrubland Park, Suffolk.

STILT HEDGE A clipped hedge with bare trunks showing at the base. Good specimens at Hidcote.

SUNDIAL Many fine examples, some bearing interesting mottoes — Sudeley Castle, Barrington Court, Ascott, Penshurst Place and so on. An **armillary sundial** has a set of linked hoops.

SUNKEN GARDEN A planted area of the main garden, created below the level of the surrounding ground. It is not linked with any particular period of history; there were Tudor sunken gardens and there are modern ones.

TAPIS VERT A long rectangular strip of turf ('green carpet') between canals or driveways.

TEMPLE Building of classical shape and with classical columns. Good examples at Studley Royal, Stourhead, Alton Towers and many other places.

TERRACE The level space between house and garden. Returned to the British garden early in the 19th century after its banishment by Capability Brown.

TERRACED GARDEN The conversion of a sloping site into a series of attractive and plant-adorned terraces. Powis Castle, Bodnant and Ascott are famous examples.

THÉÂTRE DE VERDURE An open-air stage of turf and neatly-trimmed hedges. Good specimens at Hidcote, Bodnant and Dartington Hall.

TOPIARY The clipping of trees and shrubs into geometrical or fanciful shapes. See pages 80-82.

TREILLAGE Trellis used to produce an elaborate architectural feature such as an arbour or pergola. Iron may be the material used, as in the Melbourne 'Birdcage'.

TRELLIS A framework of crossed slats or wires upon which plants can be trained.

TROMPE L'OEIL A feature designed to enhance the appearance or size of the garden by optical illusion. The most popular *trompe l'oeil* is the narrowing of the far ends of beds and borders.

URN A large ornate vessel which is narrow-mouthed and generally lidded. A common feature in the grand garden.

VASE A decorative container, usually wide-mouthed, often used as a finial. The use of vases as plant containers was reintroduced at the beginning of the Victorian era.

VISTA An attractive view stretching into the distance but with little width (compare prospect).

WALL A fundamental feature of early gardens. There are many variations — some were of practical use like the heated wall to protect tender plants (as at Packwood) and others were decorative. A **serpentine wall** can be seen at Bury St. Edmunds Abbey and a **scalloped wall** at Alton Towers.

WELL-HEAD An ornamental feature, although a few do stand over wells. The best ones are Venetian, and there are good specimens at Castle Ashby and the Queen's Garden, Kew.

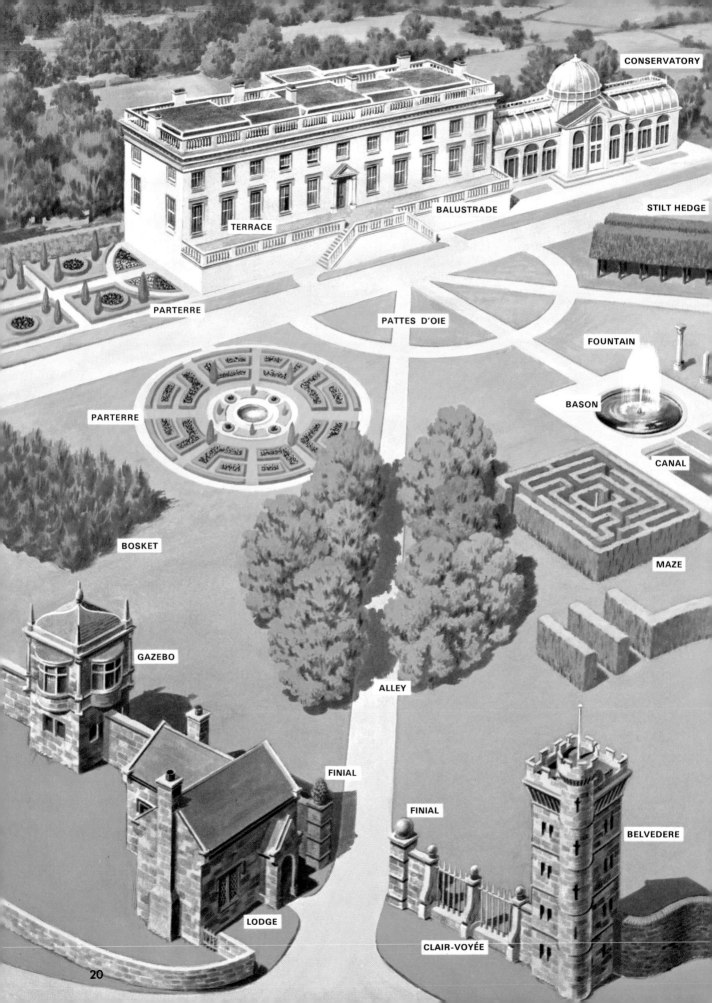

CONSERVATORY

STILT HEDGE

BALUSTRADE

TERRACE

PARTERRE

PATTES D'OIE

FOUNTAIN

PARTERRE

BASON

CANAL

BOSKET

MAZE

GAZEBO

ALLEY

FINIAL

FINIAL

BELVEDERE

LODGE

CLAIR-VOYÉE

20

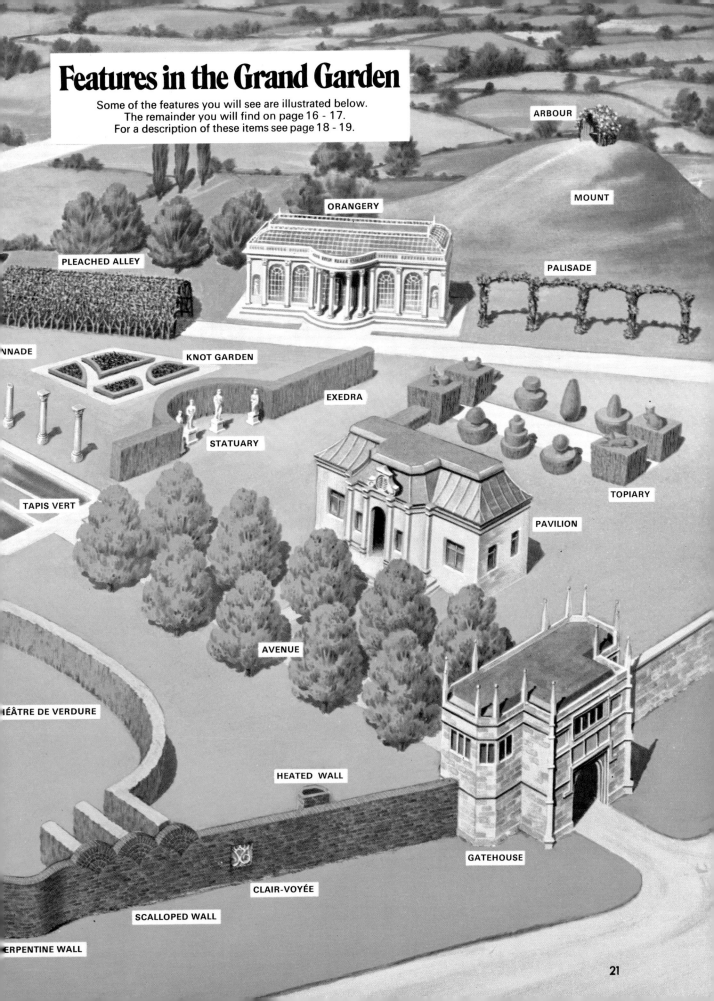

Features in the Grand Garden

Some of the features you will see are illustrated below.
The remainder you will find on page 16 - 17.
For a description of these items see page 18 - 19.

ARBOUR

MOUNT

ORANGERY

PLEACHED ALLEY

PALISADE

NNADE

KNOT GARDEN

EXEDRA

STATUARY

TOPIARY

TAPIS VERT

PAVILION

AVENUE

IÉÂTRE DE VERDURE

HEATED WALL

GATEHOUSE

CLAIR-VOYÉE

SCALLOPED WALL

ERPENTINE WALL

Grand Gardens

KEY

NT National Trust
NTS National Trust for Scotland

STYLES

* Style present in the garden. may be a reconstruction ; th guide book will tell you.
K Created by William Kent
B Created by 'Capability' Brov
R Created by Humphry Repto

	GARDEN	MAIN STYLES TO BE SEEN (see page 24-25): ROMAN	MEDIAEVAL	TUDOR	ELIZABETHAN	JACOBEAN	FRENCH	DUTCH	LANDSCAPE	VICTORIAN	MODERN	SPECIAL FEATURES	VISITORS PER YEAR
	Abbotsbury (Dorset)										*	ST T	40,000
	Alton Towers (Staffs.)									*			355,000
NT	**Anglesey Abbey** (Cambs.)						*				*		28,000
NT	**Ascott** (Bucks.)									*	*	W	12,000
	Ashridge (Herts.)		*						R			I	5,500
	Athelhampton (Dorset)									*	*		20,000
NT	**Attingham Park** (Salop.)								R				2,000
	Audley End (Essex)								B				90,000
NT	**Barrington Court** (Som.)										*		2,500
NT	**Bateman's** (Sussex)										*		32,000
	Bedgebury (Kent)										*	P	68,000
	Berkeley Castle (Glocs.)				*						*		129,000
	Bicton Gardens (Devon)						*				*	I P	110,000
	Blenheim Palace (Oxon.)						*		B			W	250,000
NT	**Blickling Hall** (Norfolk)						*		*		*		67,000
	Blithfield (Staffs.)						*						26,000
NT	**Bodnant** (Denbigh.)									*	*	A T W	81,000
	Borde Hill (Sussex)										*	T	8,100
	Bramham (Yorks.)						*					W	8,700
NTS	**Branklyn** (Perth.)										*	I	5,700
	Burford House (Salop.)										*		18,000
	Burton Agnes (Yorks.)				*						*		23,000
NT	**Buscot Park** (Berks.)							*			*	W	3,000
	Castle Howard (Yorks.)								*	*			99,000
NT	**Charlecote Park** (Warks.)								B				36,000
	Chatsworth (Derby.)						*		B	*		W	250,000
	Chiswick House (London)								K	*			28,000
	Claverton Manor (Som.)										*	I	86,000
NT	**Cliveden** (Bucks.)									*		J	39,000
	Compton Acres (Dorset)										*	I J	130,000
	Compton Wynyates (Warks.)							*		*			30,000
NT	**Cotehele** (Cornwall)									*	*	T W	30,000
	Cranborne Manor (Dorset)					*							4,000
	Crarae Lodge (Argyll)										*	T	7,000
NTS	**Crathes Castle** (Kinc.)							*			*		43,500
NTS	**Culzean Castle** (Ayr.)									*	*	P	166,000
	Dartington Hall (Devon)										*		not known
	Derry & Toms (London)										*	I	150,000
	Drummond Castle (Perth.)						*			*			600
	Duncombe Park (Yorks.)								*				98,000
	Dyffryn (Glam.)										*	I	50,000
	East Lambrook Manor (Som.)										*		5,000
	Edzell Castle (Angus)				*								9,000
	Exbury (Hants.)										*	T	38,500

KEY
SPECIAL FEATURES
A Arboretum – notable collection of trees
J Japanese garden
I Informative garden – plants clearly labelled or various garden styles on display
P Pinetum – notable collection of conifers
ST Sub-tropical garden
T Woodland garden – shrubs and trees informally planted
W Water garden

	GARDEN	ROMAN	MEDIAEVAL	TUDOR	ELIZABETHAN	JACOBEAN	FRENCH	DUTCH	LANDSCAPE	VICTORIAN	MODERN	SPECIAL FEATURES	VISITORS PER YEAR
	Fishbourne (Sussex)	*											175,000
	Frogmore (Berks.)								*	*			not known
NT	**Glendurgan** (Cornwall)										*	T	7,000
	Gt. Dixter (Sussex)										*		55,000
	Hampton Court (London)			*	*		*	*			*		649,000
NT	**Hardwick Hall** (Derby.)				*						*		61,000
	Harewood House (Yorks.)								B	*			244,000
	Harlow Car (Yorks.)										*	I	75,000
	Hascombe Court (Surrey)										*		1,500
	Hatfield House (Herts.)					*	*				*		111,000
	Heveningham (Suffolk)								B		*		21,000
	Hever Castle (Kent)									*		W	161,000
NT	**Hidcote Manor** (Glocs.)										*		54,000
	Highdown (Sussex)										*		not known
	Hodnet Hall (Salop.)										*	T W	54,000
	Holker Hall (Lancs.)									*			110,000
	Holkham Hall (Norfolk)								B	*		A	26,000
	Holt, The Courts (Wilts.)										*		1,500
	Howick Hall (N'land.)										*	T	not known
NT	**Ickworth** (Suffolk)								B	*			18,000
	Iford Manor (Wilts.)									*			650
TS	**Inverewe** (Ross.)									*	*	I ST	123,000
NT	**Killerton** (Devon)									*	*	A P ST	17,000
	Kirby Hall (Northants.)						*						12,900
	Knightshayes Court (Devon)									*	*	W	3,500
NT	**Lanhydrock** (Cornwall)									*	*		36,500
	Leonardslee (Sussex)										*	P T	45,000
	Levens Hall (W'land)				*			*					36,000
	Lochinch (Wigtown.)										*	P ST T	9,000
	Longstock (Hants.)										*	W	5,000
	Ludstone Hall (Salop.)					*						W	1,304
	Luton Hoo (Beds.)								B	*			40,000
	Melbourne Hall (Derby.)						*						14,000
NT	**Montacute House** (Som.)				*	*					*		24,000
NT	**Mount Stewart** (Co. Down)										*	ST	7,000
	Muncaster Castle (Cumb.)									*	*	T	51,000
	New Place, Stratford (Warks.)				*								81,000
	Newby Hall (Yorks.)										*		80,000
	Newstead Abbey (Notts.)		*						*	*		J	112,000
	Northbourne Court (Kent)				*								950
NT	**Nostell Priory** (Yorks.)									*			44,000
NT	**Nymans** (Sussex)										*	P	30,000
NT	**Oxburgh** (Norfolk)					*				*			19,500
NT	**Packwood** (Warks.)					*							24,000

Continued on page 26

ARRANGING
YOUR VISITS

You will need to buy several paperback annuals if you plan to take garden visiting seriously. The basic guide is

HISTORIC HOUSES, CASTLES & GARDENS
published every January and available from booksellers and newsagents price 30p, or from the publishers ABC Travel Guides Ltd., 40 Bowling Green Lane, London EC1 (37p post paid).

This ABC guide lists most of the grand gardens together with admission prices and times. Note that you have to make an appointment to visit some of the properties.

Despite its comprehensiveness, some famous gardens are not present. You will not find Julians, Dartington Hall, Exbury or St. Paul's Waldenbury in its pages. These gardens, and many others, are normally private and are only opened by their owners on one or several days each year for charity.

So you will need the 'yellow book' –
GARDENS OF ENGLAND AND WALES
published every March and available from booksellers and newsagents price 20p, or from The National Gardens Scheme, 57 Lower Belgrave St., London SW1W OLB (28p post paid).

This lists about 1200 gardens and the day or days when they are open. Most of the money raised from the admission charges is used to help elderly district nurses in financial need. The remainder goes to the National Trust.

Scotland has its own scheme and its own 'yellow book' –
SCOTLAND'S GARDENS
published every March and available from Scotland's Gardens Scheme, 26 Castle Terrace, Edinburgh EH1 2EL (25p post paid).

It now remains for you to obtain a copy of the 'green book' –
GARDENS TO VISIT
published every March and available from booksellers and newsagents price 10p, or from the Gardener's Sunday Organisation, White Witches, Claygate Rd., Dorking, Surrey (13p post paid).

This catalogue of the gardens which are open each Sunday from March until October in aid of the Gardeners' Royal Benevolent Society and the Royal Gardeners' Orphan Fund completes your library of garden lists. They all suffer from the drawback of having only sketchy accounts of the gardens to be visited, and unfortunately the choice of detailed and illustrated guides to Britain's grand gardens is limited – perhaps the best is GARDENS TO VISIT IN BRITAIN by Arthur Hellyer (Hamlyn £1.75).

If you wish to go on an organised tour of famous gardens in Britain, consult the Journal of the Royal Horticultural Society as several garden tour operators advertise regularly. Also there is the Gardens and Castle Cruise arranged every year by the National Trust of Scotland, visiting places like Tresco Abbey, Jersey, Bodnant and Brodick Castle.

Finally, remember to join the National Trust, as your membership card is the open sesame to so many of the grand gardens of Britain.

If you think in terms of the ten basic styles listed below, then you should be able to understand the architecture of most of the grand gardens you visit. This chart is, of course, a simplification of a very complex subject and many gardens consist of a mixture of styles (see pages 22, 23 and 26). Some of the features described may be new to you; use the picture dictionary on pages 16-21. Some styles are named after but do not quite fit in with the reign of monarchs.

ROMAN   before 400
None in existence. Excavated site at Fishbourne in Sussex ha simple geometric design and the artist's impression shows hedges, roses, specimen trees, turf and gravel paths. Fruit, v and some vegetables were grown in these courtyard gardens.

MEDIAEVAL   before 1530
Monasteries had a cloistered courtyard ('Paradise') with pa dividing simple beds or turf. The herb garden and fishpond w nearby. Authentic example at Newstead Abbey. Non-chu gardens were enclosed; features included raised beds, pathwa treillage, arbours, orchards and turf-topped seats.

TUDOR   1530-1560
No complete gardens exist, but Tudor features can be found several localities. The basic parts were the mount (with a pavil on the summit), the maze, raised walls with balustrades, pain wooden rails and figures, fountains and knots.

ELIZABETHAN   1560-1610
Elizabethan features remain or have been reconstructed in a f gardens, but little or nothing is left of the original magnific gardens of the age – Theobalds, Holdenby, etc. Best auther touches found at Montecute. Designs were similar to those Tudor gardens, but on a larger scale.

JACOBEAN   1610-1660
Basically similar to the Elizabethan and Tudor gardens, but lar and simpler. Mounts and carved beasts were no longer popu 'Greens' (evergreen trees and shrubs) were now in demand a green-houses and orangeries were built to house tender variet during winter.

FRENCH   1660-1730
The central view was all-important . . . over the elaborate parter and lakes, along the radiating avenues to the woods beyo The surrounding walls carried great wrought-iron gates. Statu abounded, and trimmed hedges were popular. Melbourne is best example.

DUTCH   1690-1700
The Dutch pattern was smaller and fussier than the French gard Water was more extensive; hedges and fantastic topiary increas at the expense of grass and gravel. Features included orange tr and other 'greens' in tubs, massed bulbs and lead statues.

LANDSCAPE   1730-1830
Unmistakable with its complete lack of surrounding walls a absence of straight lines or hedges. Hills and lakes may be ma made, but with planted trees, winding paths and scattered buil ings, there is a natural landscape-painting effect. A ha-ha a terrace may be present.

VICTORIAN   1830-1870
Formal and generally based on the ideas of 15th century Ita Terraces, statues, fountains and steps abound. The strictly ge metrical beds or parterres are bedded out, and topiary is genera present. Trentham Gardens and Cliveden are good examples.

MODERN   after 1870
Many types. Trees and shrubs are always important, and m dominate as at Bodnant, Sheffield Park and Rowallane. T general pattern is for gardens within a garden – formal desig with some ornaments and informal planting. There is nearly alwa a wild area and a series of attractive views. These features a present at Hidcote, Sissinghurst Castle and Dartington Hall.

Grand Garden Styles

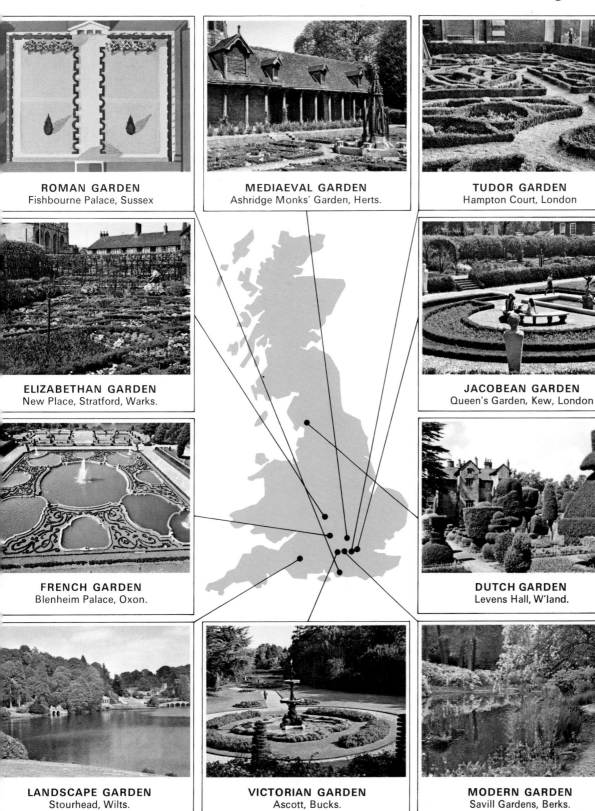

ROMAN GARDEN
Fishbourne Palace, Sussex

MEDIAEVAL GARDEN
Ashridge Monks' Garden, Herts.

TUDOR GARDEN
Hampton Court, London

ELIZABETHAN GARDEN
New Place, Stratford, Warks.

JACOBEAN GARDEN
Queen's Garden, Kew, London

FRENCH GARDEN
Blenheim Palace, Oxon.

DUTCH GARDEN
Levens Hall, W'land.

LANDSCAPE GARDEN
Stourhead, Wilts.

VICTORIAN GARDEN
Ascott, Bucks.

MODERN GARDEN
Savill Gardens, Berks.

Grand Gardens

continued from page 23

Many of the most importa[nt] grand gardens in the Unit[ed] Kingdom are listed on this pa[ge] and on pages 22 and 23. The k[ey] to the symbols appears on pag[es] 22 and 23.

	GARDEN	MAIN STYLES TO BE SEEN (see page 24-25)										SPECIAL FEATURES			VISITORS PER YEAR
		ROMAN	MEDIAEVAL	TUDOR	ELIZABETHAN	JACOBEAN	FRENCH	DUTCH	LANDSCAPE	VICTORIAN	MODERN				
	Penjerrick (Cornwall)										*	P	ST	T	not known
	Penshurst Place (Kent)				*						*				77,000
NTS	Pitmedden (Aberdeen.)						*								14,000
NT	Polesden Lacey (Surrey)								*		*		A		69,000
NT	Powis Castle (Mont.)							*							22,000
	Prior Park, Bath (Som.)								*						not known
	Rockingham Castle (Northants.)									*	*				19,200
	Rousham House (Oxon.)								K						4,500
NT	Rowallane (Co. Down)										*		T		13,000
	Rudding Park (Yorks.)								R		*		T		14,000
	St. Paul's Waldenbury (Herts.)						*								2,500
NT	Saltram House (Devon)								*						26,500
	Sandringham (Norfolk)							*	*	*					85,000
	Savill Gardens (Berks.)										*	I		W	86,000
NT	Scotney Castle (Kent)								*	*		A		T	33,000
	Seaton Delaval (N'land.)						*								5,000
NT	Sheffield Park (Sussex)								B		*	A	T	W	122,000
NT	Sissinghurst Castle (Kent)										*				79,000
	Somerleyton Hall (Suffolk)									*					37,000
	Spetchley (Worcs.)								*	*					10,000
NT	Stourhead (Wilts.)								*			A		W	106,000
	Stowe (Bucks.)								K						1,200
	Studley Royal (Yorks.)								*				W		204,000
	Sudeley Castle (Glocs.)									*					152,000
	Syon House (London)								B	*	*	I		P	250,000
NT	Tatton Park (Ches.)								R	*			J		139,000
	Thoresby Hall (Notts.)									*					38,000
NTS	Threave (Kirkcud.)										*		I		23,000
NT	Trelissick (Cornwall)										*	ST		T	31,000
NT	Trengwainton (Cornwall)										*	ST		T	8,000
	Trentham Gardens (Staffs.)								B	*			I		400,000
	Tresco Abbey (I. of Scilly)										*	I		ST	20,000
NT	Upton House (Warks.)										*		W		5,000
NT	Waddesdon Manor (Bucks.)									*			W		70,000
NT	Wakehurst Place (Sussex)										*		T		46,000
	Warwick Castle (Warks.)								B						330,000
NT	Westbury Court (Glocs.)							*					W		opened 1973
	Weston Park (Salop.)								B	*					48,000
	Westonbirt (Glocs.)										*		A		not known
	Wilton House (Wilts.)								*	*			A		68,000
NT	Winkworth (Surrey)										*		A		50,000
	Wisley (Surrey)										*	I	P	W	217,000
	Woburn Abbey (Beds.)								R						not known
	Wrest Park (Beds.)				*				B	*			W		24,000

See page 40 for Botanic Gardens

2. The Home Garden

> " I haven't a garden. You see I . . .
> She gave me a swift, keen look, sharp as an eagle.
> 'You haven't a garden !' she cried scornfully.
> 'Then why are you an Englishman ? "
> *Gone Rustic* (Cecil Roberts 1934)

There is an almost universal belief that the Englishman cannot do without his tea or his garden. The latter point, at least, is supported by recent surveys. Eighty per cent of all households in Britain have a cared-for garden.

Of course, some people who can afford it do employ a part-time gardener to do the heavy work, but this practice appears to be dying out. In 1967 3 per cent of all gardens were looked after by a professional gardener. By 1971 this figure had fallen to 1 per cent. This desire to care for one's own garden is not based on financial necessity. The 1972 Institute of Directors Survey revealed that gardening was easily the most popular hobby amongst company directors.

So it's up to the gardener in the family to do the work and this is by no means a purely male activity. It was laid down in the first home gardening guide printed in English (*Hundred Good Points of Husbandry*, 1557) that the husband and wife should share the work:

"In March and in April, from morning to night,

In sowing and setting, good housewives delight"
And the good housewives have been doing their share ever since. In 31 per cent of our gardens it is the wife who does most of the work, and in 26 per cent of them she does as much as her husband.

Now we must examine the end-product of all this hard labour – the Home Garden. There are four basic styles, as described on page 31, and it is obvious that these have nothing in common with the numerous grand garden styles listed on page 24. Of the four styles, one – the Suburban Garden – dominates the whole scene, for this is the garden we see on every car trip or train journey.

The standard Suburban Garden – similar in principle, different in detail – is found everywhere. It occurs within the city limits and out in the Green Belt, but it has become associated with suburbia, where there are neither paved town gardens nor old-world cottage gardens to relieve the row after row of this standard semi-formal layout. The lawn is dominant, and around this are the beds, herbaceous border, shrub border and rockery. At the back are the vegetables, greenhouse and informal plantings if the garden is large enough. It is a grass-and-earth place where you can show off your skill with flowers and as such has given incalculable pleasure to generations of home gardeners.

Yet the ordinary gardener hasn't the slightest idea how the style originated. People from all walks of life were asked if they had heard of some of Britain's great gardeners. More than 45 per cent had heard of 'Capability' Brown and knew that he was Britain's 'greatest gardener', but it was this man's determination to turn every estate into a pastoral scene that destroyed hundreds of formal gardens and banished all flowers to be hidden behind brick walls. His near-vandalism changed the grand garden scene forever, but in cottage gardens and small manor houses this landscape movement meant nothing and the devotion to flowers lived on.

In contrast to Brown's fame, only 1 per cent had heard of Mr. & Mrs. Loudon. And yet it was the books and magazines of this couple in the middle of the nineteenth century which first taught the middle class how to garden. The next two names in the survey fared little better – only 1 per cent had heard of William Robinson and 3 per cent knew of Gertrude Jeckyll. But it was this couple who evolved the Suburban Garden as we know it, and which is rather surprisingly a twentieth century creation.

The home gardeners of the last century had mixed the teachings of the Loudons with Victorian taste and their gardens grew fussier and more cluttered as time went on. Statues, pots, ironwork, carpet bedding were everywhere, and it was Robinson and Jeckyll who replaced them with the shrubbery, herbaceous border, rose beds, rockery and uncluttered lawn. Bedding-out, however, remained as the connecting link with the past.

Moving out of suburbia we see examples of the other home garden styles. The town garden represents the Architectural style – stone, ornaments, decorative pots, etc.; plants are *part* of the garden, not the purpose of it. At the other end of the scale is the Cottage Garden, tumbling over itself with old-fashioned flowers and with no time or room for grand lawns or fussy new varieties.

And so to the future. The leading landscape designers predict that our gardens will become more architectural, that we shall create outdoor living rooms with covered areas, highly decorative plants and modern building materials. As noted on page 29, the outdoor living room is a long time coming. It is a highly desirable concept for some, but once again there is a fear that the pride of place for flowers could be threatened. Your guideline should be to listen to Gertrude Jeckyll "A garden is for its owner's pleasure, and whatever the degree or form of that pleasure, if only it be sincere, is right and reasonable."

27

THE TYPICAL HOME GARDEN

ROCKERY

An area of garden containing rocks which is used for growing plants. If natural rock formation is copied, correct term is **Rock Garden**. True **alpines** are from mountainous areas, growing above the level at which trees can flourish. Term is now used for rock plants in general, and 7% of gardeners buy some each year.

HERBACEOUS BORDER

A **border** is a plot of cultivated ground, used for growing plants, which can generally be viewed from one direction only.

The **herbaceous border** is planted exclusively with hardy perennial plants, and is an important feature of British gardens

Dividing up plants and obtaining cuttings from friends remains an important way of stocking the border. Only 8% of households with a garden bought herbaceous perennials in 1971. Average number purchased – 22.

Most perennials have a fairly short flowering life, so many plants are required for an all-season colour display. This means a border should be at least 4 ft. wide and 30 ft. long. If less, a **mixed border** is recommended – annuals, bulbs etc. being included with the hardy perennials.

SHRUB BORDER

A 20th century innovation aiming to give a succession of colour from rhododendrons in spring to hydrangeas in autumn. Labour-saving and much praised, but popularity has not grown at expected rate. Only 9% of gardeners buy flowering shrubs each year. Average number purchased – 6.

ROSES

Present in 85% of gardens. Average number per garden – 10.

Each year 4 million gardeners plant out some new roses. Average number purchased – 9. Woolworths is the largest single supplier, and the Hybrid Tea remains the most popular group. More than 90 per cent are bush roses; the remainder are climbers, standards etc.

GREENHOUSE

Present in 2 million gardens. Most popular size is 10 ft.× 8 ft.

Most greenhouses are made of wood and were built by the gardener himself.

Nearly half of the houses are heated, oil and paraffin being the most popular fuels. But only 41% are used all year round.

Tomatoes are grown in 74% of greenhouses; cuttings and seedlings in 55% and chrysanthemums in 34%.

THE GARDEN

More than 80% of all the households in Britain have a cared-for garden.

The average size of these $14\frac{1}{2}$ million gardens is 2000 sq. ft. ($\frac{1}{20}$ acre). Only 1 in 20 is more than $\frac{1}{2}$ acre.

Total garden area is 710,000 acres.

REGIONAL DIFFERENCES		% households with a cared-for garden	% gardens where husband does most of the work	% gardens with a greenhouse	% gardens with a shed	% gardens using manure	% gardeners who call at a garden centre	% gardeners who find catalogues useful
	Scotland	68	49	7	40	15	22	76
	Northern England	72	36	11	36	9	36	67
	Midlands and Wales	86	36	14	47	14	32	74
	Southern England	84	32	15	55	11	30	63

ORNAMENTAL TREE

…ree grown for its blossom, its attractive leaves …shape. When planted singly as a focal point it …comes a **specimen tree.**

…stigiate: Column-like growth, branches …ight.

…eeping: Branches hang vertically, by training …naturally.

…andard: Main trunk bare: most usual tree …m.

…ly 5% of gardeners buy ornamental trees each …ar. Average number purchased — 5.

OUTDOOR LIVING AREA

…t yet present in the typical home garden in …tain, but often forecast for the future.
…re is little evidence of any major swing at …sent towards the 'outdoor living room' idea. …ly 6% of gardens have any decorative walling, …n 10 has a patio (paved terrace which is large …ough to use as a sitting-out area) and less than …have a garden table. Only 1% have a barbecue. …ere has been a marked increase in the purchase …aluminium-framed chairs — the number has …re than doubled in 4 years. But these are …nly used on the lawn, as is the garden …brella.

LAWN

…sent in 82% of all gardens. Grass covers an …rage of 1000 sq. ft., which is half the total …den area.
…o methods are available for establishing a lawn …eed sowing and laying turf. In 1971 grass seed …s sown in 11% of gardens, turf was laid in 3%. …5m is spent each year on lawn mowers. More …n 2 million gardeners have a power mower, …million have a hand mower.
…e lawn is traditionally the English garden …ture most admired on the Continent. "The …ss plots are so exquisite a beauty, that in …nce we can scarce ever hope to come up to …A. J. d'Argenville (1709).

BED

…plot of cultivated ground, used for growing …nts, which can generally be viewed from all …gles.
…and bed: Tallest plants in centre, dwarf types …r front.
…ised bed: Surface above surrounding level.
…rmal bed: Outline (circle, square, oval etc.) …d planting strictly geometrical.
…ds are often associated with bedding plants …e page 103-108). They are bought for 6½ …lion gardens every year (average number …chased — 45) and countless millions are …ed from seed.

THE TOOLS

UNIVERSAL (owned by more than 80% of gardeners)

Fork
Spade
Rake
Hoe
Trowel
Hand fork

COMMON (owned by 40–80% of gardeners)

Lawn mower
Secateurs
Watering can
Hedge shears
Hose pipe

UNCOMMON (owned by 20–40% of gardeners)

Lawn rake
Lawn sprinkler
Scythe
Wheelbarrow
Sprayer
Long-handled shears

RARE (owned by less than 20% of gardeners)

Lawn edger
Tree pruner
Hedge trimmer
Roller
Cultivator
Cloches
Incinerator

VEGETABLES & FRUIT

A vegetable plot is present in about half our gardens, and seedsmen have reported a sharp rise in sales of vegetable seeds. Economic necessity does not seem to be the reason — seeds are more often bought for large gardens (57% buy them) than for small ones (22%). The advent of home deep freezing is probably an important factor.

Items purchased (% of gardens)	
Vegetable seeds	34
Tomato plants	17
Vegetable plants	16
Onion sets	14
Seed potatoes	13

The most popular seeds are lettuce, runner beans, peas, carrots and onions.

A surprisingly high proportion of Britain's vegetables are home grown:

	% of 1970 consumption which was home-grown	% change in home output since 1961
Cauliflower	6	−42
New potatoes	7	−62
Maincrop Potatoes	7	+ 2
Onions, Leeks	8	−12
Tomatoes	10	+52
Carrots	11	+125
Brussels sprouts	14	+32
Celery	15	+61
Cabbage	16	−38
Lettuce	19	+ 1
Beetroot	24	−11
Peas	36	− 3
Beans	54	0
Broccoli	55	− 9
Rhubarb	70	−29

Fruit is grown in 34% of gardens. Soft fruit bushes (strawberry, currant, raspberry etc.) are bought by 2% of gardeners each year; average number purchased — 8. Fruit trees (apple, pear, plum etc.) are bought by same number of gardeners; average number of trees purchased — 4.

	% of 1970 consumption which was home-grown	% change in home output since 1961
Apples	17	+91
Soft fruit	40	+ 2

THE GARDENERS

More than 26 million people in Britain work in the gardens attached to their homes. For about 4 million of them gardening is an important part of their home life. This importance appears to increase with age and marital responsibility:

	% leisure time spent gardening
Single man, aged 23–30	1
Married man, aged 23–30	4
Married man, aged 23–30, with children	8
Married man, aged 31–45, with children	12
Married man, aged 46–60, with children	15
Married man, over 60	20

The practical side of gardening may be the responsibility of the husband, but it is equally likely to be the wife's job. It is more likely to be a husband and wife affair in the richer homes:

Responsible for looking after the garden	% of all families	% of richest families	% of poorest families
Husband	35	29	38
Wife	31	32	36
Husband and Wife	26	30	17
Gardener	1	6	—
Other person	6	3	9

ROYAL HORTICULTURAL SOCIETY SURVEY 1972

The Fellows of the Royal Horticultural Society (see page 42) are probably the most influential and include some of the most dedicated gardeners in Britain. Their gardening habits were revealed in the 1972 Survey carried out by the RHS Journal.

Plants grown	% of Fellows
Bulbs	95
Lawn	91
Roses	91
Herbaceous perennials	85
Shrubs	84
Annuals	74
Bedding plants	71
House plants	70
Fruit trees	66
Geraniums	66
Dahlias	65
Gladioli	64
Rhododendrons	64
Alpines	61
Leaf vegetables	58
Chrysanthemums	57
Fruit bushes	51
Root vegetables	47
Rough grass	37
Carnations	36
Cacti	28

THE PROBLEMS

The main problems are greenfly, slugs, mildews, *botrytis* (grey mould) and weeds in paths, beds and lawns.

	% of gardens where the product is used
Greenfly spray	32
General weedkiller	22
Lawn fertilizer	21
Peat	20
Lawn weedkiller	16
Bonemeal	15
Rose fertilizer	15
Slug killer	10
Tomato fertilizer	10
Growmore fertilizer	9
Ant killer	6
Lime	5
Rose fungicide	5
Caterpillar killer	3

THE CATALOGUES

The first fully illustrated catalogue was published in 1730. Today the range seems almost limitless, with beautiful flower pictures and helpful hints on selection, planting and after-care.

About 50% of households receive at least one plant catalogue. Only 1 in 5 are actually sent for, 8% are picked up in a shop or garden centre and 5% are obtained from another gardener. So most catalogues are unsolicited.

The facts and figures in this section were drawn from many sources, but special acknowledgement is made to the following: Contimart · Mintel · The Royal Horticultural Society

Home Garden Styles

COTTAGE GARDEN

The cottage garden has been an essential part of our rural scene for centuries, but it is becoming rarer each year as old houses disappear. Everything about it is old-fashioned . . . the plants themselves are age-old varieties raised in the garden. Little or nothing is ever bought.

There is neither clear design nor any formality. Flowers are crowded together and new introductions are planted wherever there is any room. These plants may be grown from cuttings given by friends, from wedding bouquets or even from funeral wreaths. Annuals and biennials are often raised from self-sown seed.

Pots and old sinks, winding narrow paths and substantial walls make up the framework of the cottage garden. Within this framework scented plants such as jasmine, pinks, old roses, lavender, rosemary and southernwood are important, but the main feature is the massed jumble of colours and shapes beneath old trees and climbing over house and trellis work.

SUBURBAN GARDEN

The suburban garden is a particular style which in less than a hundred years has become the standard pattern for home gardens. Obviously its mixture of formal and informal features fits in with the British character. The informal shrub border, the rockery and the wild area in the larger garden provide a feel of the countryside, a return to nature. On the other hand the geometric flower beds, the straight paths and the trimmed lawn edges give the neat and orderly look close to the house which popular taste demands.

This style has several basic features. The lawn is of prime importance, and is often placed centrally in the garden. Next comes the herbaceous border, with its motley collection of hardy perennial flowers. Roses and flower beds complete the basic picture.

Some trees and shrubs are grown, and there may be a few ornaments, but it is the flowers which dominate. This gives the style its charm in summer, and its bareness in winter.

ARCHITECTURAL GARDEN

In the architectural garden the designer sets out to produce a permanent skeleton which will look attractive in summer *and* in winter, and into which plants are introduced to add living colour and living shapes.

Here paths, walls and containers are designed to be decorative and not simply functional; page 139 illustrates some of the modern materials available. Trees and shrubs are chosen for their shapes and bark colour as well as for their blooms. It is a return to the ancient idea that the garden is a 'paradise' in which one lives, but it would be naive to forget that this idea flowered in areas well away from the British climate.

The best examples of this style can be seen in the modern Town Gardens. There are decorative concrete paved areas and a general three-dimensional effect through using raised terraces and attractively planted containers set at different levels. The famous landscape architects of today, such as John Brookes and Sylvia Crowe are masters of this style but the ordinary householder building his own garden cannot find it easy.

MISCELLANEOUS GARDEN

Practically all home gardens have been created by the owners and are not the work of professional landscape architects. This means that there have been no rules laid down and no accepted standards of good taste.

The result is that a wide variety of layouts, ranging from the beautiful to the bizarre, can be found which do not fit in with the three basic styles described above. They are classed as *miscellaneous gardens.*

The garden may be purely decorative, as when the whole area is devoted to roses, dahlias, heathers or the Scandinavian pattern of grass and conifers. Or it may be strictly functional with all of the land turned over to vegetables. A style now fast disappearing is the Victorian garden still to be seen in our cities. There are complex beds, iron seats and flower vases, laurel bushes and monkey puzzle trees.

The most depressing type of miscellaneous garden is the neglected plot, representing 5 per cent of all gardens.

Hyll 1579

Tusser 1593

Lawson 1656

Parkinson 1629

Gerard 1597

Loudon 1822

Sweet 1833

Miller 1731

Warner 1891

Robinson 1883

Jeckyll 1900

Nicholson 1900

Middleton 1951

Pearson 1948

R.H.S. 1956

Hay & Synge 1969

Hessayon 1968

Reader's Digest 1968

Marshall Cavendish 1969

Hellyer 1972

Perry 1972

Both the quantity and quality of gardening books in Britain have dramatically risen during the past 15 years. The knowledge and the ability of the authors might not have changed, but there is now much more of a desire to communicate at all levels, and a desire to produce attractive pages as well as learned text. Colour is the new ingredient, and there are recent flower books which can be admired as works of art, and all-colour gardening encyclopaedias which are examples of superb condensation and simplification.

These publications are a long way from the first British gardening book, but we cannot with certainty name this original volume as this would call for a precise definition of gardening itself and that is quite impossible.

Perhaps the best contender is the first work to describe flowers and gardens as things to give pleasure as well as produce. On this basis the title goes to *De Naturis Rerum*, written in verse by Alexander Neckham in 1213. Another book written during the same period was *De Re Rustica* by Bishop Grosseteste of Lincoln. Destined to be one of the basic guides for over 200 years, it was really a translation of the work of a fifth century writer.

In this story of the British gardening book we shall find further examples of revered works which were nothing more than translations or ill-fitting adaptations of foreign books. Sometimes the source was not even acknowledged, and one of the most famous of all botanical books was guilty of this. But that comes later in the story.

The first booklet written in English was *The Feat of Gardening* by Master Ion Gardener. This collection of verses, written in 1400, described the flowers, trees, vegetables and herbs of the mediaeval garden, but the credit for the first practical English gardening book usually goes to Thomas Hyll, Londoner. His *A most brief and pleasant treatise teaching how to dress, sow and set a garden* was published in 1563. It is regarded as one of the foundations of gardening literature, and yet Hyll made it quite clear on the title page that his writing was "gathered out of the principallest authors in this art". So we are really looking at the work of Palladius, Cato, Columella and so on.

Thomas Tusser's book, on the other hand, was English through and through. His *Five Hundred Points of Good Husbandry* (1573) gave down-to-earth advice to the husband and wife working in the small Elizabethan garden. The rhyming couplets gave instructions on what to do, when to do it and how to save money . . . "One seed for another to make an exchange, With fellowy neighbours seemeth not strange". This was the first-ever best seller, reaching 13 editions before the end of the century. But, like his predecessors, Tusser had not produced a truly comprehensive gardening book. This was still to come.

The sixteenth century ended with Gerard's *Herbal* (1597). This is one of the best known of all early books on garden plants, and it is still being reprinted. Its influence has been immense, but it was not an original work. The great Belgian botanist Rembert Dodoens wrote a popular local flora of Dutch plants and this was translated by Dr. Priest into English. Gerard took the lot, without any acknowledgement, for his *Herbal*. Some snippets were added, such as descriptions of the potato and African marigold.

Books became much more plentiful in Jacobean times. William Lawson was the most influential of the early seventeenth century writers, and his *Country Housewife's Garden* (1617) and *A New Orchard and Garden* (1618) were very popular. This was the gardener and not the translator writing about things he had gleaned from "48 years and more experience in the North part of England".

Lawson's friend was Gervase Markham, a prolific and popular author who appears to have used the technique of issuing the same book under several different titles in order to increase sales! His works included *The English Husbandman* (1613) and *La Maison Rustique* (1616) which was a guide for the cottage garden.

In 1629 John Parkinson wrote his *Paradisi in Sole Paradisus Terrestris*. Some historians, such as Miles Hadfield, feel that the *Paradisus* was the first great English gardening book. Others, like Eleanour Rohde, believe that it will always remain the greatest. Parkinson described his book as a "speaking garden". It set the standard.

Between the *Paradisus* and Loudon's great *Encyclopaedia of Gardening* there are 200 years of gardening literature. Some of the books are milestones, like John Evelyn's translation of De La Quintinye's *The Complete Gardener* (1693) and the monumental *Gardener's and Florist's Dictionary* (1724) by Phillip Miller. This latter work remained the standard authority for a hundred years.

And then came the Loudons, whose prolific writings established the rules for the Victorian garden. *The Suburban Gardener and Villa Companion* appeared in 1838 and was the first book to take gardening to the middle class millions. Another book which influenced suburbia was the *Gardener's Assistant* (1859) written by Robert Thompson. The form of the present-day gardening textbook was now being crystallised.

Before listing the standard works on modern gardening we must first look at the books which started the trend. William Robinson's *The Wild Garden* in 1870 called for natural gardens planted with shrubs and trees. His most famous book *The English Flower Garden* advocated the sort of garden we know today. Equally influential was the writing of Gertrude Jeckyll, who wrote the first popular books on colour in the garden, flower arranging and gardening for children. Her *Home and Garden* remains a classic.

Today there are thousands of books from which you can choose. Easy-to-follow guides for the beginner, erudite tomes on a single species for the expert. You can pay 15p or £15. If you want a comprehensive textbook, there is the *Amateur Gardener* by A. G. L. Hellyer in black and white or the Reader's Digest *Gardening Year* in colour. There are many other admirable ones by Percy Thrower, Frances Perry, Roy Hay etc. Penguin, Pan and Hamlyn have published series of paperbacks.

The standard encyclopaedia is the 4 volume *R. H. S. Dictionary of Gardening*. Even larger is the 20 volume *Marshall Cavendish Encyclopaedia of Gardening*. The best-selling series (over 8 million) are the '*Be Your Own Expert*' gardening booklets.

For the identification of flowers, the standard works are *The Dictionary of Garden Plants* by Roy Hay and Patrick M. Synge, and the *Reader's Digest Encyclopaedia of Garden Plants and Flowers*. Perhaps the most attractive from the artistic viewpoint is *Flowers of the World* by Frances Perry and Leslie Greenwood. This beautiful book well illustrates the saying that in gardening everything turns full circle. The pictures are similar in brilliance to the best of the hand-painted drawings which our great-grandfathers enjoyed in their books . . .

BRITISH RECORDS

One of the most remarkable British records is the length of time that the craze for growing record-breaking fruit and vegetables has been popular. Even 450 years ago gardening caused "strife and contention between street and street", and this competitiveness reached its peak last century in the dirty back streets of the industrial cities. The annual competitions were held in local public houses and prizes went to the largest leeks, onions or gooseberries. The tradition is maintained today by the annual *Garden News* Giant Vegetable and Fruit Contest, from which many of the records listed below are taken.

HEAVIEST

Tomato 3 lb. B. Austin, Uttoxeter

Carrot 7 lb. 7 oz. A. Garwood, Blidworth

Potato 7 lb. 1 oz. J. H. East, Spalding

Apple	3 lb. 1 oz.	1965
Artichoke	8 lb.	1964
Beetroot	24 lb.	1971
Broccoli	28 lb. 15 oz.	1964
Brussels sprout	7 lb. 10 oz.	1966
Cabbage	123 lb.	1865
Carrot	7 lb. 7 oz.	1970
Cauliflower	52 lb. 12 oz.	1966
Celery	27 lb. 8 oz.	1970
Cucumber	10 lb. 2 oz.	1967
Leek	9 lb. 4 oz.	1968
Lemon	1 lb. 12 oz.	1969
Lettuce	16 lb. 2 oz.	1966
Marrow	60 lb.	1963
Onion	5 lb. 13 oz.	1965
Parsnip	9 lb. 4 oz.	1962
Pear	1 lb. 12 oz.	1966
Potato	7 lb. 1 oz.	1963
– crop from 6 tubers	1701 lb.	1971
Pumpkin	204 lb. 8 oz.	1970
Radish	16 lb. 8 oz.	1966
Savoy	38 lb. 8 oz.	1966
Shallot	1 lb. 7 oz.	1962
Strawberry	6 oz.	1968
Tomato	3 lb.	1964
– truss	14 lb. 8 oz.	1972
– plant	34 lb.	1957
Turnip	38 lb.	1972

TALLEST

Brussels sprout plant		7 ft.	1966
Kale plant		12 ft.	1950
Rhubarb plant		5 ft. 1 in.	1968
Sunflower plant		16 ft. 6 in.	1972
Tomato plant		20 ft.	1957
Tree :	Douglas fir at Powis Castle (Mont.)	181 ft.	
Broadleaved tree :	Lime tree at Duncombe Park (Yorks.)	154 ft.	
Trimmed hedge :	Beech trees at Meikleour (Perth.)	85 ft.	

OLDEST

Tree :	Yew at Aberfeldy (Perth.) reputedly 1500 years old.
Broadleaved tree :	Oak tree at Hatfield Broad Oak 800 years old.
Nursery :	Rivers of Sawbridgeworth (Herts.) founded 1725.

LARGEST

Runner bean 33¾ in. A. Bratton, Ryton

Broad bean pod		23⅜ in. long	1963
Carrot		15 in. long	1970
French bean pod		14½ in. long	1970
Lemon		4¾ in. diameter	1969
Mushroom		17¼ in. diameter	1957
Parsnip		50 in. long	1959
Pea pod		10⅛ in. long	1964
Runner bean pod		33¾ in. long	1966
Chrysanthemum bloom :	'Shirley Primrose'	12½ in. diameter	
Charm Chrysanthemum :	2100 blooms		1972
Dahlia bloom :	'Donald van der Mark'	17 in. diameter	
Oak tree :	Chirk (Denbigh.) Trunk is	12 ft. 10 in. diameter	
Private park :	Woburn Abbey (Beds.) 3000 acres		
Seed list :	Thompson & Morgan (Ipswich) catalogue – approx. 4500 varieties		
Vine :	Great vine at Hampton Court. Average yield ½ ton.		

3.The Allotment

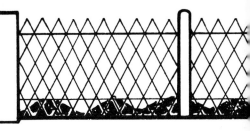

The 'industrious poor' of the nineteenth century were given the means to grow their own food by the first Allotments Act. This compelled local councils to rent small plots of land if a few 'registered parliamentary electors or ratepayers' demanded them. Allotments were born out of poverty and were fostered by two World Wars. In recent years there has been neither war nor mass poverty, and so the number of holdings has steadily fallen.

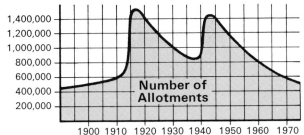

In our cities there are 'allotment gardens' – small plots on which the tenant is obliged to grow mainly vegetables and fruit for his own family. Sixty years ago the standard 10 rod (300 sq. yd.) plot was evolved, and rents remain at about 50p – £1.00 per year.

In country districts there is the true 'allotment', providing up to 5 acres and the right to use it as a farm or garden. So land is available in town and country at rates which are perhaps the lowest in Europe. More than 99 per cent of all urban areas have allotments to offer, and yet nearly one in five stands idle. Why?

There are several reasons. One of the most important is the strange fact that owning an allotment appeals to only a small and highly specific section of the community. Working in the garden appeals to all . . . young and old, rich and poor. But more than 82 per cent of allotment holders are over forty, only 3 per cent are women, and three in every four are either the sons of allotment holders or were born in the country.

The appeal to young married people living in flats has been surprisingly small. It is only the middle aged or retired man, who usually has a garden at home and has a tradition of working on the land, who is attracted by the idea of simple farming away from home.

The economic returns are not particularly good – about £50 net value in return for 500 hours per year. The satisfaction is tremendous, but the effort cannot be justified on economic grounds alone.

The attitude of some councils has helped the downward trend. Allotments are either not advertised or are neglected. In our city allotments only 50 per cent have piped water, 93 per cent have no toilet facilities and only 5 per cent have a car park. One in every three is not even properly fenced, and the fear

or effects of vandalism has caused many allotments to be surrendered.

Another reason quoted for giving up is insecurity of tenure. Notice of 3–12 months must be given and compensation paid for crops, manuring and disturbance. But this is little reward for a lifetime's work.

In short, there are about 60,000 acres of allotment land in Britain, one tenth of the total garden acreage maintained by a dwindling band of devotees. Once there were over a million of them, now there are about 400,000. Some experts believe that only an improvement in the sites is required to check the drift. Good roads, lock-up sheds, toilets, security of tenure, adequate fencing – these are claimed to be the answer. There are some encouraging signs to support this view; the model sites are attracting young homeowners and there are waiting lists at some of them.

It would seem that this is not enough. The 1969 Thorpe Report firmly stated that nothing less than a radical change in the present law would do. Professor Thorpe and his committee felt that we could no longer insist on food production – today's need is for leisure and so we should create leisure gardens. Their great success on the Continent is described on earlier pages. These weekend homes on the edge of town, with flowers, lawns and chalets, give city dwellers the chance to garden as a family. The Allenbank site at Cardiff was an early leisure garden experiment, and has been followed by other sites, notably at Birmingham and Coventry.

But some critics believe this Continental idea will never successfully cross the Channel. They quote vandalism, sleepy councils and the English seaside mania, but nobody *knows*. We must wait until the law is changed to see if Thorpe was right.

CITY versus CITY

The councils which look after our cities have an understandable pride in the flowers, lawns and trees which bedeck their streets and squares. Each one, of course, provides its standard public parks but some cities have tried to go one better. Glasgow has developed a pedestrian walkway system between its parks, one of which possesses a unique grove of fossil trees. Sheffield has created nature trails, one of which runs through its largest park.

All cities have been involved in a recent innovation – the attempt to brighten the whole urban area with plants and flowers by involving *everyone* – schools, shops, offices, factories and private gardens as well as the Parks Department. To reward the efforts of cities which work actively in this way there is a national competition held each year – *Britain in Bloom*.

This city versus city competition is organised by the British Tourist Authority and part of its purpose is obviously to make this country look more attractive to the tourist. But the London regional leaflet makes a good point – "Our visitors see us briefly, but we are here all the year round to see and appreciate London in Bloom."

Bath, Somerset

Each year nearly 300 cities, towns and villages compete for the Britain in Bloom awards. These entrants range from mighty conurbations to tiny hamlets, each one striving to be the best in its class.

Regional and inter-regional competitions result in 15 winners, and these go forward to the national competition which is judged by a panel of experts in September. The winning city becomes the "Floral City" for the year, and two places have been outstanding since the competition began in 1964. Bath has won the top award three times, Aberdeen four times.

Since 1970 there have also been "Floral Town" and "Floral Village" awards, and the Gordon Ford Trophy goes to the place where commercial enterprises have made the best efforts during the year. Here Bath has again been a trophy winner.

Everybody supports the basic aim of the Britain in Bloom campaign – "to encourage greater use of flowers, trees and shrubs in public and private decoration, and general improvement." Three sections are taken into equal consideration when judging – the public sector, commercial premises and private gardens.

Towns and cities with branches of national companies rather than local traders find it more difficult to get active support, and garden-conscious places find it harder each year to report spectacular improvements. So not all cities enter.

Support, however, is steadily growing and there is now more interest than ever in the announcement of the awards each October by the Chairman, Mr Roy Hay. All 33 of London's boroughs compete in the regional contest known as London in Bloom, and a commemorative plaque goes to the winner. The City of London has shown the way by being a prize-winner in the Britain in Bloom contest in every year from 1965 to 1971.

One of the features of the summer scene in Brighton is the line of 14 flower beds along the roadside at Preston Park, each one bedded out to a plan submitted by a town or horticultural society.

In early August the judging takes place, and trophies are awarded to the best displays. Towns in northern Britain have been well represented in recent years, and there is an International section in which Rotterdam and Canberra have been recent winners.

4. The Botanic Garden

The basic purpose of the Botanic Garden is the scientific study and collection of plants. The value of these institutions to the world has been enormous – the rubber industry of Asia was founded on the seedlings raised at Kew about 100 years ago.

The ancient Greeks and Romans and the monasteries had their collections but the first truly scientific garden was laid out at Padua in 1545. By the time Oxford Botanic Garden was opened in 1621 there were several flourishing establishments in Italy, Holland, Germany and France.

Some of Britain's Botanic Gardens are not open to the public, but you can write for permission to visit Aberystwyth, Bristol, Exeter, Leeds and Reading. Fortunately the greatest collections are open, and here you can see the superb displays of clearly labelled trees, flowers and exotic greenhouse plants from all over the world. The Royal Botanic Garden at Kew is one of the greatest horticultural sights of Europe, with over one million visitors coming to see the 25,000 different varieties of plants each year. Next comes the Royal Botanic Garden at Edinburgh which attracts about ½ million visitors each year.

A few of the Great Gardens of Britain, such as the Bedgebury National Pinetum, Westonbirt Arboretum, Harlow Car Gardens, Tresco Abbey Gardens and the Wisley R.H.S. Garden are sometimes classed as Botanic Gardens. The dividing line is a narrow one.

Palm House,
Royal Botanic Gardens, Kew

BOTANIC GARDENS OPEN TO THE PUBLIC

BOTANIC GARDEN	TOWN	OWNERSHIP	ACREAGE	SPECIAL FEATURE
Cruickshank Botanic Garden	Aberdeen	University	11	Alpine plants
Bath Botanical Gardens	Bath	Municipal	7	Chalk-loving plants
Birmingham Botanical Gardens	Birmingham	Private	17	Tropical plants
Bradford Botanic Garden	Bradford	Municipal	2	Economic and medicinal plants
University Botanic Garden	Cambridge	University	39	Winter garden ; rockery
Younger Botanic Garden, Benmore	Dunoon	National	100	Conifers ; rhododendrons
Royal Botanic Garden	Edinburgh	National	61	15,000 varieties of plants
Glasgow Botanic Gardens	Glasgow	Municipal	41	Orchids and ferns
University Botanic Garden	Hull	University	16	Ferns
Royal Botanic Gardens	Kew	National	296	Largest collection in UK
Garden of L. M. Mason	King's Lynn	Private	22	Greenhouse plants
Beaumont Hall	Leicester	University	7	Trees ; Elizabethan garden
City of Liverpool Botanic Garden	Liverpool	Municipal	126	Greenhouse plants
S. London Botanical Institute	London	Private	1	British wild flowers
Liverpool University Botanic Garden	Ness	University	43	Conifers ; heathers
University Botanic Garden	Oxford	University	5	Variegated plants
University Botanic Garden	St. Andrews	University	20	Alpines ; succulents
Logan Botanic Garden	Stranraer	National	14	Sub-tropical plants outdoors
University Botanic Garden	Swansea	University	4	Trees and shrubs
Museum Gardens	York	Private	10	Trees

GETTING INFORMATION...

...on gardening in general

The first step is to buy a good **Book** dealing with all aspects of home gardening. This will tell you what to do, when and how to do it and why it is necessary.

Encyclopaedias of this type come in a wide range of prices and sizes. A list of some of the more popular textbooks appears on page 33; your local bookseller or librarian will gladly give you further information. For a comprehensive list of gardening books, plus very brief comments, write to Landsmans Bookshop, Buckenhill, Bromyard, Herefordshire for their catalogue, price 10p. Do *buy* your basic guide rather than trying to work with a borrowed copy . . . it is frustrating to have to return your source of information to the library just as a problem arises!

Whether you buy or borrow the additional books which you will no doubt require depends on your keenness and your pocket. Two outstanding gardening libraries are the R.H.S. Library, Vincent Square, London SW1 and the Worshipful Company of Gardeners Library, Guildhall, London EC2.

Alongside your general textbooks you will need a picture guide to show you what to grow. Here the **Plant Catalogue** is the essential item for your book collection. Send for or pick up seed and plant catalogues; the coloured illustrations, brief descriptions and cultural notes will be invaluable. In addition there are excellent books you can buy or borrow, such as the *Oxford Book of Garden Flowers, Dictionary of Garden Plants in Colour* and the *Reader's Digest Encyclopaedia of Garden Plants and Flowers*.

However well-informed you are, it will still be necessary to keep up with new ideas, new discoveries and new varieties, as the gardening scene is constantly changing. This calls for reading regularly at least one **Gardening Magazine** (see page 40). Some magazines publish annuals – there are the *Do-it-Yourself Gardening Annual, Amateur Gardening Annual* and *Popular Gardening Annual*.

Don't forget the **Gardening Page** in your daily newspaper, local newspaper or woman's magazine. The Royal Horticultural Society Survey showed that 47 per cent of their members read the gardening column in their national paper and 27 per cent read the horticultural item in their local newspaper. The **Advertisements** on the gardening pages are a good source of information on what is new and what is available for your garden.

Books and magazines are not the only way of learning about gardening. Your local further education authority probably runs an **Evening Course** on General Horticulture for the amateur, and such courses are excellent for the beginner who finds it hard to learn from books. Some people find a **Correspondence Course** useful; if you want details write to I.C.S., Intertext House, London SW8.

For everyone, beginner and expert alike, there is the popular **Radio** programme *Gardeners' Question Time* (2.00 – 2.30 Sunday, repeat Tuesday, Radio 4). About $1\frac{1}{4}$ million people listen each week to the panel of experts answering questions posed by members of a local horticultural society.

Words, whether spoken or written, are not enough. Many cultural practices have to be seen in order to be understood. **Television** has been a great help here; *Gardeners' World* with Percy Thrower is shown weekly on BBC 2 during the growing season and 100,000 viewers watch this admirably practical programme. **Demonstrations** are held at the R.H.S. Gardens, Wisley between February and November, and deal with subjects such as sowing, planting, pruning and pest control. Demonstrations are also occasionally held at garden centres and public parks.

Join your local **Horticultural Society.** In this way you will find experienced gardeners to answer your questions. Furthermore, there will be **Lectures** to attend and **Shows** to visit.

This list of ways to acquire more knowledge about gardening is a long one. Use as many as you can if you wish to become an expert.

...on designing your garden

The trouble with building a new garden is that you have no chance to practise the art. In most cases it is the homeowner's first experience in garden-making, and mistakes are costly in terms of patience, time and money.

So do collect as much information as possible before you start. Look at other people's gardens for good and bad points, walk around garden centres to see what is available and read design articles and suggestions in magazines. There is a Penguin book called *Garden Design* (K. Midgeley) and Garden News publishes a handbook on the subject.

Most gardeners are prepared to adapt but are not willing to follow exactly a plan from a book or magazine. If you would like to have your garden individually designed by an expert, then you will have to pay for the plan. You cannot expect a company, magazine or newspaper to design a garden just for you as part of their free advisory service.

One magazine, *Homes and Gardens*, offers an inexpensive **Garden Planning Service.** A form appears in each issue, and after completion it is sent with a rough scale drawing, photographs and the fee of £3.50 to the magazine. You will receive a detailed plan of your new garden, drawn to scale with planting suggestions.

You may wish to employ a qualified **Landscape Architect.** He (or she) will visit the site, discuss your ideas and prepare a detailed plan. If you feel you need and can afford such a service, write to the Institute of Landscape Architects, 12 Carlton House Terrace, London SW1.

The basic problem of the new homeowner may still be unanswered – who is going to do the work? If you want a plan drawn and carried out by one company, then you need a **Landscape Gardener.** Many of the larger garden centres have an experienced landscaping department. Local newspapers often carry advertisements but do be careful; there are many unskilled beginners. A good plan is to write to the British Association of Landscape Industries, 44 Bedford Row, London WC1. They will send you the name of some local members, and you will have the safeguard that their work and experience is good enough to qualify them for membership of B.A.L.I.

. . . on a special group of plants

Your local library will undoubtedly be able to obtain a book for you on the particular plant you have chosen to study. Send for the R.H.S. Publications List, as most of their books are of a specialised nature. Above all, join the appropriate specialist society (see page 43). These groups, which often have less than 1,000 members, show a friendliness and willingness to help which is quite outstanding.

. . . on cut flowers and pot plants

Florists, garden centres, nurseries and other suppliers usually have a selection of free **Leaflets** which illustrate the popular varieties of house plants and tips on how to care for them. Inexpensive coloured guides are also available.

Dial 01 499 4191 for the **F.P.C. Telephone Service.** Listen to the advice on the weekly best buys of flowers and indoor plants, and information on their care. The recorded message is changed every Friday.

. . . on a gardening problem

Problems are inevitable. The first step is always self-help, looking through your books and pamphlets to see if the answer is there. For solving pest, disease and weed problems the free **Pest Charts** published by the major pesticide companies are invaluable. Try to obtain copies *before* problems arise.

The most popular method of problem-solving is to seek help from a **Keen Gardener.** This can be a neighbour, colleague or fellow member of a horticultural society. If the problem remains unsolved then there are several ways of obtaining help.

The **Advisory Bureau** of your gardening magazine will probably be able to provide the answer if the query can be put simply into words and is the type which has a definite solution. Pesticide companies, fertiliser manufacturers, seed houses, large nurseries and the gardening correspondents of newspapers run a similar service. If you need to send specimens, wrap them carefully. Sometimes it is easier to talk rather than write about a problem; your local garden centre or nursery will probably have somebody on the staff who can help.

If you live in a large town your **Parks Department** might run an advisory service for residents. The facilities offered vary widely from one town to another. Some offer leaflets, detailed advice, soil analysis and even lectures for club meetings. Glasgow, Liverpool, Manchester and Sheffield are outstanding in this respect. Other towns feel that skilled advice is already available from other sources.

The **Royal Horticultural Society** will try to answer any gardening query, and is able to call on highly skilled experts. Write to the R.H.S. Gardens, Wisley, Ripley, Surrey. Plant identification and pest or disease recognition are their strong points. A charge is made for manure analysis, soil analysis, fruit identification and garden inspection.

Perhaps the best single source of advice is your **County Horticultural Adviser.** Write to him at the following address:

ENGLAND

BEDFORDSHIRE:	Education Dept., Shire Hall, Bedford.
BERKSHIRE:	Agric. Education Section, 5 Abbott's Walk, Reading.
BUCKINGHAMSHIRE:	County Offices, Aylesbury.
CAMBRIDGESHIRE:	Shire Hall, Cambridge.
CHESHIRE:	Cheshire School of Agriculture, Reaseheath, Nantwich.
CORNWALL:	County Hall, Truro.
CUMBERLAND:	Cumberland and Westmorland Farm School, Newton Rigg, near Penrith.
DERBYSHIRE:	Derbyshire Farm Inst., Broomfield Hall, Morley.
DEVONSHIRE:	County Hall, Exeter.
DORSETSHIRE:	County Farm Inst., Kingston Maurward, Dorchester.
CO. DURHAM:	School of Agriculture, Houghall, Durham.
ESSEX:	Essex Inst. of Agriculture, Writtle, Chelmsford.
GLOUCESTERSHIRE:	County Farm Inst., Hartpury House, near Gloucester.
HAMPSHIRE:	County Farm Inst., Sparsholt, near Winchester.
HEREFORDSHIRE:	Herefordshire Education Committee, County Offices, Bath St., Hereford.
HERTFORDSHIRE:	Hertfordshire Inst. of Agriculture and Horticulture, Oaklands, St. Albans.
ISLE OF WIGHT:	County Hall, Newport.
KENT:	Kent Farm and Horticultural Inst., Swanley.
LANCASHIRE:	County Inst. of Agriculture, Hutton, Preston.
LEICESTERSHIRE:	Brooksby Hall Farm Inst., near Melton Mowbray.
LINCS (Holland):	Education Dept., County Hall, Boston.
LINCS (Kesteven):	Kesteven Farm Inst., Caythorpe Court, Grantham.
LINCS (Lindsey):	Education Dept., County Offices, Lincoln.
NORFOLK:	Burlingham Horticultural Station, near Norwich.
NORTHAMPTONSHIRE:	Northamptonshire Inst. of Agriculture, Moulton.
NORTHUMBERLAND:	20 Westbourne Av., Grange Park, Gosforth, Newcastle-upon-Tyne 3.
NOTTINGHAMSHIRE:	Nottinghamshire Farm Inst., Brackenhurst, Southwell.
OXFORDSHIRE:	Agricultural Education Dept., 23 Park End St., Oxford.
SHROPSHIRE:	Education Office, County Buildings, Shrewsbury.
SOMERSET:	Somerset Farm Inst., Cannington, near Bridgewater.
STAFFORDSHIRE:	Farm Inst., Penkridge, Stafford.
SUFFOLK:	Manor House, Bury St. Edmunds.
SURREY:	County Hall, Kingston-on-Thames.
SUSSEX (E.):	East Sussex School of Agriculture, Rodbaston, Plumpton, near Lewes.
SUSSEX (W.):	County Hall, Chichester.
WARWICKSHIRE:	22 Northgate St., Warwick.
WESTMORLAND:	See Cumberland.
WILTSHIRE:	Lackham School of Agriculture, Lacock.
WORCESTERSHIRE:	Agricultural Education Office, Royal George Buildings, Hanbury Rd., Droitwich.
YORKSHIRE (E. Riding):	County Hall, Beverley.
YORKSHIRE (W.Riding):	County Education Offices, Bond St., Wakefield.

WALES

ANGLESEY:	Coleg Pencraig, Llangefni, Anglesey.
BRECONSHIRE:	Education Offices, 4 Glamorgan St., Brecon.
CAERNARVONSHIRE:	Glynllifon Agricultural Inst., Clynnog Rd., Caernarvon.
CARMARTHENSHIRE:	Government Buildings, Carmarthen.
CARDIGANSHIRE:	Government Buildings, Lampeter.
DENBIGHSHIRE:	Llysfasi Farm Inst., Ruthin, Denbighshire.
FLINTSHIRE:	Flintshire Horticultural Inst., Northop.
GLAMORGANSHIRE:	Tregroes, Glamorgan School of Agriculture, Pencoed.
MERIONETHSHIRE:	County Offices, Penarlag, Dolgellau.
MONMOUTHSHIRE:	Monmouthshire Inst. of Agriculture, near Usk.
MONTGOMERYSHIRE:	Agriculture Education Office, Newtown.
PEMBROKESHIRE:	County Offices, Haverfordwest.
RADNORSHIRE:	Education Offices, County Hall, Llandrindod Wells.

SCOTLAND

EAST:	Edinburgh and East Scotland College of Agriculture, West Mains Rd., Edinburgh 9.
NORTH:	North of Scotland College of Agriculture, 581 Kings St., Aberdeen.
WEST:	West of Scotland College of Agriculture, Blythswood Sq., Glasgow C2.

CHANNEL ISLANDS

GUERNSEY:	States of Guernsey Horticultural Advisory Service, Hort. Expt. Station, P.O. Box 72, St. Martin's.
JERSEY:	States' Experimental Station, Howard Davis Park, Trinity.

NORTHERN IRELAND

Write to the Horticulture Advisory Service, Ministry of Agriculture, Dundonald House, Upper Newtonards Road, Belfast 4.

MAGAZINES

Reading a gardening magazine can be a pleasant way of passing half an hour on a bus or train journey. We are told what jobs to do at the weekend and the brightest annuals to sow in the spring. But the regular periodical has always had a more important job to do than merely presenting pages from the textbook.

Above all, it is the magazine's job to tell the gardener about important developments and trends – the new plants, new techniques, new designs and new equipment. Undoubtedly the *Gardener's Chronicle* deserves pride of place from the historical point of view. It began in 1841 as the first of the weeklies with a mixture of advertisements and articles. Right from the outset it provided the professional and keen amateur with information on current gardening trends. It is still being published, but it has been transformed into a trade journal.

Two magazines have actually started major trends in gardening. The first of all regular journals designed for the man in the street was the *Gardener's Magazine*, founded by John Claudius Loudon in 1826. This played an important part in revealing the secrets of practical gardening to the urban middle class for the first time, and it helped to dictate the pattern of the Victorian villa garden.

It was another magazine, *The Garden* started in 1871 by William Robinson, which persuaded people to move away from this Victorian style. For more than 50 years its pages poured scorn on highly formal design, and Robinson's magazine undoubtedly helped to foster the less formal style we see today.

Alongside the popular magazines there have always been the journals devoted to scientific horticulture. The *Botanical Magazine* founded by William Curtis in 1787 has straddled the centuries. Its glorious illustrations and detailed descriptions of garden plants made it world famous; the plates were still being hand-coloured in the 1930s. Detailed descriptions of new and interesting plants also appear in the *Journal of the Royal Horticultural Society*.

So many journals have come and gone – *Gardening Illustrated*, *The Rose*, *Home Gardener* and so on. Many good magazines remain, and the big five are listed below. Apart from these there are important specialist journals such as *Rose Bulletin* and *Flower Arranger*. In addition there are regional magazines, such as *The Gardener* which caters for Scotland and the North of England.

Frequency	Weekly	Weekly	Weekly	Monthly	Monthly
Price	6p	6p	7p	16p	Sent to members
Circulation (1972)	171,200	164,400	98,500	80,100	70,000
Founded	1884	1898	1958	1960	1804
Editor	Peter Wood N.D.H.	Fred Whitsey	Frank Ward	Stanley Russell	Elspeth Napier
Style	Glossy covers in full colour, appealing to the keen hobbyist gardener. Contributors include Percy Thrower, Roy Hay, Bob Woolley and Arthur Billitt.	Magazine format, with lots of pictures, advertisements and some colour. All subjects covered – flowers, vegetables, garden design and flower arrangement.	Lively newspaper format. Lots of Horticultural Society news. Specially caters for small garden and allotment holders, and exhibitors.	Essentially practical approach presented pictorially and entertainingly, with wide use of colour. Special features on readers' gardens.	Articles on growing and collecting garden plants for amateurs and professionals. Book reviews. Detailed descriptions of award plants.
Services	Extensive Gardening Advisory Service. Overseas tours, mainly in collaboration with Percy Thrower. Awards Scheme for flower shows.	Readers' Enquiry Bureau. Occasional supplements and special offers.	Readers' Advice Bureau – 300 queries per week. Overseas tours of horticultural interest.	Free Advice Service. Awards offered for gardening club shows.	News of forthcoming R.H.S. events and announcements of services available to members.

5. The Public Park

Britain, like the other countries of Europe, has a multitude of public parks – those areas of land owned by local authority, state or crown in which people can sit, walk or play. These areas provide a refuge from the noise and congestion of the towns in which they are sited, and a vital factor in their make-up is the combination of grass, trees and flowers.

Perhaps no other feature of the gardening scene in Britain has aroused so much criticism as the antiquated design of the average municipal park. As one authority wrote recently, it is the product of Victorian minds administering nineteenth century parks when the nineteenth century public had long since gone.

At the forefront of this criticism have been the architect, the landscape designer and the plantsman. But the ordinary public does not appear to be upset by the Victorian-style bedding, the bandstand, the iron seats and the 'keep off the grass' notices. A survey in London has indicated that seven out of ten people regularly go to a park and at least half the park visitors call in every week.

Leaving aside the over-discussed and over-criticised park bedding there is much to see, from the Gardening Demonstration Grounds in Sheffield to the 'Gardens of Greeting' competition held in Preston Park, Brighton, each year. There are the famous rose displays at Saughton Park, Edinburgh; Roath Park, Cardiff; Vivary Park, Taunton and of course at Queen Mary's Rose Garden in London with one of the largest public displays of roses in Europe. There is the superb rockery in Brighton, the peat garden in Harrogate and the landscaped cactus garden in Alexandra Park, Manchester.

Some of the better parks have removed many of the railings so beloved by the original designers. There is, of course, a saving in upkeep (Manchester spends more than £10,000 each year painting and repairing its park fences). Even more important is the indication that vandalism drops as the prohibitive barriers disappear and the standard of upkeep is improved. Convictions for park vandalism in England and Wales fell from nearly 2,000 in 1961 to 308 just six years later.

Maybe the young, like the planners, know that we must keep our parks. As overcrowding increases, so does the need for open spaces in which to escape . . . and that is how the public park began.

The workers in the mills and mines of the early nineteenth century needed air. The first Corporation-owned park was the Derby Arboretum, presented by a benefactor in 1840. A few years later the first park built by a town was opened at Birkenhead and soon the other industrial cities followed suit. By 1870 every sizeable town had its own park – part landscape as if built by Repton and part ironwork and flower beds in all their Victorian glory.

The royalty of Germany and Austria had created a number of public gardens before the opening of the Derby Arboretum, but the idea of town-owned parks for the working classes was a British idea. It spread to the Continent, and the municipal parks of Paris expanded from 50 to 4,500 acres in less than twenty years.

Now we must learn from Europe. Greater London has five acres of open space for every 1,000 people, Manchester has less than four. This area must not be allowed to shrink, and new parks are needed.

There are hopeful signs. Work has started on the 6,000 acre Lee Valley Regional Park, London, which is due for completion in 1985. In the New Towns there is an abundance of park and open space: 7 acres per 1,000 people in Harlow, 13 acres in Stevenage and 36 acres in Peterlee.

Many towns have notable parks – you will find them in Bath, Brighton, Eastbourne, Edinburgh, Birmingham, Norwich, Liverpool, Glasgow, Sheffield, Southport, and Stratford. But Parks Departments do more than maintain their show gardens; they also maintain that other vital piece of the British garden scene – the tiny gardens and squares within the heart of the city.

Royal Pavilion Gardens, Brighton

SOCIETIES & ORGANISATIONS

There are thousands of societies and organisations concerned with the many facets of the gardening scene – and nobody knows how many. New clubs appear each week, others close down, but the trend is definitely upwards as the interest in indoor and outdoor gardening grows. About 350,000 people belong to the National Trust, nearly 30 belong to the Pot Plant Growers Association. Between these two extremes lie the membership figures for other national societies.

Local horticultural and flower arrangement societies dominate the picture in terms of both numbers and members. It has been estimated that there are about 6,000 local societies with a total membership of 1 million. They arose, rather surprisingly, out of the early Industrial Revolution. The millworkers were still farm hands at heart, and they set up flower clubs to create judging standards and competitions for the plants they lovingly grew. The gardeners of the new industrialists set up professional associations. From these two sources came today's horticultural societies of village, factory and town.

Nearly all of the important local societies are affiliated to the Royal Horticultural Society, which was founded in 1804 to "collect every information respecting the cultivation of all plants and trees and to foster and encourage every branch of horticulture".

There are specialist societies which cater for specific sections of horticulture. The Royal National Rose Society has about 100,000 members, and no other specialist group can begin to approach such support. But they all do a valuable and important job by fostering interest in and improving standards for their particular subject.

NATIONAL ASSOCIATION OF FLOWER ARRANGEMENT SOCIETIES OF GT. BRITAIN

N.A.F.A.S. was founded in 1959 as the official organisation of the flower arrangement movement throughout Britain. You cannot join the National Association; its job is to look after the 20 Area Associations made up of local societies and clubs.

There are about 1,000 of these societies with nearly 100,000 members. They welcome newcomers although some have waiting lists. Men are still a rarity – more than 99 per cent of members are women. If you wish to join them the National Secretary, N.A.F.A.S., 21a Denbigh St., London SW1 will put you in touch with the nearest society. She will also send you a booklet if you want to start one in your area.

The *Flower Arranger* is published quarterly, price 15p. It is distributed exclusively through the local societies and is read avidly by 25,000 enthusiasts. Included in the magazine is an order form for the many N.A.F.A.S. publications, which include the *Show Handbook* and the *Handbook of Schedule Definitions*. The training of judges, demonstrators and teachers is a vital part of the National Association's duties.

Equally important is raising money for charity. More than £$\frac{1}{4}$ million has been collected by members during the past 12 years, and many displays are created for hospitals and churches.

N.A.F.A.S. is affiliated to clubs all over the world – in Japan, U.S.A., New Zealand, Canada, Africa and so on. But only Gibraltar, Malta and Monaco are affiliates in Europe. It is most surprising that the sales of cut flowers are appreciably higher in many Continental countries than in Britain, and yet the standards and interest in flower arranging as a hobby are much lower. At the moment N.A.F.A.S. leads the field in Europe.

ROYAL HORTICULTURAL SOCIETY

For a basic fee of £4.50 per annum anyone interested in gardening can become a Fellow of the Royal Horticultural Society. You need neither a proposer nor a seconder, nor do you have to pass an examination. Simply write for an application form to The Secretary, The Royal Horticultural Society, Vincent Square, London SW1P 2PE.

In return for the fee you will receive a Fellow's Ticket. This will admit you to all of the shows held at the Society's Halls in Westminster. These take place during every month except December, and lectures are usually given in conjunction with the shows.

In May your Fellow's Ticket will admit you to the Chelsea Flower Show, and there is a special 'Private View' card attached for admittance on Fellows Day. Finally, your Ticket will admit three persons to the Society's Gardens at Wisley (see page 44).

Young people under 18 who are recommended by a parent and a Fellow may be admitted as Junior Members. The subscription is £1.05 per annum. Many Fellows find that one ticket is not enough, and they pay a £7.00 subscription in order to receive two Fellow's Tickets.

There are several additional privileges apart from entry to shows and Wisley. You can use and borrow books from the R.H.S. Library. This houses 38,000 volumes and is probably the most distinguished gardening library in the world. Also, a Fellow can participate in the scheme for the distribution of surplus seeds from the Society's Garden. Advice on horticultural problems is freely available, but a charge is made for chemical analysis and garden inspection. Each month the R.H.S. Journal is mailed to Fellows.

Full advantage is taken of these privileges. A recent survey showed that 93 per cent of Fellows have been to Chelsea, 90 per cent to Wisley, 83 per cent to the Westminster Shows and 80 per cent keep their Journals for reference. More than one in four have written for advice, and 128,000 seed packets were distributed in 1972.

Part of the Society's function must be, of course, to serve the 68,622 membership and 2,396 affiliated societies. But it also has a much wider role to play – the furtherance of the cause and science of horticulture in Britain. Detailed answers are given to gardening queries by any member of the public. Honours are awarded to distinguished horticulturalists – there are 63 holders of the Victoria Medal of Honour (VMH) and 100 Associates of Honour.

The Society is the International Registration Authority for Daffodils, Dahlias, Delphiniums, Dianthus, Lilies, Orchids, Rhododendrons and Dwarf Conifers. It is responsible for recording the names of new cultivars of these plants.

Finally, the R.H.S. serves as the Examining Body for the National Diploma in Horticulture, the Teachers' Diploma in Horticulture for Schools, and the General Examination in Horticulture. The teaching of the young is well catered for, but the attraction of the young to the Society remains a major problem. Less than 5 per cent of Fellows are under 35, and Junior Members number just 71.

NATIONAL TRUST

In 1895 a woman, a knight and a churchman founded the National Trust for Places of Historical Interest or Natural Beauty. Buildings and land were steadily disappearing under the wheels of industrial progress, and the simple idea was for a group of private citizens to acquire places worth preserving and then hold them forever as trustees for the nation.

In 1907 the Government granted to the National Trust the right to declare its properties inalienable. This means that they can never be sold or compulsorily purchased without Parliament's permission.

The Government has given the Trust unique rights, but it is the public which must provide most of the money. Despite the generosity of many official organisations, it relies largely on members' subscriptions, gifts, legacies, covenants and rents.

The National Trust is the largest private landowner in Britain, and owns 200 historic houses and 100 gardens in England, Wales and Northern Ireland. The gardens are seen by more than two million visitors each year, and many of these people are members of the Trust.

Application forms are available at all properties, or write to National Trust Membership Dept., P.O. Box 30, Beckenham, Kent BR3 4TL. Ordinary membership is £3 per year. Family membership costs £3 for the first member and £1.50 for each additional member. Scotland has its own scheme (National Trust for Scotland, 5 Charlotte Square, Edinburgh EH2 4DU). Your membership card is a season ticket providing free entry to all the Trust properties in England, Wales, Northern Ireland and Scotland. You also get a full list of National Trust properties, three Newsletters a year and the Annual Report.

There are 350,000 members. Nearly 300 schools are corporate members and about 400,000 acres have been preserved for the nation, together with 300 miles of coastline. Many of Britain's great gardens belong to the National Trust (see page 22–26) and here it is more than just preservation. Neglected gardens such as Westbury Court, Castle Ward and Farnborough Hall are being restored to their former glory. For a full description of the N.T. Gardens, see *The National Trust Guide*, price £4.50.

The place of the National Trust in the British garden scene is summed up in the 1971 Annual Report – "Its properties will continue to offer solace and escape to millions".

FLOWERS AND PLANTS COUNCIL

In 1958 the F.P.C. was formed to encourage the greater use and enjoyment of fresh flowers and decorative plants. It is maintained by contributions from growers, wholesalers and florists.

Under its active Information Officer it has produced a number of informative free leaflets, but the F.P.C. Telephone Service has been the Council's biggest success. Newspaper advertisements invite the public to ring for information on plant care and the best buys (see page 38 for details). About 2,000 calls are received each week.

CENTRAL GARDENS ASSOCIATION FOR NORTHERN IRELAND

Many Ulster societies and organisations, including the Tourist Board and Civic Trust, are federated with the Central Gardens Association. This association arranges the "Best-Kept" competition for towns and villages, provides speakers for local meetings and publishes the annual *Ulster Garden Handbook.* Information is available from the Secretary, 2 Annadale Av., Belfast.

WORSHIPFUL COMPANY OF GARDENERS

The Gardeners Company is steeped in more than 600 years of tradition and service to the "trade, crafte and misterie of gardening". Once its power was immense – by the Royal Charters of 1605 and 1616 it controlled the standards of professional horticulture and for many years it was an offence to break these rules. At one time only the Freemen of the Company were allowed to trade as gardeners within the City of London.

Now its power has largely gone, and its role in setting standards has been taken over by the Royal Horticultural Society. But the strong spirit of ceremony remains. The Worshipful Company has the privilege of providing the Queen's bouquet at her coronation, and the bridal bouquet at the marriage of a Royal Princess. Five Court Dinners with distinguished guests are held each year. The grades of membership – Liveryman, Freeman, Patrimony Candidate, Apprentice – have the ring of a bygone age.

Nevertheless, the Gardeners Company is not a museum piece, and from its offices in Compter House, 4-9 Wood St., London EC2 it involves itself in many ways in the garden scene of today. It presents scholarships, administers floral competitions within the City and supports a number of London and horticultural charities. Its extensive gardening library in the Guildhall is open to all. Horticultural and floral arrangement societies can apply for Diplomas or Certificates of Merit for their annual shows.

Membership of the Gardeners Company is a sought-after honour. The maximum number of Liverymen is restricted to 250, and the waiting list is both long and distinguished.

SPECIALIST SOCIETIES

For the addresses of the begonia, cactus, chrysanthemum, dahlia, house plant, pelargonium and rose societies see the appropriate chapters.

ALPINE GARDEN SOCIETY: 58 Denison House, 296 Vauxhall Bridge Rd., London SW1
BRITISH FUCHSIA SOCIETY: 72 Ash Lane, Hale, Altrincham, Cheshire.
BRITISH GLADIOLUS SOCIETY: 25 Kimpton Av., Brentwood, Essex.
BRITISH IRIS SOCIETY: 72 South Hill Park, London NW3 2SN.
BRITISH NATIONAL CARNATION SOCIETY: 1 Woodham Rd., Catford, London SE6.
BRITISH PANSY AND VIOLA SOCIETY: 43 Northfield Lane, Horbury, Wakefield, Yorkshire.
BRITISH PTERIDOLOGICAL (FERN) SOCIETY: 46 Sedley Rise, Loughton, Essex.
DELPHINIUM SOCIETY: 5 Park Lane, Sevenoaks, Kent.
GARDEN HISTORY SOCIETY: 5 St. Margaret's Close, Berkhamsted, Hertfordshire.
HARDY PLANT SOCIETY: 10 St. Barnabas Rd., Emmer Green, Reading, Berkshire.
HEATHER SOCIETY: Yew Trees, Horley Row, Horley, Surrey.
INTERNATIONAL CAMELLIA SOCIETY: Bodnant Gardens, Tal-y-Cafn, Denbighshire.
NATIONAL SWEET PEA SOCIETY: 33 Priory Road, Rustington, Sussex.
NORTHERN HORTICULTURAL SOCIETY: Harlow Car Gardens, Harrogate, Yorkshire.
ORCHID SOCIETY OF GREAT BRITAIN: 87 Brookman's Av., Brookman's Park, Hertfordshire.
ROYAL CALEDONIAN HORTICULTURAL SOCIETY: 44 Melville St., Edinburgh 3.

 BRITAIN

LONDON

Nearly 1 in every 5 British residents live in London. More than 4 in every 5 tourists to Britain spend some time in the capital. There are a wealth of gardening sights to see– hop on a bus or tube in central London and you can quickly reach some of the outstanding gardens of Europe.

SYON PARK

The Gardening Centre at Syon Park has recently changed its image. It has brought in new family attractions such as the Transport Museum and no longer aims to be completely comprehensive in the horticultural field. But it remains a superb place for the gardener to visit. There is 'Capability' Brown's famous landscape, many rare trees and superb displays of houseplants and roses. See page 46 for further details.

SOCIETIES

There are many local horticultural societies in the London area and some of these are affiliated to the London Gardens Society (20 Buckingham St., London WC2).

Membership of the L.G.S. is open to all, and visits to various gardens in the area are arranged, window boxes and gardens on housing estates are judged, and the Noel-Buxton Cup goes to the best garden "cultivated under exceptional difficulties".

The Metropolitan Public Gardens Association (296 Vauxhall Bridge Rd., London SW1) strives to promote the creation, acquisition and preservation of land for public use within the Greater London area.

ROYAL BOTANIC GARDENS, KEW

Kew holds a special place in the study of plants. It houses the largest botanical library in the world, it has the most comprehensive collection of dried plant specimens in its herbarium and there are about 100,000 different living plants in its gardens and glasshouses. Yet most of the million visitors who come each year know little about scientific botany; for them Kew is a garden.

Part of the 300 acres is woodland. The northern part is more formal, and here you will find the Rock, Iris, Herb and Aquatic gardens. In the Herbaceous Ground the plants are grouped in families for the scientifically minded; a reminder that Kew has a school for student gardeners.

There are a number of notable buildings – the Pagoda, Orangery, Palace and Museums. Above all, perhaps, are the many glasshouses with their spectacular collections.

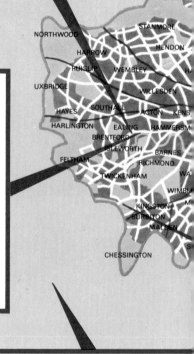

THE LONDON PLANE

For nearly 200 years this hybrid of the western plane and the oriental plane has graced the parks and squares of London, and is now the capital city's best known tree.

The flaking bark makes it easy to recognize, and it can reach a height of 100 ft. The finest specimens are to be seen in Berkeley Square, and were planted in 1789.

R.H.S. GARDENS, WISLEY

Just off the London–Portsmouth road (A3) between Cobham and Ripley you will find the R.H.S. Gardens. Its 200 acres contain the most complete collection of garden plants in Britain. It is open all year round and the 62 page guide book is crammed with things to see. You can look at demonstration home gardens, inspect trials in the Portsmouth Field, obtain advice on horticultural problems and watch how-to-do-it demonstrations. There is a School of Horticulture here, and Wisley is correctly described in the leaflet as "one of the finest gardens in the world".

Visit it more than once if you can. In the spring for the extensive display of bulbs and alpines, in summer for the roses and herbaceous borders.

DERRY & TOMS ROOF GARDEN

Although taken over by Biba in 1973, the Roof Garden remains on top of Derry & Toms, 100 ft. above the traffic jams and busy shoppers in Kensington. One and a half acres of lawns, ponds and magic in the middle of London – the Tudor garden, Spanish garden and Woodland garden. There are vines, peaches and palms as well as everyday plants and trees.

LONDON SQUARES

Dotted throughout central London are small green oases in the heart of busy streets. These rectangular areas of closely-mown turf, spring bulbs, summer bedding plants and trees were created to bring the country to the grand town houses built around the periphery. In Chelsea and Kensington some squares are still privately owned, and only the residents have keys. The remainder are public squares, serving as miniature parks for residents and tourists.

CITY OF LONDON GARDENS

Within the square mile of the City of London lies the commercial and historical heart of the capital city. In 1963 the *Flowers in the City* campaign was launched, and it has been an outstanding success. Business houses have provided window-boxes and have undertaken forecourt plantings, and there are about 80 small gardens and open spaces administered by the Corporation. These range from Finsbury Circus with its bandstand and bowling green to the flower bed in Cheapside with a couple of trees and some bedding plants. The standards have been high enough to win two Civic Trust Awards and a succession of prizes in the *Britain in Bloom* competition.

The City of London Corporation owns or administers large parks and open spaces outside its own square mile – Highgate Wood, Burnham Beeches and the 6,000 acres of Epping Forest are examples.

CHELSEA FLOWER SHOW

Britain's most important Flower Show draws people from all over the country. More than 60 per cent of the visitors travel to London especially for this late May show, held each year in the grounds of the Royal Chelsea Hospital. The first day (Tuesday) is for Fellows of the Royal Horticultural Society; Wednesday to Friday are for everyone. Not quite everyone – children under 5 are not admitted. This could account for the relative absence of young married couples; 85 per cent of visitors are over 30 years old.

At the centre of the show is the $3\frac{1}{2}$-acre marquee, with trade exhibits of flowers and vegetables competing for gold and other medals. There are many other things to see– a scientific exhibition, a horticultural information bureau, a floral display area and scores of garden equipment and sundries stands. You cannot buy plants and equipment at Chelsea – orders are taken for subsequent delivery.

HAMPTON COURT

Hampton Court Palace Gardens were the first of the grand gardens of Britain, and still remain the most popular. The 200-year old Great Vine continues to fascinate the Sunday crowd, and struggling through the Grand Maze is part of growing up in London.

It is here you must come if you want to turn the pages of the picture book of our gardening history. There is an ancient pleached alley and the 'Kinges Beastes' of Henry VIII stand guard. Apart from these Tudor touches, there is the Broad Walk in the Grand French manner and the Great Fountain Garden of Dutch William. Today's fashion in gardening is represented by the magnificent herbaceous border – 1,000 ft. long and perhaps the best in the country.

Fifty five acres of tradition, which even two centuries ago was strong enough to prevent the Landscape School from bringing in the lakes, hills and temples which changed so many gardens.

LONDON PARKS

Pitt described the parks as the lungs of London, and since his day they have continued to be a vital part of the scenery. They have impressed visitors for more than a century; Napoleon III redesigned the Bois de Boulogne in Paris in order to rival Hyde Park which he had seen during his exile.

Hyde Park and the adjoining Kensington Gardens (630 acres) make up the largest public park in central London. This is considerably smaller than other Royal Parks on the outer fringes of the capital – the 4,800-acre Windsor Great Park (which includes the superb Savill Garden) and the 2,400-acre Richmond Park where deer still roam.

In addition to these parks administered by the Ministry of Works, there are 7,500 acres under the control of the Greater London Council and 33,000 acres owned by London Borough Councils. The total number of parks runs into hundreds, and for details of where to go and what to see, obtain *Parks of Greater London* (3p) and *Parks for all Seasons* (35p) from the G.L.C. Bookshop, County Hall, London SW1.

45

6. The Flower Show

The annual Summer Flower Show is an important event in the life of towns and villages throughout Britain. This unique aspect of our national scene involves the show secretaries of the local horticultural society and allied clubs. It is their duty to painstakingly arrange the displays and of course the heart of the show – the exhibition of flowers, fruit and vegetables competing for prizes.

The exhibitors are not a small and select group of expert gardeners – no fewer than 750,000 people compete in these shows. If you wish to become an exhibitor, your first task is to obtain and carefully read the *schedule* well in advance of the show date. Some of the terms you may find, such as cultivar, saladings, corolla etc., may be new to you. Check in books or with the secretary. From this schedule select one or more *classes* in which you wish to compete. Then submit your entry form by the appointed day.

If you want to take exhibiting seriously, or if you wish to improve your chances of winning a prize, then you must obtain a copy of the exhibitor's bible – *The Horticultural Show Handbook* published by the Royal Horticultural Society, price 50p.

The motive for exhibiting is certainly not money. In most cases the prize is very small – a few pence or a box of fertiliser. The Handbook advises the would-be exhibitor that "there is more honour in exhibiting well in a strongly contested class without winning a prize than in winning a prize in a class where there is little or no competition." But there can be little doubt that the main driving force is the desire to win that cherished card stating First Prize, Second Prize, Third Prize, Fourth Prize, H C (Highly Commended) or C (Commended).

The local show is generally a pleasant Saturday afternoon affair. The city or national show may last for two days or even longer, and the prizes are much more valuable – gold and silver gilt medals, silver cups, medals and salvers.

A regular series of shows are held at the R.H.S. Halls in Westminster. There is an Opening Flower Show in January and the year ends with the November Flower Show. Some of these exhibitions are staged by specialist societies – the National Orchid, Dahlia, Rose and Chrysanthemum Shows are held at Westminster. The appeal is to the more knowledgeable gardener, and the total yearly attendance is 82,000.

SYON PARK GARDENING CENTRE

Queen Elizabeth the Queen Mother opened the Gardening Centre in June 1968 and the dream of many people came true. Britain at last had its own National Exhibition of Gardening.

The 55 acres of display grounds were crammed with items of interest. More than 400 varieties adorned the 6 acre rose garden; house plants, cacti and orchids filled the 382 ft. conservatory; the whole range of modern equipment, sundries and plants were there to be admired and bought. Bookshop, technical advice bureau . . . truly a place to spend a day with all of the family.

But the dream surprisingly faded. The average visitor was over 45 and unaccompanied by children. The annual attendance was 250,000 – not the expected 1 million. So in 1973 Syon Park became a beautiful grand garden and an active garden centre. But the idea of a comprehensive National Exhibition of Gardening was abandoned.

TRENTHAM HORTICULTURAL CENTRE

Trentham Gardens have recently taken on the mantle of a National Horticultural Centre. Many show gardens have been created, 12 model home gardens have been laid out, flowering shrub trials can be seen and there is one of the largest bedding displays in Europe. Trentham Gardens have successfully fostered the "complete one-day package holiday" idea with boating, swimming, funfairs, miniature railway and 500 acres in which to walk and picnic. Annual attendance is 400,000.

R.H.S. GARDENS, WISLEY

Wisley remains the true mecca for the keen gardener. Without claiming to be Britain's Gardening Centre, here is one of the greatest horticultural exhibitions in the world. Annual attendance is 217,000; see page 42 for further details.

SHOW OR EXHIBITION	MONTH	ANNUAL ATTENDANCE
Daily Mail Ideal Home Exhibition, London	MARCH One of Europe's great house & garden exhibitions	960,000
Scottish Spring Flower Show, Edinburgh	MARCH	10,000
Harrogate Great Spring Flower Show	APRIL	40,000
Spalding Flower Parade	MAY A mile of tulip-decorated floats	250,000
R.H.S. Flower Show, Chelsea	MAY Britain's most famous flower show; see page 44	147,000
National Rose Show, London	JUNE	20,000
Leeds Flower Show	JULY	15,000
Liverpool Show	JULY	110,000
Newcastle-upon-Tyne Summer Exhibition	AUGUST	145,000
Shrewsbury Musical & Floral Fete	AUGUST	75,000
Southport Flower Show	AUGUST	110,000
Ayr Flower Show	AUGUST	19,000
Birmingham City Show	SEPTEMBER	78,000
Scottish Autumn Flower Show, Edinburgh	SEPTEMBER	10,000
Cardiff Horticultural Show	SEPTEMBER	15,000

7.The Supplier

❝ I cannot omit nor spare to deliver my mind, concerning the great and abominable falsehood of those sorts of people which sell garden seeds... **❞**
Profitable Instructions for Manuring, Sowing and Planting of Kitchen Gardens (R. Gardiner 1603)

The first gardening catalogue warned the reader about the unscrupulous nurseryman and seedsman. Today such warnings are not necessary as we have a highly responsible industry and the gardener is protected by a number of laws. Perhaps the most important is the Trade Descriptions Act 1968, as this makes it an offence to offer an item for sale with a false description. So "Two year old bushes, guaranteed to flower" must be 2 years old and money must be refunded if they fail to bloom. The Seeds Act 1920 spells out the minimum purity and minimum germination rate for vegetable seeds. The Fertiliser and Feeding Stuffs Act 1926 states that any product which is claimed to be a fertiliser must declare the nitrogen, phosphates and potash content, and this statement has to be correct. Finally, the Farm and Garden Chemicals Act 1967 obliges the pesticide manufacturer to state the active ingredient on his bottle or box.

Up to twenty years ago there was a stable arrangement for the supply of garden needs. There were two mainstays – the nurseryman supplied plants at the appropriate time of the year, either by post or at the nursery; the corn and seed shop sold seeds and sundries as well as plants. In addition Woolworths was important, and so were Boots, the ironmonger, the department store and the florist.

This pattern was disturbed when the garden centre arrived. By the early 1960s this idea from Australia and the U.S.A. was taking root and by 1970 there had been a rapid development in both numbers and quality. Many factors have contributed to this growth but two are outstanding. The container-grown plant means that active selling can take place throughout the year and the garden centre can sell its wares on Sunday because they are perishable. So seven-day-a-week, year-round selling is possible, and about 30 per cent of the gardening population call during the year. About one in every two makes a purchase.

The number of establishments now selling gardening supplies has expanded enormously. It is not just garden centres – there are supermarkets, cash and carry stores, even breakfast cereal companies with premium offers. It is estimated that 150,000 outlets sell or have sold one or more gardening items, and of these 2,000 specialise in gardening. The vast majority of sales go through about 4,000 retailers.

Despite Britain's preoccupation with horticulture, no national chain of specialised gardening shops has appeared. It is arguable whether this is a strength or a weakness.

The supplier side of gardening has always been highly individualistic and has had more than its share of great characters. These people have done more than satisfy the customers' wants – they have created the pattern and the plants. It was the London and Wise nursery at Brompton Park which stamped French gardening all over Britain in the eighteenth century. From James Veitch & Sons Ltd. at Chelsea came nearly 500 new hybrids and many new plants brought back by their plant hunters in the nineteenth century.

THE MARKET

1970 estimates of retail sales	£ million
Cut flowers	45
Pot plants	15
Bulbs	12
Roses	11
Bedding plants	10
Seeds	8
Other plants	5
Lawn mowers	25
Chemicals/fertilizers	18
Tools	16
Sheds	5
Greenhouses	5
Miscellaneous items	10

HORTICULTURAL TRADES ASSOCIATION

This organisation was founded in 1898 to represent all of the various trades which serve the gardener. It deals with the Government on questions of legislation, it seeks to publicise all aspects of gardening and it organises Proficiency Tests for shop assistants. The HTA sets out to keep its 1000 members informed of trends and events which affect the horticultural industry.

Garden Gift Tokens are available where you see this sign. They can be exchanged for plants, seeds or other garden requisites at any shop, nursery or garden centre where the sunflower symbol is displayed. These tokens are becoming increasingly popular.

INTERNATIONAL GARDEN CENTRE ASSOCIATION (British Group)

In 1970 the Garden Centre Group of the Horticultural Trades Association decided to join the International Garden Centre Association. Within a couple of years the British Group of the IGCA became the largest and most powerful section of the Association. Its members represent about one half of all of the garden centres in this country, and when you see the symbol displayed you know that certain standards are being met. These are checked regularly. As a minimum, there must be toilet and parking facilities, an employee who can give advice, a comprehensive range of products and adequate displays of hardy plants, house plants and sundries.

A PICTURE GUIDE TO

*"Classes AX, A and B are available in
the following separate colours: crimson,
scarlet, salmon, rose ..."*
Begonia Catalogue

But exactly what colours *are* crimson, scarlet,
salmon and so on? Tests have shown that few
people can with confidence select scarlet or
vermilion from a pack of assorted red cards.

The naming of flower colours is notoriously
difficult and many charts have been produced in
Europe. In Germany there is the classification by
Hickethier with its 1000 colours and until
recently the standard British authority was the
Horticultural Colour Chart published in 1941.
These systems generally rely on naming and
numbering each basic colour together with tints

(lighter versions of the same colour). Darker
versions of a colour are called shades.

Unfortunately some common terms, such as
mauve and lemon, cover a wide range of tones. So
in 1966 the Royal Horticultural Society Colour
Chart was introduced. This relies solely on a
combination of letters and numbers for identification, and has proved invaluable to the
specialist and scientist.

But the gardener must continue to rely on
words, and the guide below illustrates some of
the colour names found in plant catalogues.

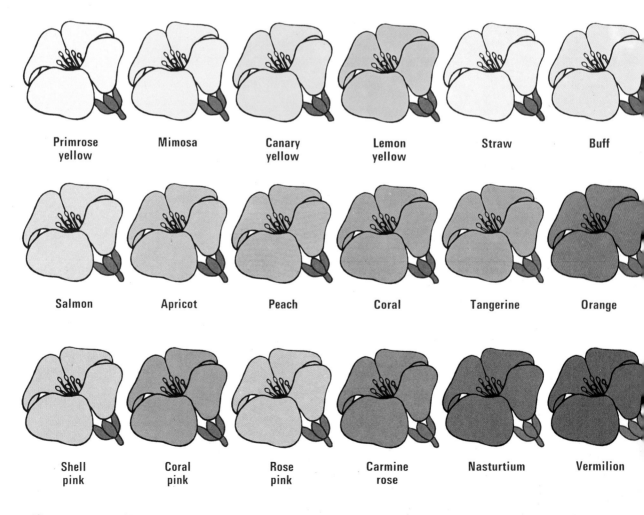

Primrose yellow	Mimosa	Canary yellow	Lemon yellow	Straw	Buff
Salmon	Apricot	Peach	Coral	Tangerine	Orange
Shell pink	Coral pink	Rose pink	Carmine rose	Nasturtium	Vermilion

Brick red

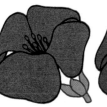

Scarlet

Blood red

Crimson

Magenta

Ruby

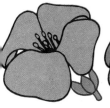

Mauve

Lilac

Cyclamen

Petunia

Violet

Heliotrope

Sea blue

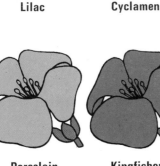

Porcelain blue

Kingfisher blue

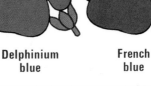

Delphinium blue

French blue

Gentian blue

BLUE—the colour that got away

There are many beautiful blues in the flower world — the gentian, the delphinium and the cornflower. But this colour is missing from some of our most important garden flowers. A blue begonia is still awaited. There is no blue-flowered cactus, although *Cereus chalybaeus* and several others have deep blue stems when young. The real interest, however, is in finding the blue rose and the blue dahlia.

The blue rose

According to Sam McGredy, the first true blue rose should earn a million pounds for its raiser. His grandfather is reputed to have thrown one away, and we shall never know whether this was really the elusive true blue or merely a lavender or violet like today's so-called "blue" roses. The first of these was the hybrid tea 'Prélude', bred by Meilland in 1954. 'Sterling Silver' with its silvery lilac petals marked another step forward and in 1964 Tantau introduced 'Blue Moon', the most popular of all the near-blue roses. The lavender-coloured 'Silver Star' (Kordes 1966) is perhaps the best to date.

The blue dahlia

Ever since 1840 plant breeders have been searching in vain for the blue dahlia. A prize of £1000 was offered about 100 years ago, and it remains unclaimed. Millions of seedlings are raised every year in the hope of finding this elusive colour. There are a number of mauve and lilac-coloured dahlias — 'Meiro', 'Amethyst', 'Bonny Blue' and so on. The best of these is the giant decorative 'Nearest Blue', raised by Britain's most distinguished dahlia breeder, H. Stredwick. But its flowers are really mauve, and many experts believe that pure blue is impossible. Despite this, the search goes on.

Petals plain

The petals of most wild flowers are **self-coloured**, which means that there is little or no variation in the single colour which covers the surface. In our modern garden flowers we find countless varieties where one or more extra colours have been introduced into the petals, and the word **fancy** is sometimes used to describe outstanding examples of such flowers.

There is a host of specific terms for the various colour combinations, and there is a great deal of confusion as to the exact meaning of *laced*, *tipped*, *flamed*, *painted*, *suffused*, *flushed* and so on. It is impossible to define all of the terms which have been used (and misused!) but below is a simple guide to the three main groups.

and fancy

BLENDED FLOWERS

In a blended flower the petals possess two or more colours, with one gradually merging into the other. The basic factor here is that there is no sharp dividing line between one colour and the next. In many cases one colour disappears as the other takes over; in other blends the ground colour remains and is said to be **tinted, flushed, suffused** or **overlaid** with the second colour.

BICOLOURED FLOWERS

Flowers showing two quite different colours, such as the red dahlia 'Mrs. McDonald Quill' with its white-tipped petals, are sometimes described as bicolours. In roses, however, the term has a specific meaning – the bicolour here has petals in which the inside colour is distinctly different from the outside. Popular examples are 'Caramba', 'Tzigane', 'Piccadilly', 'Ideal Home', 'Rose Gaujard' and 'Gail Borden'.

VARIEGATED FLOWERS

In a variegated flower the petals possess two or more colours with a fairly distinct dividing line between them. There are, of course, scores of variations. The ground colour can be **tipped** by the second colour, or it can be **spotted, striped, splashed** (broken stripes of various sizes), **flaked** (broad stripes running inward from the edges) or **blotched** (irregularly scattered patches).

In a **picotee** the ground colour of the petal is white or pastel, and there is a narrow but distinct band of colour around the edge. If the strip of colour is more than ⅛ in. wide it is called heavy-edged, if less then the bloom is a wire-edged picotee. Picotee varieties are popular in both carnations and begonias.

In a **feathered** flower the petals have coloured edges which are fringed with fine lines extending inwards. Examples are found in both crocuses and virus-infected ('broken') tulips. Where in addition there is a band of solid colour extending up the centre of the petal then the bloom is described as **flamed**.

A PICTURE GUIDE TO
Pelargoniums

G is for geranium in the horticultural ABC of Europe. This plant, with its umbels of red, pink or white flowers is found in gardens, window boxes, balconies, glasshouses and on window sills everywhere from Scandinavia to Spain. But, as any botanist will tell you, the bedding "geranium" is not really a geranium at all; it is the zonal pelargonium.

Look closely at the leaves. You will find a distinctive horseshoe marking or "zone" in nearly all varieties and that is where the name comes from. With the fancy-leaved group this leaf marking is more decorative than the flower. The zonal pelargonium can be made to bloom at any time of the year providing the temperature is at least 50°F. and that the light is bright enough. With care you can have specimens in bloom in the greenhouse for nine months or even more each year.

The universally-known zonal pelargonium has an aristocratic relation – the regal or show pelargonium. These are the beauties of the pelargonium world with their shrubby growth, saw-edged leaves and large, bi-coloured ruffled flowers. But they do have their problems. They are not suitable for bedding outdoors and are only used for indoor display. Also their flowering period is often limited to about two or three months during early summer.

Another relative is the ivy-leaved pelargonium, which is a highly adaptable plant widely used by the European gardener. Its long pliable stems make it suitable for weeping over hanging baskets, window boxes, balconies, etc., or training up canes and trellis work.

The scented-leaved varieties are the final major group. These were the darlings of the Victorian age, grown in cottages and conservatories for their property of producing a strong fragrance when the foliage is crushed. In the home the leaves were used for garnishing, jam making, etc., and in industry are still used to produce substitutes for more expensive flower oils.

You don't need green fingers to succeed with pelargoniums. They have few pests or diseases and even fewer fussy demands. All they need is plenty of light and a free-draining soil. Remove the dead flower heads to prolong the flowering period and pinch out the growing points occasionally to keep the plants bushy. Indoors the pots should be kept regularly watered and fed in summer, with some shading if they are displayed in the greenhouse. In winter store the pots in a cool but frost-free place, and water sparingly.

Propagation is as easy as cultivation, and it is a shame that so many people buy their stock afresh each spring. You can sow seed, but the standard method is to strike cuttings (3-inch stem tips) in pots of Cutting Compost in August or September.

The old favourites, Paul Crampel and Gustav Emich, still dominate the displays in Britain, but there are now many types from which you can choose. There are dwarf varieties which reach only 8 inches. There are stellars, irenes, rosebuds and deacons. Miniature pelargoniums grow less than 5 inches tall; standards can reach 6 ft. To see a selection of modern varieties go to a large garden centre, Syon or the Royal Parks. Best of all visit a specialist nursery such as Clifton Nurseries (Chichester), Morden Nursery (near Wimbledon), Cypress Nursery (Birmingham), or Wyck Hill Geraniums (Stow-on-the-Wold).

In Britain there has been a pelargonium revival. The British Pelargonium and Geranium Society (129 Aylesford Av., Beckenham, Kent) is flourishing, and its 1,800 members receive bulletins, advice and a year book for their £1.00 subscription. Yet the pelargonium is never truly at home in Britain. It must be lifted from the garden before the first frosts and allowed to sleep indoors until the end of May. Only in rare western spots such as the Scilly Isles can it grow outdoors as a perennial, and in wet seasons it tends to produce more leaves than flowers.

In the dry and frost-free areas of southern Europe the pelargonium comes into its full glory. Here the ivy-leaved varieties can be seen cascading as shrubby perennials from balconies and pots, and on the hillsides the zonal pelargonium has become naturalised in a home which reminds it of its native South Africa.

ZONAL PELARGONIUM

Other names: Geranium
Bedding geranium

Fancy-leaved varieties

Flowers ½–1 inch across.
White, pink, salmon, red, purple

single   double   cactus

Marechal MacMahon   Distinction   Mrs Henry Cox

Caroline Schmidt   Happy Thought   Mrs Pollock

Verona   Miss Burdett Coutts   Black Cox

REGAL PELARGONIUM

Other names: Show pelargonium
Show geranium

Carisbrooke   Muriel Harris   Elsie Hickman   Zulu King

Flowers 1½–2 inches across.

SCENTED-LEAVED PELARGONIUM

**P. karooense
(P. capitatum)**
scent: rose

P. crispum
scent: lemon

P. graveolens
scent: rose

P. tomentosum
scent: peppermint

P. odoratissimum
scent: apple

IVY-LEAVED PELARGONIUM

derived from *P. peltatum*

Fancy-leaved varieties

Flowers are usually double.
White, pink, mauve, red

Crocodile   L'Elégante

THE GARDEN SCENE
IN FRANCE

VERSAILLES

Grand gardens in the French style

In 1661 at Vaux-le-Vicomte the French Style of grand gardening, *le jardin français*, burst into flower. At his first attempt André Le Nôtre had perfected a new formula for achieving grandeur, and for a century France was destined to reign supreme over the European gardening scene.

Before 1661 the gardens around the châteaux of France were generally divided by hedges, walls or trellis work into various compartments such as the flower garden, the vegetable garden and the symbolic garden. The gardens were places for quiet enjoyment or meditation. They have been swept away by the waves of later fashions, like the French Style or English Landscape, but you can travel back into history at **Villandry,** a few miles from Tours. At this world-famous château you can see a twentieth century reconstruction of a pre-Le Nôtre garden. There are 12 acres set on four levels, and the visitor looks down from the terrace on to the much-photographed symbolic garden with its intricately planted box hedges representing the four different kinds of love. Of equal interest is the *potager*, or kitchen garden, which in those early days was set out as a place of colour and beauty as well as food production.

But the wealth and pomp of the Sun King era wanted more than a place for meditation, and Le Nôtre provided the answer with his grand French Style. The garden was transformed into a vast outdoor drawing room, for music, entertaining, masked balls, flirtations, intrigue but certainly not for smelling the flowers or cutting the vegetables.

Vaux-le-Vicomte, an hour's drive from Paris, will show you how this was achieved, for the gardens were restored to the Le Nôtre pattern in 1875. Here you will find the great parterres, the long magnificent vistas, the pools and strict geometry which characterise *le jardin français*. Grander still is **Versailles** with its mile-long Grand Canal, its Royal Alley lined with marble vases, its vast parterres. There are 250 acres of this breathtaking grand garden; do not miss the Parterres du Midi, Orangerie, Bassin de Neptune and the Parterres d'Eau. On several Sundays between May and September the fountains are switched on and this display is one of the sights of Paris.

It is often debated whether Vaux-le-Vicomte or Versailles was Le Nôtre's masterpiece, but today's visitor cannot judge. Both gardens have changed considerably since their creation – much of Vaux-le-Vicomte went to Versailles and at Versailles many of the statues, fountains and hornbeams have gone, whilst other features have been added.

The French Style can be seen without leaving home. Melbourne Hall in Derbyshire is Britain's best example. In Spain there is La Granja, in Russia there is the Peterhof. Many European countries created *les jardins français*, and good examples remain, but perhaps the style is only truly at home in its native France. Here many grand gardens in the La Nôtre tradition were created during the seventeenth and eighteenth centuries, especially in the Ile de France and Loire Valley, and outstanding examples are described later in this chapter.

Suddenly it was France's turn to copy. In the middle of the eighteenth century the Landscape Garden, *le jardin anglais*, became fashionable all over Europe. The French, however, never set about the wholesale destruction of their formal heritage as occurred in Britain and Germany. Instead a pastoral landscape was set within the formal garden, as at Versailles, or built alongside the *jardin français* as can de seen today at the Château de Lunéville. And so many grand gardens in the French Style remain, as places where you will want to stand back to admire the view rather than lean forward to smell the flowers.

Le Nôtre – GARDEN MASTER OF EUROPE

In 1613 André Le Nôtre was born, and from his baptism he was continually surrounded by gardening tradition. His father was the Royal Gardener at the Tuileries; his godmother was the wife of Claude Mollet, one of France's great garden designers.

At 20 he went to work in the Tuileries where he was a diligent but unspectacular gardener. At 40 the world had still not heard of his name.

Then his chance came. In 1656 the young and corrupt Finance Minister, Nicholas Fouquet, employed him to design the gardens for the new château at Vaux-le-Vicomte. At last Le Nôtre was able to create his vast vistas and living geometry, and the French Court was spellbound at its opening in 1661. Fouquet was jailed for life by a jealous King.

Now Le Nôtre became the Royal Gardener, commissioned by Louis XIV to design the greatest garden in the world at Versailles. He was almost 50 when he started the task and it took more than 16 years to complete. Year after year Le Nôtre patiently laboured and watched the 36,000 workmen creating the ultimate *jardin français,* destined to inspire designers throughout the world.

The Garden Master of Europe died in 1700, a Frenchman and not a European. He travelled little — to Italy when a youth, to Rome when ordered by Pope Innocent XI to improve the Vatican Gardens. But France was his canvas and his masterpieces were many — St. Cloud, Fontainebleau, Rambouillet, Sceaux, St. Germain-en-Laye. And the one he liked best of all, Chantilly.

THE FRENCH HOME GARDEN

About 45 per cent of the households in France have a garden. The area of these gardens, as in all countries, differs widely with the wealth of the occupant and the area in which it is located. Over 30 per cent are smaller than the British average of 2,000 sq. ft.; 4 per cent are more than 16,000 sq. ft. In 1971 the average French garden was 5,000 sq. ft.

The gardener

Gardening is regarded as a man's job and very few products or tools are designed for the woman of the house.

Outside help is used much more often than in Britain – 13% of all households with a garden employ either part-time or full-time help.

How the garden is used

All the surveys immediately reveal a basic difference between the French and British home garden scene. In France it is the food crops which are dominant, compared to the lawn, roses and bulbs of Britain.

	% of gardens where they are grown
Vegetables	74
Fruit trees	55
Shrubs	39
Lawns	38
Climbers	37
Ornamental trees	32
Conifers	32
Fruit bushes	29

Less than 20 per cent of French gardeners express an interest in lawns. Even in the average ornamental garden where no food crops are grown the grass area covers only one third of the area of the garden.

On the other hand more than 75 per cent of all gardens have a vegetable/fruit section and this sets France apart from other European countries. But the pattern is changing quite rapidly – gardens are getting smaller and the trend is towards the purely ornamental garden :

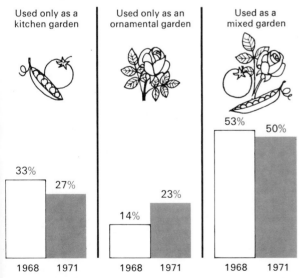

Used only as a kitchen garden		Used only as an ornamental garden		Used as a mixed garden	
33%	27%	14%	23%	53%	50%
1968	1971	1968	1971	1968	1971

Lawns are slowly becoming more commonplace, but the universal close-shaved look of British lawns is not general in France. More than one third of the lawn owners leave two or more weeks between mowings. Roses remain the most popular flower and sales continue to increase.

The changes continue, but it is still as impossible as ever to define the 'typical' French garden. The plots vary from the kitchen gardens of the country districts to the semi-tropical floral estates near the Mediterranean. Nowhere else in Europe is the pattern quite so variable, as illustrated by the chart below :

	Used only as a kitchen garden	Used only as an ornamental garden	Used as a mixed garden	Other uses or untended garden	No garden
	% of all households				
Rural areas	43	5	25	11	16
Small towns	21	7	20	6	46
Average towns	12	8	20	9	51
Large towns	5	15	10	8	62
Paris area	3	11	8	11	67

The suburban home

The garden scene around Paris and Lyons has been carefully investigated by the Comité National Interprofessionnel de l'Horticulture, Rue de Séminaire, 94 Min Rungis. As with the national picture only 20 per cent of the gardens are looked after by the woman of the house. In these urban gardens flowers rival vegetables in popularity – 80 per cent grow roses and spring-flowering bulbs, 83 per cent raise vegetables.

The second home

As shown on page 58 the purchases of garden plants and products have increased rapidly in recent years. One of the causes is the increase in popularity of second homes for holidays and weekends. The owners of these weekend retreats live mainly in the Paris, Lyons, Marseilles and Burgundy areas and they try to create a labour-saving garden with conifers, shrubs, ornamental trees and roses.

	Number of households with a second home
1954	500,000
1962	1,000,000
1967	1,200,000
1972	1,800,000

Le potager

The *potager,* or kitchen garden, is at the heart of the French domestic garden scene. Most gardens have one ; in the standard pattern the front garden is the *jardin d'agrément* (ornamental garden) and the area at the back of the house is devoted to the *potager*. In country districts it is common for the whole of the plot to be used as a kitchen garden.

The fruit and vegetables are grown in square or rectangular plots divided by paths – quite different from the British vegetable plot with its long straight rows of plants. The traditional walls surrounding the *potager* are now disappearing, but the small area set aside for growing cut flowers remains.

Potatoes are rarely grown in urban areas nowadays. The most popular vegetables are the salad crops such as lettuce ; pears are more popular than apples.

PARIS

Within 40 miles of the centre of Paris are many of the great gardens of France, and no other capital city in Europe can offer such a wealth of horticultural showpieces on its doorstep. Some can be reached by metro or taxi; for others you will need a car or excursion bus.

BAGATELLE
A world-famous garden, with 60 acres to delight the flower lover. The display begins in April and May with 200,000 tulips and in summer there are 20,000 roses to see. There is a notable collection of water lilies and the 18th century design of the garden has been carefully preserved.

COURANCES (33 miles)
The most famous feature of this Le Nôtre garden is water – its great pools, moat, waterfalls and fish-ponds. There is a small Japanese Garden at Courances.

ST. CLOUD
This magnificent park of 1,000 acres is open to the public. From the terrace there is a sweeping view of Paris and everywhere there is Le Nôtre's garden – lakes, statues, flower beds. The Great Waterfall is a famous feature, and so is the 'flower mosaic'.

FLEURISTE MUNICIPAL
This is the nursery which raises over 1 million plants each year for the City of Paris, and it is one of the greatest flower displays in the world. There is an arboretum of rare trees in the 32 acre garden, but the great sights to see are in the 94 greenhouses. In these you will find orchids, palms, succulents and house plants of every description. Open all the year round, it should not be missed.

VAUX-LE-VICOMTE (31 miles)
For details see page 54. Illustration on page 2–3.

CHANTILLY (26 miles)
A famous Le Nôtre garden, created before he turned his hand to Versailles. Here are the parterres, grand canal and statuary of the *jardin français*. Other interesting features are the Hamlet, Sylvia's House and the English Garden.

VERSAILLES
For details see page 54. Illustration on page 53.

FONTAINEBLEAU (38 miles)
Tourists who visit Fontainebleau go mainly to see the Palace, for many French sovereigns lived there and it is steeped in history. But the gardens are also of great interest, and over the centuries they have been created as separate compartments. There is the Jardin de Diane, the Cour du Cheval Blanc, the English Garden and the parterre laid out by Le Nôtre.

DAMPIERRE (33 miles)
The garden of this 17th century château in the Chevreuse Valley is another example of Le Nôtre's work.

JARDIN DU MUSEE RODIN

The gardens surrounding the Rodin Museum at the Hôtel Biron have been beautifully restored to their 18th century design. Here you can see some of the world's greatest statues, such as The Thinker and the Burghers of Calais, in an old-world rose garden containing 2,000 bushes.

QUAI DE LA MEGISSERIE

V. de Vilmorin opened a seed shop on this street on the banks of the Seine in 1747. So Vilmorin became the first seedsman in France and the Quai de la Mégisserie was destined to become the main shopping area for plants, seeds and garden sundries. Here, between the Louvre and Notre-Dame, you will find the shops of the great nurseries, such as Delbard, Truffaut and Vilmorin-Andrieux.

JARDIN DES PLANTES

Officially the National Museum of Natural History, this 70 acre site is one of the most popular gardens in Paris. The reason is that everyone is catered for – the scientifically minded can look around the museums and the children can watch the lions in the zoo. For the gardener there is the famous Herb Collection, the Winter Garden of cacti and tropical plants, and the Alpinum with its rare flora from the Alps, Arctic, Himalayas and Pyrenees.

JARDIN ALBERT KAHN

A $7\frac{1}{2}$ acre collection of gardening styles. Best known is the Japanese Garden with its bridges, bonsai, lanterns and tea houses. There is also a French Garden and a Mountain Garden.

L'HAY LES ROSES

For details see page 91.

SCEAUX

A Le Nôtre garden of 450 acres, restored after the war and now one of the finest in the Paris region. The waterfalls, grand canal, orangery and large dahlia collection are popular attractions.

RAMBOUILLET (23 miles)

The château is the summer residence of the President of France, and its garden is the classical *jardin français* with canals and tapis vert. Popular attractions are the Queen's Dairy and the shell-covered pavilion.

CHAMPS

This garden with its wonderful examples of 'embroidered' parterres was created by Claude Desgots, nephew of Le Nôtre. The main vista extends to the River Marne.

THE PARKS OF PARIS

JARDINS DU LUXEMBOURG

One of the loveliest parks in Paris. Its 62 acres are mainly formal – flower beds, octagonal lake, the Medici fountain. There are also informal gardens and many tree-shaded paths for the students and children who congregate here.

JARDINS DES TUILERIES

A *jardin français* in the centre of Paris, designed by Le Nôtre and left unchanged. Nearly every tourist passes through this 60 acre park, gay all summer long with flower-filled parterres.

BOIS DE BOULOGNE

A vast park of 2,180 acres in which you can walk or drive. There are many things to see along its 60 miles of pathways; in the 'Bois' there are 7 lakes and many flower gardens. Visit the Pré Catelan where you will find the Shakespeare Garden, the Poets' Garden and a 160 year old beech – "the most beautiful tree in Paris".

PARC MONCEAU

An example of the 18th century 'folly' garden. The pyramid, grotto, tomb and colonnade remain. Parc Monceau is noted for its many beautiful trees.

BOIS DE VINCENNES

The largest park in Paris – more than 2,300 acres. The Tropical Garden is open on Thursday afternoons.

THE SUPPLIERS

Since 1965 the money spent on garden plants and supplies by the average French household has risen steadily by about 11 per cent each year. In 1972 the expenditure was 170F (£15) per household.

In France there are much larger regional differences than in Britain, as shown below:

Average French household expenditure on garden plants and supplies 1972

It is obvious that the Paris suburbs and N.E. France are the keenest areas, and for the gardener there is an exceptionally wide choice of suppliers from which to choose.

First of all there are the traditional seed merchants, 6,000 shops scattered throughout France. Nearly a third of these are owned by Vilmorin-Andrieux, who with Truffaut and Clause dominate the French garden supply industry.

Many types of outlet sell garden seeds — the grocer, tobacconist, baker, chemist and the ironmonger. For plants the main source of supply remains the nursery, and mail order is important for both seeds and plants. Truffaut sends out nearly 700,000 catalogues each year.

Two major innovations in recent years have begun to transform the picture. *Les Centres-Jardinières* have appeared — large horticultural selling areas attached to supermarkets and their big brothers, hypermarkets. Carrefour is the great hypermarket name in France, and their superstores have selling areas of up to $\frac{1}{4}$ million sq. ft. A large range of gardening articles are stocked and these are sold self-service, like the biscuits and the bifsteks.

Les Garden Centres are the second innovation. In 1965 there were 20, now there are nearly 200. The average *Garden Centre* is similar to its British counterpart, but there are several outstanding examples. Florélites 20, not far from Paris on the R.N. 20, is Europe's largest garden centre, with flamingos on the lawn and a wide range of fully-furnished show homes which can be bought to go with the lawn mower!

PLANTS IN THE HOME

Window boxes, plants in pots and balcony gardens are much more popular than in Britain and the red geranium is a great favourite. Cut flowers and pot plants are also popular, but here the average number purchased is not much higher than in Britain, and appreciably lower than in those great indoor plant nations — Holland, Germany and Scandinavia.

There are many florists to cater for this trade, but the open-air flower stall remains the main place for the bunch of roses or clump of violets. The place to go in Paris is the Place Louis-Lépine.

Société **N**ationale d' **H**orticulture de **F**rance

The French National Horticultural Society (84 rue de Grenelle, Paris 7) was founded in 1827 to encourage amateur gardening. It plays many parts — it has its own library and trial grounds, it arranges shows, exhibitions and conferences, it answers queries from the press and the public, and it gives out long-service awards.

It is similar to Britain's R.H.S. in these respects, but there are several important differences. The S.N.H.F. full membership is only 7,000, although the subscription is not excessive — 25F per year (35F for overseas members). One of the reasons is that it has adopted the policy of working through affiliated societies, which may be local or specialist groups, and there are about 137 of these affiliates. In 1967 this represented more than 1,100,000 members.

One of the attractions for a society to become affiliated with the S.N.H.F. is the *Amis de 'Jardins de France'* scheme, whereby its members receive a discount of 10 – 15 per cent on garden plants, books and sundries from some suppliers. Also, the members can join one of the *Voyages de la S.N.H.F.* to see and learn about gardens overseas. The Society magazine, *Jardins de France,* is published monthly.

Société d'Horticulture et des Jardins Populaires de France

This is by far the most popular horticultural society in France, with more than 800,000 members. It was created in 1867 to look after the interests of allotment holders, but now it caters for both the home garden owner as well as the man with an allotment.

The annual subscription is only 3.80F, and for this each member receives the Society magazine *Pour nos Jardins.*

ALLOTMENTS

Allotments have been an important part of French gardening since the 19th century. On these plots of about 250 sq. yds. *les ouvriers* (the workmen) of Northern France have traditionally raised their potatoes, beans and saladings, and the old name *jardin ouvrier* is still widely used.

Changes are taking place. The use of allotments as leisure gardens is increasing, and the term *jardin familial* is now used frequently for allotments, thus removing the working-class image. But the change-over from kitchen garden to a place for lawn, chalet and roses is occurring much more slowly than in Holland, Germany and Scandinavia.

The land belongs to local authorities and industry, and La Ligue Française du Coin de Terre et du Foyer is responsible for the issuing and management of *les jardins ouvriers.* Another important provider of allotments is the S.N.C.F. (French National Railways). These *jardins du cheminot* are leased to their personnel.

MAGAZINES

Garden magazines are slightly more popular in France than in Britain. *Pour nos Jardins* is by far the most widely read.

Mon Jardin et ma Maison
    Monthly.   Circulation 175,000
L'Amis des Jardins & de la Maison
    Monthly.   Circulation 133,000
Rustica
    Weekly.   Circulation 205,000
Horticultural Society Journals:
Jardins de France
    Monthly.   Circulation 15,000
Pour nos Jardins
    Bimonthly.   Circulation 820,000
Le Jardin du Cheminot
    Bimonthly.   Circulation 110,000
Le Jardin Ouvrier de France
    Bimonthly.   Circulation 17,000

FLORAL ROUTES

The *Routes Fleuries* are an outstanding example of the way a nation can improve its horticultural image to the outsider. A large number of roads have been turned into tourist attractions as Floral Routes as a result of massed plantings and floral displays along the roadside by householders, local authorities and various organisations.

Examples are :

Seine-Maritime Floral Route The 150 mile circular route from Rouen through Barentin, Dieppe, Fécamp and Cany.

Médoc Floral Route The road through the vineyards from Blanquefort to Saint-Suerin-de-Cadourne. Roses have been planted at the end of each row of vines.

Midi Floral Route The coastal road from Nice to Menton has been planted with flowers and flowering shrubs for a number of years.

Pas-de-Calais Floral Route The 45 mile road from Le Touquet to Frévant was the first of the northern showpieces.

Paris Floral Routes The long road from Paris to Deauville has been transformed into a Floral Route, and the road from Paris to Provins (R.N. 19) is the famous *Route des Roses.* Further down the R.N. 19 is another Floral Route between Villeneuve-au-Chêne and Lignol-le-Château.

Anjou Floral Route The road between Angers and Saumur was turned into a Floral Route in 1964.

This list is by no means exhaustive. You will find these Floral Routes in many other districts — Brittany, Champagne, Alsace, Auvergne, the Loire Valley — almost anywhere the tourist is likely to go.

FLEURIR LA FRANCE

In 1959 the French Government Tourist Office began the 'Make France Flower' Campaign. Towns and villages throughout the country compete for the annual awards, which are based on the way flowers are used to adorn buildings, roadsides and public parks. Thousands of places in every corner of France are involved each year in this event.

THE FLOWER SHOWS

International Flower Shows are occasionally held in France — the Paris Floralies in 1969 attracted more than 3 million people. There are numerous national shows held each year in various parts of the country, but these tend to be rather small and deal with specific plants — the Azalea Show in April and the Chrysanthemum Show in October at the Fleuriste Municipal in Paris, the Rose Show at Saverne and the Dahlia Show at Sélestat are examples. But there is nothing to dominate the exhibition scene like Chelsea in England or the Bundes Gartenschau in Germany.

BOTANICAL GARDENS & TREE COLLECTIONS

Compared with the average German or British Botanical Garden the French equivalent is surprisingly small. Despite this limitation in size there are many excellent collections.

BESANÇON BOTANICAL GARDEN Bog garden. Collection of alpine plants. 4 acres.

CAEN BOTANICAL GARDEN Wild flowers of Normandy. Rock garden. 1 acre.

ALPINE INSTITUTE (Col du Lautaret). About 50 miles from Grenoble, 6,000 ft. above sea level. More than 3,000 alpine varieties ; many rare. 4 acres.

GENERARGUES BOTANICAL GARDEN Contains the world's finest collection of bamboos. Privately owned. 100 acres.

GRIGNON BOTANICAL GARDEN Ecological garden and collection of chalk-loving plants. 4 acres.

LILLE JARDIN DES PLANTES Orchids and succulent plants. 26 acres.

LYON BOTANICAL GARDEN A fine display of alpines, shrubs, conifers, ferns and camellias. Well worth a visit. 15 acres.

MONTIGNY LES METZ BOTANICAL GARDEN Noted for its collection of roses, succulents and iris. 9 acres.

MONTPELLIER JARDIN DES PLANTES Oldest Botanical Garden in France. Alpine, succulent and orchid collections. 12 acres.

NANCY BOTANICAL GARDEN Special features are medicinal plants and grasses. Noteworthy iris collection. $2\frac{1}{2}$ acres.

NANTES BOTANICAL GARDEN Good collections of bulbs, orchids, camellias, conifers and local plants. 17 acres.

ARBORETUM DES BARRES (Nogent-sur-Vernisson). 700 acre collection of trees — more than 250 different conifers. Write to the Director for permission to visit.

ROUEN BOTANICAL GARDEN Specialises in the flora of Normandy. 25 acres.

LES CEDRES BOTANICAL GARDEN (Saint-Jean-Cap-Ferrat). An outstanding private collection of subtropical plants. 35 acres. Write to the Director for permission to visit.

FIFTEEN GRAND GARDENS

Nearly all the grand gardens of France are gardens of châteaux. Hundreds of these castles and mansions have opened their gates to the public, and some hold spectacular 'Son et Lumière' performances during the summer.

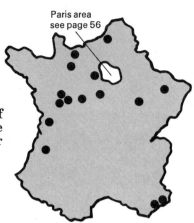

Paris area
see page 56

BAGATELLE (Abbeville)
The gardens were created in the transition period between the grand French Style and the *jardin anglais.* It has both styles, a formal garden with parterres close to the house and a landscaped park beyond.

BUSSY-RABUTIN (Bussy-le-Grand)
A fine example of a *jardin français,* designed by Le Nôtre. The legend is that Compte de Bussy-Rabutin tried to copy Versailles after being exiled by Louis XIV.

CANON (Mézidon)
A famous garden but a private one, so write for permission to visit; the address is Château de Canon, Mézidon, Calvados. It is a water garden, with statuary everywhere. Look for the Chartreuses — walled gardens filled with spring flowers.

CHENONCEAUX (Loire Valley)
One of the fine Loire Valley château gardens with elaborate parterres, topiary and a long canal. Son et Lumière performances are held in the garden.

LANGEAIS (Loire Valley)
Delightful French Style garden (illustrated below) with outstanding parterres. One of the oldest castle keeps in France stands in the park.

LUNEVILLE
The garden of this château is usually quoted as the best example of the 'transitional style' in which the geometric lines of the *jardin français* change into the informal landscape garden away from the house. The formal garden was created by a rival of Le Nôtre, Yves des Hours.

MAINTENON
A Le Nôtre garden. In the grounds stands the viaduct which was used in a vain attempt to carry water to the canals and pools of Versailles. This venture cost the lives of several thousand workmen.

MALLE (Preignac)
This garden in the Gironde district was created in the Italianate Style. There are terraces, fountains and abundant statuary.

MUSEE ILE-DE-FRANCE (Saint-Jean-Cap-Ferrat)
Large sub-tropical garden with several smaller sunken gardens in various national styles.

PARC FLORAL (Orléans-La Source)
A superb 35 acre horticultural show ground. Half a million bulbs, the largest rose garden and the largest iris garden in Europe, hundreds of thousands of bedding plants. It is a place for a family day out, with wildlife, outdoor amusements and souvenir shops alongside the million plants.

ROCHE COURBON (Saint-Porchaire)
A vast garden with terraces and lily ponds, reconstructed in 1930.

SASSY (near Carrouges)
A distinctive garden with a series of balustraded terraces leading down to the long canals. The parterres have an intricate 'embroidered' design.

USSE (Rigny-Ussé)
Large garden designed by Le Nôtre. Perrault used the castle and its grounds as the model for his story 'The Sleeping Beauty'.

VILLA ROQUEBRUNE (Cap Martin)
A plantsman's garden on the edge of the Mediterranean, with masses of flowers and none of the stiff formality of the *jardin français.*

VILLANDRY (Loire Valley)
For details see page 54. Aerial view below.

A PICTURE GUIDE TO
Plants in the Home

The post-war boom in plants and flowers for the house is graphically illustrated in recent official statistics. Nearly £100 million is now spent each year in Britain by householders and commercial organisations on cut flowers and plants in pots. This is more than twice the expenditure on all garden plants and seeds, and yet Britain lags behind Scandinavia, W. Germany, France and Benelux in the number of plants found in the home.

The boom goes on. The market is growing by 20 per cent each year in Belgium, 15 per cent in W. Germany, Holland, Norway and Italy, and 10 per cent in Britain. Denmark, which spends more than £6.00 per head each year on plants for indoors, seems at last to have reached its peak.

One of the results of all this interest has been an outpouring of books on indoor gardening. These tell the housewife in simple language how to choose, arrange and care for her pots and cut flowers, but they all omit the fascinating history of how the boom developed.

The biggest surprise in this story is the relative newness of the major features of indoor gardening. The hobby of arranging cut flowers is a twentieth century phenomenon in Europe. Furthermore, nearly all of today's most popular house plants were unknown in Britain until after the Second World War.

The roots, however, go back to the beginning of civilization. From time immemorial flowers such as roses, violets, lavender and oxslip have been strewn on floors to mask the odours of an insanitary world. Growing plants were also used – a 400 year old textbook listed nearly forty herbs and flowers for growing in windows.

The use of indoor flowers and plants for decorative purposes began in the sixteenth century, and indoor flowers can be found in some of the paintings by the Dutch Masters. The Victorian age saw the full flowering of this fashion, and Britain led Europe for the first and last time. The *epergne* (large silver or china bowl) was filled with flowers at table, and the fern-filled Wardian cases gave way to the parlour palms, the aspidistras and the plant tables.

With the turn of the century a new idea was in the air – the artistic arrangement of cut flowers in a glass vase instead of massed displays of assorted flower-heads in a bowl. The European pioneers of this new hobby for women were Constance Spry in England and Franziska Bruck in Germany. New in Europe, but the first rules for the stylish and symbolic art of Ikebana (Japanese flower arranging) had been laid down 1300 years before in China.

General interest in indoor pot plants had faded with the passing of the Victorian era, and only in cottage windows and grand conservatories did they continue to flourish. The revival began in Britain in the early 1950s and here we lagged well behind Scandinavia and the United States, where a whole new generation of spectacular foliage house plants had been developed. The pioneer was the nurseryman Thomas Rochford, who in 1947 was asked by Constance Spry to raise some novelties for her to sell in her London florist shop. These plants were *Cissus antarctica* and decorative ivy, and demand soon exceeded the supply. Mr. Rochford introduced additional varieties of these *Grøner Glader* (Green Pleasures) from Scandinavia – *Philodendron*, *Fatsia*, *Monstera*, *Aphelandra*, *Pandanus* and *Peperomia*, and he coined the English name "house plants" for them. Common plants now, but novel enough to win a Chelsea Flower Show medal in 1952.

From this brief history it should be clear that there have always been plants in the home, but never before in such variety and with such varied uses. On pages 62 and 63 fourteen separate facets are described. Some of these may be new to you and others you may wish to ignore. But the basic lesson you have to learn if you wish to understand indoor gardening is the difference between a house plant and a pot plant. A house plant is capable of being a permanent resident in an ordinary room, provided certain basic requirements are met. It may be grown for its leaves alone (foliage house plant) or for its flowers as well as its leaves (flowering house plant). A flowering pot plant is a temporary visitor and after the flowering period is over it must be transferred to the greenhouse, garden or discarded.

The Fourteen Faces of

FLOWERING HOUSE PLANTS

The foliage of these varieties remains alive throughout the year and in some cases (e.g. *Aphelandra, Aechmea* and *Anthurium*) may be most attractive. But they are principally grown for their flowers, and plants in this group can be expected to flower and to live under room conditions if their needs are met. They can be regarded as permanent residents and therefore should not be confused with Flowering Pot Plants. The chart on page 66 lists the popular flowering varieties which belong to this group.

FOLIAGE HOUSE PLANTS

The foliage of these varieties remains alive and attractive throughout the year. All of them will live permanently under room conditions provided that their needs are met. For some these needs are very simple — some light and a watering every week or two. At the other end of the scale are the delicate varieties which require carefully controlled light, water, air moisture and temperature conditions if they are to survive. The chart on page 66 will help you to choose the right plants for the conditions in your room.

FLOWERING POT PLANTS

These plants can be kept in flower for a considerable time under room conditions. Spring, summer and autumn blooming types are available, as well as the winter *Azalea, Poinsettia, Cyclamen* and *Solanum.* The flowering span will depend on the conditions provided and the variety chosen, but the time must come when the flowers fade and the leaves fall. Then the plants are usually thrown away, although many varieties will bloom again if you have the necessary greenhouse and green fingers.

BONSAI

A bonsai is a tree or shrub which is tall-growing under natural conditions but which is grown indoors and kept permanently dwarfed by the careful and balanced pruning of both roots and branches. Conifers are the easiest types to train into the attractive shapes associated with these miniature trees, but almost any tree can be grown the bonsai way. Mature specimens are expensive, so always obtain detailed cultural instructions when you buy. These will call for plenty of light, fresh air and occasional feeding.

Plants in pots

BULBS AND CORMS

Many bulbs and corms will grow and flower under room conditions when planted in bulb fibre, soilless compost or soil and kept at the appropriate temperature during the early stages of growth. Choose varieties which are recommended for growing indoors and the bulbs should be good-sized and firm. 'Prepared' bulbs are available for August-September planting for flowering at Christmas. Bulbs cannot be grown as pot plants for more than one season, so plant them out in the garden after flowering.

ANNUALS FROM SEED

Indoor plants are generally raised from cuttings, not seeds. But there are about five flowering annuals which are sometimes grown in pots to provide a bright display during the summer months. Choose from *Schizanthus wisetonensis* (Butterfly Flower), *Tropaeolum peltophorum* (Climbing Nasturtium), *Ipomaea tricolor* (Morning Glory), *Thunbergia alata* (Black-eyed Susan) or *Cobaea scandens* (Cup and Saucer Vine). Sow seeds in soilless compost during March and cover the pot with a polythene bag. Feed regularly with liquid plant food when flower buds begin to appear.

CACTI AND SUCCULENTS

Succulent varieties are a distinct group of house plants, easily identified by the swollen and fleshy nature of their stems and/or leaves. Some succulent plants belong to the cactus family; others (the 'succulents') do not. Page 116 shows you how to tell the difference.
All of the popular varieties will live permanently and may flower under room conditions. As a general rule they need a sunny window-sill, plenty of water during summer with little or no water and no frost in the winter.

PIPS

The pips and stones of many fruits (orange, lemon, tangerine, grapefruit, date, apricot, peach and avocado) can be used to provide miniature trees for indoors. Plant the pip in soilless compost and keep the pot covered with a polythene bag. Leave in a warm, dark spot until germination occurs; this may take many weeks. Move the seedling to a well lit site and keep the compost moist by watering regularly. One disappointing feature is that you cannot expect your home-grown trees to bear fruit under ordinary room conditions.

Plants in the Home

BOTTLE GARDENS

Bottle gardens are an excellent way of providing a moist atmosphere and draught-proof home for delicate plants. The traditional bottle is the 10-gallon carboy, but these are becoming quite rare. Any bottle will do, however, as long as small plants can be pushed through the neck. Use a soilless compost which is moist but not wet and place 5–6 inches in the bottom of the bottle. With a fork and a spoon tied to bamboo canes plant half a dozen small plants. Varieties of *Calathea, Maranta, Peperomia* and ferns are excellent, but avoid cacti and flowering plants. If the bottle is stoppered, no water will be necessary for months.

INDOOR GARDENS

An indoor garden is a collection of three or more plants removed from their pots and planted in a bowl. The important thing to remember is to place together only plants with the same cultural requirements. Cacti and succulents cannot grow happily with plants requiring moist conditions all year round. When planting mixed groups always aim for variety in colour, texture and shape. If the plants are left in their pots when grouped together in a deep container they become a *trough garden.* Sometimes small plants and models are used to produce a *miniature garden* with small-scale garden features such as lawns and pools.

POT-ET-FLEUR

This French phrase describes an arrangement of foliage house plants with cut flowers. When the bowl is being planted with its permanent residents (the house plants) a small water-holding container is inserted. Make sure that it is hidden by the foliage. A few blooms are then put into the container to add colour to the bowl. Tulips, daffodils and carnations are particularly successful. As the houseplants provide a green background, all leaves on the cut flowers should be removed. Remember to check the arrangement each day as the flower holder is unlikely to hold much water and will need to be topped up frequently.

Plants in groups

Arrangements

FLOWERS FROM THE GARDEN

The garden owner is fortunate in having flowers freely available for cutting during the growing season. Always cut in the morning or evening – never in the heat of the day. Don't use a flower basket; stand the cut blooms in a bucket of water.

Once indoors remove all the leaves which will be below the water line in the final arrangement, and then condition the blooms. This means filling the stems with water to prevent wilting. To do this cut off the ends of the stems and then immerse them up to the neck of the blooms in tepid water for several hours.

CUT FLOWERS

Cut flowers bought from a shop or market are the basic source material for arrangements in the home. It is essential, however, to shop wisely. Purchase tulips, daffodils, irises and lilies in tight bud. Double flowers such as chrysanthemums and carnations should not be showing their stamens. When buying flowers which have several blooms on a stem, ensure that only the bottom bloom or two has already opened. As soon as shop flowers arrive home, recut all stems on the slant and place in a bucket of water.

DRIED PLANTS

Dried leaves, flowers and grasses can be bought in natural shades, bleached or dyed in brilliant colours. There are special varieties of easily grown annuals ("everlasting" flowers) which retain their colour and form after cutting and drying. However, many ordinary garden plants can be quite simply dried at home. One of the best methods is to place the ends of the stems in a mixture of one part glycerine to two parts water for several weeks. Plants preserved in this way are pliable, richly coloured and may last for years. All grasses and some flowers may be air-dried by hanging them upside down in a warm room, but this material can be rather brittle.

Leaf guide to Plants in pots

1. *Pteris cretica*
2. *Begonia* 'Cleopatra'
3. *Begonia rex*
4. *Begonia masoniana*
5. *Cyclamen* 'Silver Leaf'
6. *Monstera deliciosa*
7. *Platycerium*
8. *Sansevieria trifasciata*
9. *Chlorophytum capense*
10. *Acorus gramineus*
11. *Dracaena sanderiana*
12. *Ficus pumila*
13. *Gynura sarmentosa*
14. *Laurus nobilis*
15. *Scindapsus aureus*
16. *Philodendron scandens*
17. *Rhoicissus rhomboidea*
18. *Ficus elastica decora*
19. *Selaginella*
20. *Zygocactus truncatus*
21. *Saxifraga sarmentosa*
22. *Aphelandra squarrosa*
23. *Dieffenbachia arvida*
24. *Impatiens sultanii*
25. *Hedera helix*
26. *Hedera helix* 'Glacier'
27. *Hedera helix lutzii*
28. *Hedera helix* 'Green Ripple'
29. *Hedera canariensis*
30. *Grevillea robusta*
31. *Jasminum polyanthum*
32. *Adiantum cuneatum*
33. *Asparagus sprengeri*
34. *Calathea insignis*
35. *Codiaeum*
36. *Philodendron melanochrysum*
37. *Aglaonema treubii*
38. *Cissus antartica*
39. *Aralia elegantissima*
40. *Fatsia japonica*
41. *Vriesia splendens*
42. *Cryptanthus roseo-pictus*
43. *Columnea*
44. *Pilea cadierei*
45. *Pilea* 'Moon Valley'
46. *Dracaena godseffiana*
47. *Maranta makoyana*
48. *Fittonia verschaffeltii*
49. *Kalanchoe*
50. *Coleus*
51. *Fatshedera lizei*
52. *Peperomia glabella*
53. *Peperomia caperata*
54. *Peperomia hederaefolia*
55. *Peperomia magnoliaefolia*
56. *Neanthe bella*
57. *Syngonium podophyllum* 'Emerald Gem'
58. *Saintpaulia*
59. *Anthurium scherzerianum*
60. *Zebrina pendula*
61. *Tradescantia* 'Quicksilver'
62. *Setcreasea purpurea*

Caring for House Plants

House plants are the group which can be permanent residents in your home, if you give them the right conditions. This means that their needs for heat, light, water and air must be met, and these needs vary widely between one plant and another. The bright sunlight which would kill a fern might be sufficient to keep some cacti happy. The cool winter conditions needed by an Aralia could kill a Finger Aralia. Pick the right plants for your room – the table below will guide you.

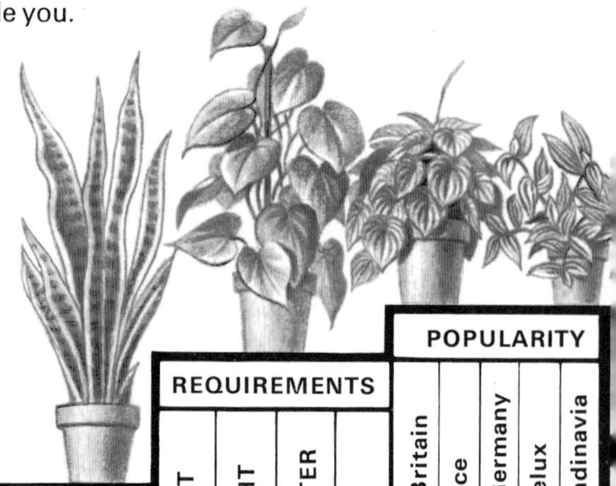

KEY

HEAT
A Keep at 60°-80°F
B Keep at 50°-70°F
C Keep at 40°-60°F

LIGHT
A Keep in full sun
B Needs semi-shade
C Will grow in shade

WATER
A Water freely
B Water when soil begins to dry
C Avoid overwatering

AIR
A Needs very high humidity
B Needs moderate humidity
C Tolerates dry air

POPULARITY
🏵 One of the five best-selling house plants in the country

LATIN NAME	COMMON NAME	HEAT	LIGHT	WATER	AIR	Gt. Britain	France	W. Germany	Benelux	Scandinavia
Abutilon		B	A	B	B					
Acorus		C	B	A	B					
Adiantum	Maidenhair Fern	C	C	A	B					
Aechmea	Urn Plant	A	B	B	A				🏵	
Aglaonema commutatum	Chinese Evergreen	A	C	A	A					
Anthurium scherzerianum	Flamingo Flower	A	B	A	A					
Aphelandra	Zebra Plant	A	B	A	B					
Aralia elegantissima	Finger Aralia	A	B	B	A					
Araucaria	Norfolk Island Pine	C	C	B	C					
Asparagus plumosus	Asparagus Fern	B	B	A	B					
Aspidistra	Cast Iron Palm	C	C	B	B					
Begonia rex		A	B	A	A					
Beloperone guttata	Shrimp Plant	B	A	A	B					
Cacti (Desert varieties)		C	A	C	C					
Calathea	Peacock Plant	A	B	B	A					
Ceropegia	Chinese Lantern	B	C	C	B					
Chlorophytum	Spider Plant	B	C	B	B	🏵				
Cissus antarctica	Kangaroo Vine	B	C	B	B			🏵		
Citrus mitis	Calamondin	B	A	B	B					
Clivia miniata	Kaffir Lily	C	B	B	B					
Codiaeum	Croton	A	B	B	A					🏵
Coleus	Flame Nettle	A	A	B	B					
Columnea		A	B	B	B					
Cordyline		B	B	B	B					
Crassula		C	A	C	C					
Cryptanthus	Earth Star	B	B	B	A					
Cyperus alternifolius	Umbrella Plant	B	B	B	A					
Dieffenbachia	Dumb Cane	A	B	A	A					
Dracaena	Dragon Plant	B	B	B	B					
Echeveria		C	A	C	C					
Epiphyllum	Orchid Cactus	B	B	B	B					
Euphorbia splendens	Crown of Thorns	C	A	A	C					
Fatshedera lizei	Fat-headed Lizzie	C	C	B	B					
Fatsia japonica	Aralia	C	C	C	B					
Ficus benjamina	Weeping Fig	A	B	B	B					
Ficus decora (or *F. robusta*)	Rubber Plant	A	B	B	B	🏵	🏵	🏵	🏵	🏵

LATIN NAME	COMMON NAME	HEAT	LIGHT	WATER	AIR	Gt. Britain	France	W. Germany	Benelux	Scandinavia
Ficus pumila	Climbing Fig	B	B	B	B					
Fittonia		A	C	A	A					
Grevillea robusta	Silk Oak	C	B	A	B					
Guzmania		A	B	B	A					
Gynura	Velvet Plant	A	B	B	A					
Hedera	Ivy	C	C	A	B	●			●	●
Helxine soleirolii	Mind-Your-Own-Business	C	B	A	B					
Hibiscus	Chinese Rose	A	B	B	B					
Hoya carnosa	Wax Plant	A	B	B	B					
Impatiens	Busy Lizzie	B	B	A	B					
Maranta	Prayer Plant	A	B	B	A					
Monstera deliciosa	Swiss Cheese Plant	A	B	B	B	●			●	●
Neanthe elegans	Dwarf Palm	B	B	B	B					
Pandanus	Screw Pine	A	B	B	B					
Passiflora	Passion Flower	C	A	B	B					
Pelargonium	Geranium	B	A	B	B					
Pellaea	Cliff Brake Fern	B	C	B	B					
Peperomia	Pepper Elder	A	B	B	B					
Philodendron scandens	Sweetheart Plant	B	C	B	B		●			●
Pilea cadierei	Aluminium Plant	A	B	B	B					
Platycerium bifurcatum	Stag's Horn Fern	B	C	B	B					
Pteris	Ribbon Fern	C	C	A	B					
Rhoicissus rhomboidea	Grape Ivy	B	C	B	B		●	●		
Saintpaulia	African Violet	A	B	B	A	●	●	●		
Sansevieria trifasciata	Mother-in-Law's Tongue	B	B	C	C		●	●	●	
Saxifraga	Mother of Thousands	C	B	B	B					
Scindapsus aureus	Devil's Ivy	B	B	C	B					
Sedum sieboldii		C	A	C	C					
Selaginella	Tropical Moss	A	C	A	A					
Setcreasea purpurea	Purple Heart	B	B	B	B					
Sparmannia	African Hemp	C	C	B	B					
Spathiphyllum		A	B	A	A					
Syngonium	Goose Foot	B	C	A	A					
Tetrastigma	Chestnut Vine	B	C	B	B					
Tradescantia	Wandering Jew	C	B	B	B					
Vriesia		A	B	B	A					
Zebrina	Wandering Jew	C	B	B	B					
Zygocactus truncatus	Christmas Cactus	B	B	B	B					

A			A

◀ Difficult to grow under average room conditions

C			B or C

◀ Easy to grow under average room conditions

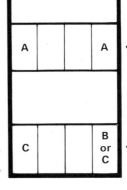

67

Flower guide to Plants in pots

1. *Aphelandra squarrosa Louisae*   (Zebra Plant)
2. *Vriesia splendens*
3. *Aechmea fulgens*   (Urn Plant)
4. *Beloperone guttata*   (Shrimp Plant)
5. *Billbergia nutans*
6. *Begonia tuberhybrida*
7. *Browallia*
8. *Exacum affine*
9. *Achimenes longiflora*   (Trumpet Achimenes)
10. *Campanula isophylla*   (Italian Bellflower)
11. *Saintpaulia ionantha*   (African Violet)
12. *Euphorbia pulcherrima*   (Poinsettia)
13. *Hippeastrum vittatum*   (Amaryllis)
14. *Tulipa*   (Tulip)
15. *Hyacinthus orientalis*   (Hyacinth)
16. *Narcissus*   (Daffodil)
17. *Dipladenia rosea*   (Pink Queen of Rio)
18. *Zygocactus truncatus*   (Christmas Cactus)
19. *Spathiphyllum wallisii*   (White Sails)
20. *Anthurium scherzerianum*   (Flamingo Flower)
21. *Fuchsia hybrida*   (Lady's Eardrops)
22. *Peperomia caperata*   (Pepper Elder)
23. *Bougainvillea glabra sanderiana*
24. *Sinningia hybrida*   (Gloxinia)
25. *Senecio cruentus*   (Cineraria)
26. *Calceolaria herbeohybrida*   (Slipper Flower)
27. *Ipomea tricolor*   (Morning Glory)
28. *Convallaria majalis*   (Lily of the Valley)
29. *Kalanchoe blossfeldiana*
30. *Columnea gloriosa*
31. *Hoya carnosa*   (Wax Plant)
32. *Begonia semperflorens*
33. *Chrysanthemum hybridum*
34. *Cyclamen persicum*
35. *Rhododendron indicum*   (Azalea)
36. *Camellia hybrida*
37. *Clivia miniata*   (Kaffir Lily)
38. *Euphorbia fulgens*   (Scarlet Plume)
39. *Hibiscus rosa-sinensis*   (Rose of China)
40. *Hydrangea hortensis*
41. *Impatiens*   (Busy Lizzie)
42. *Jasminum*   (Jasmine)
43. *Mammillaria*   (Pincushion Cactus)
44. *Passiflora caerulea*   (Passion Flower)
45. *Pelargonium*   (Geranium)
46. *Rochea coccinea*
47. *Rosa hybrida*   (Miniature Rose)
48. *Primula obconica*   (Poison Primrose)
49. *Primula malacoides*   (Fairy Primrose)
50. *Primula kewensis*   (Kew Primrose)
51. *Primula sinensis*   (Chinese Primrose)
52. *Stephanotis floribunda*   (Madagascar Jasmine)
53. *Streptocarpus hybridus*   (Cape Primrose)
54. *Thunbergia alata*   (Black-eyed Susan)

The *EuroPlant in the Home*

❶ In **GT. BRITAIN** the demand for house plants continues to increase by 15 – 20 per cent each year. The old favourites stay at the top of the list – *Ficus*, *Hedera*, *Chlorophytum*, *Rhoicissus*, *Monstera*, *Sansevieria* and recently they have been joined by *Saintpaulia*. Another recent shift has been towards the large architectural plant which can serve as a focal point in home or office. In the flowering pot plant group there has been a marked increase in the popularity of the *Poinsettia* at Christmas time.

Most people own house plants, but the Saintpaulia and Houseplant Society (82 Rossmore Court, Park Road, London NW1) has only 200 members. The flower arrangers are much more gregarious – nearly 100,000 belong to local societies. Yet cut flower sales are disappointing, they have hardly risen over the past few years, and obviously home-grown material is the standby of the flower arranger. Chrysanthemums and carnations are the most popular types purchased, but 60 per cent of the population rarely or never buy any flowers.

The best permanent indoor plant displays are at Syon Park Gardening Centre and in the Botanical Gardens at Cambridge, Edinburgh, Liverpool and Glasgow. Worthy of special mention is the Garden of Leonard Maurice Mason (King's Lynn) which is open to the public. There are good displays at many large garden centres and at the major flower shows.

Rochford Stand, Chelsea Flower Show 1973

❷ **SCANDINAVIA** is perhaps the area of greatest interest in Europe. The present vogue for house plants began there, and both Norway and Denmark spend more per head on cut flowers and indoor plants than any other European country.

There are 15 – 20 house plants in the average Scandinavian home. Flowering pot plants are popular; favourites include chrysanthemums, pelargoniums and begonias. Favourite cut flowers are chrysanthemums, roses, tulips and carnations; Denmark uses more cut flowers per head than any other country in Europe.

❸ **W. GERMANY** continues to dominate the indoor plant market of Europe with a staggering total of £330 million spent each year on flowers and plants in pots. No other country reaches even half of this figure. Sales have grown nearly six times in the past 20 years, and much of this has been due to the custom of giving flowers when calling on friends or relatives. This is most popular with the upper-income group and sales may have reached saturation here, but the use and giving of flowers and plants is still rising steadily with the lower-income groups.

❹ **FRANCE** has the British attitude towards plants in the home. Cut flowers are bought for special occasions; nearly three quarters of all sales are for this purpose.

House plants are extremely popular, and so are *Azalea indica*, *Cyclamen*, *Hydrangea hortensis* and other flowering pot plants. Over 90 per cent of households have some indoor plants and the average number is 15 per home.

❺ The **BENELUX** countries are important producers and exporters of indoor plants, but they are also keen on having plants around them in the home. In both Belgium and Holland sales are increasing at a faster rate than in W. Germany. To see Benelux plants at their best visit the Aalsmeer Flower Auction (daily), Aalsmeer Flower Shows (November and December) and Ghent Floralies (every five years).

A PICTURE GUIDE TO Conifers

We all know a conifer when we see one, and yet surprisingly there is not one characteristic which can be completely relied upon to tell you whether you are correct.

Conifers are nearly always evergreen, but larch and swamp cypress lose their leaves in autumn. Leaf shape is a good guide, for nearly all have scale-like or elongated leaves, but *Ginkgo biloba* has fan-shaped foliage. At least the presence of cones ought to be a reliable recognition factor . . . yet even here there is wide variation. *Pinus coulteri* bears cones more than 1 ft. long and several pounds in weight, and at the other end of the scale are many dwarf varieties which never bear cones at all. Yew and juniper bear fleshy fruits.

The conifer is the garden plant *par excellence*, and this was recognised at the start of European gardening. Ancient Rome had its tree barbers to clip the garden cypresses, and in the sixteenth century arbor-vitae and white pine from newly-discovered Canada were grown in the gardens of France. North America has played a vital part in the conifer story, and it was the Victorian plant hunters like Douglas who provided the raw material for today's range of garden varieties.

The prime feature of the conifer is its permanence. To the new garden it gives an immediate touch of maturity. In all gardens it remains alive and in leaf throughout the year, and with slow-growing forms the tree may change little in the life-span of the owner. The oldest living thing is the 5,000 year old *Pinus aristata* in California.

This permanent piece of garden architecture is available in many shapes. Most conifers are column-like or pyramid-shaped, but many spreading varieties are available. Mighty trees like the atlas cedar and wellingtonia can be admired in grand gardens, but they have no place in the average plot. Always check the anticipated height of any conifer before you buy it.

For the ordinary suburban garden, the rockery and the plant tub there are now many dwarf varieties. Some of these are true dwarfs, but the majority are merely slow-growing varieties which can develop into large specimens over the years.

The skill with conifers comes at the selection and planting stages, for after-care could not be simpler. There is no staking, spraying, dead-heading or leaf raking. Pruning is not necessary except in one special case – if a green-leaved branch appears in a golden or variegated variety then chop it out immediately.

So care is easy but selection is not. First of all, study the site. If your soil is slightly acid then you have no problems, but if it is chalky you will have to choose carefully. If you live in a town then pick a variety which will tolerate some air pollution. *Cupressus* varieties are the most reliable, but the range is rapidly expanding in the wake of the Clean Air Act. Conifers may soon be established in London's Royal Parks for the first time since the Industrial Revolution.

Plant the chosen specimen with care as it must be kept growing during the establishment period, and transplant in *early* autumn or *late* spring. If the roots are 'balled' with earth, do not break up the ball before planting.

If you want to see the stately conifer at its best, then go to a *pinetum*, which is a collection of coniferous trees. There is the National Pinetum at Bedgebury in Kent, and collections can be found in many grand gardens. In Europe there are great displays from the Finnish Arboretum Mustila in the north to the Lyon Botanical Garden in central France. But these are not the places to go if you want to learn more about the range of garden conifers now available; go to your garden centre or local nursery. The major flower shows and some Botanical Gardens have good displays.

Moving across Europe we find conifers in gardens from the Arctic to the Mediterranean. In northern Scandinavia the genera of the cool forests predominate – *Picea*, *Abies* and *Pinus*. In France and the Low Countries *Thuja*, *Chamaecyparis*, *Picea* and *Juniperus* are the favourite genera and in the far south only the most drought-resistant conifers (*Cupressus*, *Juniperus*, *Cedrus* and a few *Pinus* species) are able to flourish. The names change, but the basic benefits of conifers in the garden do not.

ABIES (Silver fir)

.Mostly tall and straight-growing. A few dwarf garden varieties are available. Leaves strap-like and leathery, usually grey below. Barrel-shaped cones borne upwards.

ARAUCARIA (Monkey puzzle)

One outdoor species (*A. araucana*) ; slow growing tree eventually reaching 70 ft. Leaves dark green, hard and sharp-edged. Globular cones borne on female trees.

CEDRUS (Cedar)

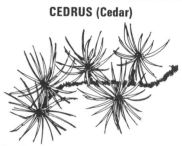

Mostly tall trees ; weeping and compact varieties also available. Leaves green or blue-grey, very narrow and mainly borne in tufts. Barrel-shaped cones borne upwards.

CHAMAECYPARIS (False cypress)

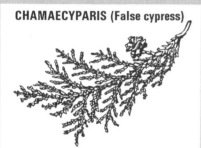

Most popular British genus. All shapes, sizes and colours – green, blue, and yellow. Leaves small and scale-like. Branchlets lie in one plane on the shoots. Cones globular, pea-sized.

CRYPTOMERIA (Japanese cedar)

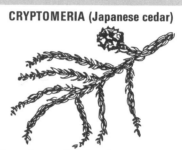

Several attractive dwarf varieties available. Leaves green and awl-shaped, generally bent close to the cord-like shoots. Foliage turns bronze in the winter. Cones globular, spiky.

CUPRESSUS (Cypress)

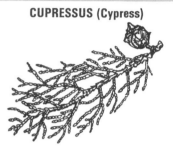

Upright trees, mainly tall growing. Leyland cypress is the most popular British conifer hedge. Leaves small and scale-like. Branchlets lie at random angles on the shoots. Cones globular, 1 inch across.

JUNIPERUS (Juniper)

Small trees ; many prostrate and upright varieties available. Tolerant of poor conditions. Two types of leaves – hard and spine-like or small and scale-like. Fruits look like berries.

LARIX (Larch)

Quick-growing tall trees, only suitable for large gardens. Leaves green, soft and needle-shaped ; borne in tufts on short spurs. Foliage falls in winter. Cones egg-shaped, small.

PICEA (Spruce)

Mostly tall conical trees (*P. abies* is the Christmas Tree) but all shapes and sizes are available. Leaves short, hard and needle-like ; green, blue or grey. Cones hang downwards.

PINUS (Pine)

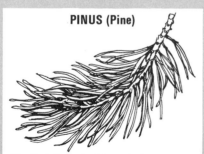

Mostly tall conical trees but numerous dwarf varieties are available. Leaves long (2 – 10 inches), needle-like and borne in bundles of 2, 3 or 5. Cones of various shapes.

TAXUS (Yew)

Bushy trees or shrubs, much used for hedging. Tolerant of poor conditions. Leaves strap-like and dark green. Golden varieties are available. Red, berry-like fruits borne on female trees.

THUJA (Arbor-vitae)

Small slow-growing trees and shrubs, similar in appearance to *Chamaecyparis*. Leaves small and scale-like, often highly aromatic. Branchlets are flattened. Cones urn-shaped, erect, 1 inch across.

THE GARDEN SCENE
IN W. GERMANY

WILHELMA,
STUTTGART

The country that came from behind

Learned books on the story of gardening tend to be hard on Germany. They point out that this country is the only nation in Europe which did not evolve a grand gardening style of its own.

When the German scholars and travellers returned from Italy in the sixteenth century they brought back the news and drawings of the spectacular and revolutionary gardens which had been created there. France moulded and refined these Italian ideas into *le jardin français*, and strode into the lead with Versailles. The German aristocracy, however, merely switched from the Italian Renaissance concepts to the new Grand French style. So the German Baroque castles were surrounded by French gardens, and you can still see them today – Nymphenburg (Munich), Charlottenburg (West Berlin), Augustusburg (Bruehl) and Herrenhausen (Hanover).

In the eighteenth century the back-to-nature movement of Brown, Repton and Kent moved from Britain to the Continent. France was cautious – the usual pattern there was to create an English park alongside the existing formal French garden. But in Germany the landscape concept was wholeheartedly accepted. Hirschfeld became the German 'Capability' Brown and as in England hundreds of French style gardens were completely destroyed and replaced with landscaped parks. Some of these transformed gardens remain today, and you can visit Grossherzogliches (Eutin), Schwöbber (near Hameln) and Philippsruhe at Hanau.

German grand gardens have always been important numerically. In the sixteenth century there were more gardens in Germany than in any other country in Europe, but over the years they have added little to the development of new ideas. Their only contribution has been a note of exaggeration added to other styles. The topiary was often more grotesque than the Dutch originals, and the 'joke' fountains more absurd than the earlier Italian versions. In their French style gardens they built pavilions and other garden buildings of unrivalled magnificence. When the landscape style arrived some of the German versions were filled with bizarre collections of sham castles, mosques, pyramids, temples and grottoes on a scale never seen in England.

So the textbooks are right; the Germans were copyists in the creation of the grand gardens around their palaces and stately homes. But it is grossly unfair to leave the story there, for the German contributions to the home garden, city park, national exhibition, indoor plant and plant breeding scenes have been immense since the war. Germany is the European country that has come from behind to take the lead in several aspects of amateur gardening.

Germany has been at the forefront of the trend towards the architectural home garden. Here stone, water and other materials are used to create a permanent non-living skeleton inside the garden and the beauty of these inanimate objects is held to be as important as the beauty of the flowers. Everywhere you will see plants and stones in partnership, and the seeds for this were sown in Germany hundreds of years ago. Joseph Furttenbach (1591–1667) wrote about his home garden at Ulm with its large terrace of paving slabs containing a series of rectangular flower beds. How like the German 'paradise' garden of today!

According to the German Horticultural Society, gardening is the most popular hobby in the Federal Republic. Millions of people belong to the various local and plant societies, and the gardener tends to be the man of the house. Gardening has become part of the rapidly expanding do-it-yourself movement, and as with painting, papering or furniture making it is something that the husband does for the wife and children to enjoy.

Women are very much involved in one aspect of horticulture — the use of cut flowers and pot plants. Much has been written about the German indoor-plant boom. Annual purchases in 1950 were £1 per person. In 1971 the figure was £5.56. This is several times higher than the British figure and about 50 per cent of the entire EEC production of cut flowers is used in Germany.

The simple reason is that cut flowers have become part of the German way of life. When calling on friends it is almost obligatory to take a bunch of flowers, and about one third of the purchases are used for this purpose. Graves are regularly dressed with flowers (especially chrysanthemums) and you will see roses, carnations, freesias etc. in offices, taxis, restaurants and everywhere that people gather. An interesting regional difference is that the southern German spends only half as much as his northern counterpart on plants and flowers.

There is a great deal of competitive spirit in German gardening, but it is significant that this is mainly based on judging the overall effect rather than the quality of groups of blooms as in Britain. The contest may be between houses in a town or city, or between offices and factories in an area. In the national 'Our Village Shall Become More Beautiful' competition about 4,000 villages compete for the gold, silver and bronze medals. In the allotment competitions the search is for the neatest plots and not the largest vegetables, and the city versus city competition (see page 78) centres around the future 'green' plans of the local authority.

These 'green' plans are an all-important part of German horticulture, and the proper utilisation of the natural resources of Germany is actively fought for by many organisations. The summer-long gardening exhibition was a German innovation, and so in the twentieth century the Federal Republic has done much to remove the impression that they have contributed little to the garden scene of Europe.

THE GERMAN HOME GARDEN

Forty nine per cent of German households have a garden around the house. This means that there are about 11 million home gardens in the Federal Republic. A further 6 per cent have a plot away from the home.

The size of the average garden is 5,000 sq. ft. The total area of land devoted to gardening is 1,250,000 acres, which is about twice the British garden area.

SHRUB BORDER
Popular throughout Germany. The list of the common shrubs is similar to the British list — Forsythia, Weigelia, Ribes, Viburnum, Deutzia, Euonymus etc. Less common in Britain but very popular in Germany is Kolkwitzia.

LAWN
Present in about 80% of all gardens. Interest in lawn care has greatly increased in recent years and sales of lawn mowers, fertilisers and weed-killers have grown accordingly.

FLOWER BORDER
More popular than in France, but not as universal as in Britain. List of commonest perennials is similar — Phlox, Delphinium, Lupin, Michaelmas Daisy, Aquilegia, Gaillardia etc.

POOL OR PLAY AREA
The recreational aspect of the garden is much more important in Germany than in most other European countries. A pool (even in small gardens) or a children's play area is present in 30% of all gardens.

PARADISE GARDEN
The *paradiesgartlein* is a German feature found in both old and new gardens. Most of the early gardens throughout Europe were 'paradise gardens' — square or rectangular grassy plots separated by straight paths. This tradition is preserved in the modern German version — a collection of square or rectangular beds in a paved area. Dwarf conifers or perennials are grown in the beds.

ORNAMENTAL TREES
Flowering trees and conifers are present in most gardens. There are 3 – 4 in the average plot. Popular genera include Acer, Prunus, Sorbus, Thuja, Picea and Chamaecyparis.

FRONT GARDEN
Flowering shrubs are popular here, especially Rhododendrons and Azaleas.

STEPPING STONES
A popular feature in the German lawn, leading from the patio to the back of the garden.

WINDOW BOX
Present on 13 per cent of all homes. Keen gardeners are more likely to have window boxes than non-gardeners — about 45% of garden magazine readers extend their flower area in this way.

KITCHEN GARDEN
About 17 per cent of the total garden acreage in Germany is devoted to fruit and vegetables. The vegetable plot is absent from most small gardens, but there may be an area close to the house for herbs and soft fruit. Strawberries are extremely popular; they are grown in more than 40% of all gardens. Potatoes are only half as popular. Greenhouses are uncommon.

ROSES
Present in most gardens; popularity is increasing. There are 6 – 7 bushes in the average garden. Roses are frequently underplanted with tulips. Common varieties include Lilli Marlene, Queen Elizabeth and Super Star.

BALCONY
One third of the homes in Germany have at least one balcony, and about 6% of them are planted with flowers.

PATIO
Present in more than 50% of all gardens; the central point of the modern German home garden (see below).

OUTDOOR LIVING IN GERMANY

Germany has pioneered the concept that the garden should be an outdoor living room as well as a place for flowers. This has meant more than laying down a floor of concrete slabs — in many new gardens you will find a wide variety of materials in this patio area, such as large smooth pebbles, rough-faced concrete, wood, dressed stone and metal. A three-dimensional effect is sought, with various levels of interest as one would find in an indoor room.

The outdoor living area is nearly always adjacent to the house and is designed for two basic purposes. There is the play aspect with sand box, swing or swimming pool and then there is the dining aspect with fixed or portable table and chairs of wood, metal or stone.

THE GRAND SIGHTS

There are many grand gardening sights to be seen in Germany. You will find formal gardens in the French tradition around the Baroque castles and palaces, and there are many *Englischer Gärten* with lakes, rolling hills, clumps of trees and artificial ruins. Then there are the twentieth century city parks, where Germany has created its own gardening tradition.

RHODODENDRONPARK (Bremen)
The most comprehensive display of rhododendrons in Europe can be seen in this attractive park in the Botanical Garden at Bremen. There are several hundred varieties on display, and June is the best month to see them.

AUGUSTUSBURG (Bruehl, near Cologne)
This splendid Baroque Schloss is surrounded by a large French style garden, designed by an apprentice of Le Nôtre. It could be in Paris or the Loire Valley – there are the typical long canals, fountains and box parterres of the *jardin français.*

PLANTEN UN BLOMEN (Hamburg)
This park is the site of the International Horticultural Exhibition (I.G.A.) held every 10 years, and between exhibitions it reverts to being one of the best public parks in Europe. There is a great deal to see – one of the finest iris collections in the world, herb gardens, tropical houses, 60,000 roses and regular flower shows. The well-known Ballet of the Fountains takes place each afternoon.

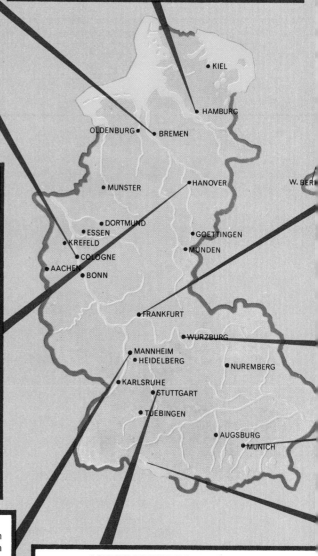

HERRENHAUSEN (Hanover)
France has its Versailles, Austria has its Schönbrunn and Germany has its Herrenhausen. It is undoubtedly the finest German Baroque garden. The gardens at Herrenhausen were created between 1666 and 1726 in the French and Dutch style. The Royal Palace of the Hanoverian kings was completely destroyed during the war, but the gardens remain in all their original splendour. There is an impressive Grand Alley (more than a mile long), the highest fountain in Germany and extensive parterres filled with flowers and coloured stones. But the main fascination of Herrenhausen is its small enclosed gardens – the Topiary garden, the Rose garden, the Island garden, the Knot garden and so on. The most famous of all its features is the *Théâtre de Verdure* which seats 800.

SCHWETZINGEN (Mannheim)
The gardens around the Schloss Schwetzingen were created when the formal *jardin français* was falling out of favour and the English landscape was taking over as the garden style of Europe. Nicholas Pigage laid out a standard French garden in 1753. About 25 years later the owner commissioned Von Skell to build an English park. The two styles butt onto each other; a mosque and imitation ruins complete the odd collection. Some experts have admired the mixture, more have condemned it.

LUDWIGSBURG (near Stuttgart)
One of Germany's great gardens, created around a perfectly preserved 18th century palace. Open from April to October, it is called *Bluehendes Barock* (Baroque in Bloom). There are roses, flower-filled parterres and a "fairy-tale" garden.

CHARLOTTENBURG (West Berlin)

The gardens around this Palace of Frederick the Great have been restored to their Baroque glory. The Great Parterre is famous.

CITY PARKS

Germany is justifiably proud of its city parks. Most of these have been enlarged and improved by the Garden Shows held there, and the transformation has provided flower-laden oases in some of the most industrialised areas of Europe. Planten un Blomen in Hamburg is outstanding, but so are the parks in Dortmund and Essen.

GROSSE TIERGARTEN (Berlin)

Destroyed during the war, the Tiergarten has now been restored. Two miles long and $\frac{1}{2}$ mile wide, this vast park contains woods, rhododendron plantations, gardens, zoo and restaurants.

RHEINPARK (Cologne)

A large park containing many plant collections — roses, iris, aquatics etc. A cable car runs over the park, so many visitors see it from above.

WESTFALENPARK (Dortmund)

A superb park, full of interest. There are demonstration areas for the home gardener, a famous Rosarium for the rose enthusiast and a Japanese garden for those in search of peace. Fountain displays take place throughout the summer.

NORDPARK (Dusseldorf)

A typical German metropolis park — big enough to provide relaxation for a large population and to house a National Garden Show attracting millions of visitors. Lawns, pools, roses, flower borders and terraces.

GRUGA PARK (Essen)

Another park in the heart of the Ruhr, well known for its dahlia display. There is a home garden demonstration area and a miniature railway for visitors. In this way the young and the elderly can see all the varied sights of this large park.

STADTGARTEN (Karlsruhe)

This park has been called the 'Green Heart of Karlsruhe'. There are lakes, fountains, zoo, rock garden and Japanese garden.

ENGLISCHER GARTEN (Munich)

One of the first landscaped parks in the English style to be created on the Continent. Winding paths criss-cross the extensive parkland, and near the northern boundary lies the large Kleinhesseloher Lake.

PALMENGARTEN (Frankfurt)

This is really a Botanical Garden under Dr. Schoser, where plants are scientifically studied. But to most visitors it is a popular park with 50 acres of roses, pools and flowers, and the big attraction is the group of 17 display glasshouses. Here you will find more than 2,000 different varieties of orchids, cacti and succulents. Open-air concerts are held during the summer months.

VEITSCHOECHHEIM (near Würzburg)

The fame of Veitschoechheim is based on its style and not on its size. It is quite small, but it is the best example in Germany of the Rococo garden. This flowery, highly ornamented style was popular in Bavaria in the 18th century, and the statues in this garden are one of the finest collections of German Rococo sculpture.

NYMPHENBURG (Munich)

A garden of Germany's past, laid out by Carbonet, a pupil of Le Nôtre at the beginning of the 18th century. At the end of the century the *jardin français* was altered and a landscaped park in the English style was added. But the grand canals, the high fountains and the geometric pathways remain. Go to Nymphenburg if you want to see the German Baroque style. Here you will see garden buildings at their glorious best — the three miniature palaces of Pagodenburg, Badenburg and Amalienburg.

MAINAU (Lake Constance)

There are few gardens in Europe which can rival the Island Garden of Mainau. The list of planting numbers is impressive — 15,000 dahlias, 25,000 roses, a million spring bulbs. But the most famous feature at Mainau is the Tropical garden, in which the visitor walks among the date palms and the banana trees. Bougainvillea, hibiscus, trumpet flowers and orchids provide splashes of colour; orange and lemon blossom scent the air.

Two factors, its owner and its climate, have combined to create this unique Grand Garden of Europe. Count Lennart Bernadotte of Sweden had the horticultural skill which was required to transform a garden of formal beds and fine trees into a flower-lover's paradise. Biographers have not missed the fact that he is descended from Empress Josephine, the great patroness of the rose. The roses at Mainau are in bloom in May, for this small island has an unusually mild climate.

77

NATIONAL GARDEN SHOWS

Every 10 years since the war a vast International Gardening Exhibition, the I.G.A. has been held in Hamburg. Between these shows Germany, unlike other European countries, has kept up the grand tradition with its own *Bundes Gartenschauen* (National Garden Shows).

These major events in the German calendar are held every two years. A city has to request permission to stage the show about 8 years ahead of the proposed date and one of its parks is transformed into the showground. A new park may be specially created for the purpose (Westfalenpark in Dortmund was built for the *Bundes Gartenschau* of 1959) or an existing park may be extended and improved. The city meets the cost and receives the income from admissions. The *Zentralverband des deutschen Gartenbaues* provides the administration.

The show lasts from spring until autumn and has none of the crowded big-tent image of the British flower show. There is a great deal of space and this is filled with a wide variety of gardens, demonstration areas, playgrounds, educational exhibits and places to rest tired feet. Floral displays are changed, of course, as the season progresses and so many visitors come again and again. Attendance at each show runs into millions – they come by the bus load and train load from all over Germany. Nearly all local horticultural societies and many organisations and factories arrange visits, but this interest is not international. The National Garden Shows attract surprisingly few tourists from abroad.

Year	Town	Attendance
1959	Dortmund	6.8 million
1961	Stuttgart	6.8 million
1963	I.G.A. at Hamburg	5.4 million
1965	Essen	5.3 million
1967	Karlsruhe	6.3 million
1969	Dortmund	6.8 million
1971	Cologne	5.0 million
1973	I.G.A. at Hamburg	
1975	Mannheim	
1977	Stuttgart	
1979	Bonn	
1981	Essen	

In addition to these *Bundes Gartenschauen* there are many horticultural exhibitions held in Germany each year. These generally only last a few days, like the internationally famous Cologne Trade Fair and the biennial *Dein Garten* show.

'GREEN SPACE' COMPETITION

Every three years hundreds of small German towns (population 3,000 – 50,000) compete for the coveted gold medals of the 'Green Space' Competition. The contest is organised by the D.G.G., and the parks department of each town has an important part to play.

Points are awarded for the present appearance of the parks and green spaces of the town, its floral displays and its future plans for the environment. State finalists go forward to the National final in the following year.

MAGAZINES

mein schöner Garten
Monthly.   Circulation 250,000

Garten als Jungborn
Monthly.   Circulation 120,000
A further 200,000 copies are
distributed by garden centres

Grün
Monthly.   Circulation 100,000

The quality of these magazines is extremely high, and they include general interest articles which are only slightly related to practical home gardening. This could explain why 58 – 62 per cent of the readers are women, whereas it is generally the man of the house who works in the garden.

DEUTSCHE GARTENBAU – GESELLSCHAFT

The D.G.G. (German Horticultural Society) speaks for gardening, the gardener and the preservation of green space in the Federal Republic. Its role in German horticulture is immense – it organises inter-factory, inter-village and inter-town competitions; it awards Quality Certificates to outstanding new varieties and presents awards to outstanding people. It holds seminars, exhibitions and most important of all, the annual Green Parliament at Mainau. At this island home of its President, Count Lennart Bernadotte, the Green Charter of Mainau was adopted at the fifth Green Parliament. This Charter demanded adequate legislative measures for the promotion and safeguarding of healthy living space. A great deal of the effort of the D.G.G. is directed towards preserving the beauty of the German landscape.

The Society has in this way taken on a more far-reaching role than its counterparts in other countries, and it has 150 years of tradition behind it. The annual subscription is 30 – 50 DM per year, and yet there is only a mere handful of individual members. Its strength lies in the fact that all the German local, state and specialist societies belong to it, and here the combined membership is a staggering 7 million people.

THE SUPPLIERS

The German garden market is an expanding one and the number of suppliers continues to grow to keep pace with the demand. There are thousands of seed merchants throughout the country and these with the plant nurseries have been the traditional outlets. Mail order is extremely important in the Federal Republic. The most important recent development has been the appearance of the *Grüne Warenhaus* (Green Department Store). Basically they are garden centres, but unlike their British counterparts they also sell a wide range of do-it-yourself materials, pet supplies, fishing equipment etc. There are 150 – 200 of these establishments and the most important chain is *Die Flora*.

KLEINGÄRTEN

In Germany, as in Holland and Scandinavia, allotments have been transformed since the war from rather dreary places used solely for food production into attractive gardens complete with chalets for family recreation.

The idea of allotments for recreation and healthy exercise rather than as charity for the starving poor is not new. More than 100 years ago Dr. Schreber of Leipzig advocated family gardens for exercise as well as food, and even to this day allotments are sometimes called *schrebergärten* in Germany.

The popular name for today's chalet gardens is *kleingärten,* and these can be found throughout the country, with the main concentrations on the outskirts of the larger towns and in the surrounding green belts. In the industrial cities there is one *kleingarten* per 20 – 30 families.

Size, rent, rules and administration vary from one locality to another. The tenant pays £6 – £12 per year to the local allotments association. In return he receives a 250 – 550 sq. yd. plot, but no long-term guarantees of tenure. He becomes a member of the association and receives its magazine.

Each *kleingarten* must have its chalet, and the tenant is responsible for its erection. These structures cost £300 – £700, and the plans must be passed by the association. The chalet is not meant to be a second home – the floor area is only 13 – 16 sq. yds. and not all sites will permit the tenant and his family to sleep there.

The old rule of $\frac{1}{3}$ vegetables, $\frac{1}{3}$ fruit and $\frac{1}{3}$ chalet, lawn and flowers is not followed. Grow what you like, but the *kleingarten* must be kept tidy or the tenant is fined or evicted. In most cases a miniature garden is created – lawn, flowers, a few roses, fruit, some vegetables and somewhere to sit. There are no walls and few dividing fences, yet vandalism and theft is surprisingly low. This is due in part to the friendly spirit in most places; the community centre is often the hub of the site.

Germany has 550,000 *kleingärten* and long waiting lists of people, many without a home garden, who want their own place in the sun.

BOTANICAL GARDENS & TREE COLLECTIONS

There are many fine Botanical Gardens in Germany, and a welcome feature in some of them is a demonstration area designed to help the home gardener.

AACHEN BOTANICAL GARDEN Large collection of local flora. $2\frac{1}{2}$ acres.

AUGSBERG BOTANICAL GARDEN Eight thousand different species to be seen in the greenhouses. $4\frac{1}{2}$ acres.

BERGGARTEN (Hanover) Very important historically; plants have been raised in its glasshouses for more than 300 years. For today's gardener there are display plots of perennials.

BERLIN BOTANICAL GARDEN A large and beautiful garden to enjoy as well as plants to study. The alpine collection is one of the best in Europe, and the cacti and orchids attract many visitors. There is an important tree collection. 100 acres, containing about 18,000 varieties.

BRAUNSCHWEIG BOTANICAL GARDEN Good collections of orchids and cacti. $3\frac{1}{2}$ acres.

BREMEN BOTANICAL GARDEN Contains the world-famous Rhododendronpark. There are model ornamental and vegetable gardens on view, and displays of annuals and shade-loving plants for the amateur. Well worth a visit. 84 acres.

DARMSTADT BOTANICAL GARDEN Notable collection of trees. $12\frac{1}{2}$ acres.

DORTMUND BOTANICAL GARDEN Famous for its flowering shrubs and heathers. Good display of orchids. 160 acres.

ESSEN BOTANICAL GARDEN Noteworthy collection of alpines, conifers and house plants. 50 acres.

GEISENHEIM BOTANICAL GARDEN This Vine, Fruit and Gardening Institute does not appear in the guidebooks, but it is of great interest to the gardener. Special displays of fruit, vegetables, ornamentals and landscape gardening. Here you can see how to use stone in the garden. 220 acres.

GOETTINGEN BOTANICAL GARDEN Recently extended to include a tree collection. Large alpine display. 72 acres.

HEIDELBERG BOTANICAL GARDEN Cacti, succulents, bromeliads and ferns housed in 10 display houses. 10 acres.

KIEL BOTANICAL GARDEN Well known for its large landscaped displays of cacti and rock plants. If you are an alpine enthusiast, Kiel should be seen.

KREFELD BOTANICAL GARDEN Large collection of Rhineland flora.

MUNDEN FORESTRY GARDEN Extensive collection of North European trees. $10\frac{1}{2}$ acres.

MUNICH BOTANICAL GARDEN Seventeen display greenhouses with orchids palms, cacti etc. Out of doors there are many plant collections, notably rhododendrons, alpines, ferns and heathers. 52 acres.

MUNSTER BOTANICAL GARDEN One of the special displays at Munster is the collection of aquatic plants. In the glasshouses there is a collection of bromeliads. $10\frac{1}{2}$ acres.

OLDENBURG BOTANICAL GARDEN Large collection of plants which are native to North-West Germany. 90 acres.

PFORZHEIMER ALPINE GARDEN (Worms) Privately-owned collection of alpines, azaleas and dwarf conifers. Open to the public. 4 acres.

TUEBINGEN BOTANICAL GARDEN Large collection of Bavarian wild flowers. Alpine collection. 25 acres.

WILHELMA BOTANICAL GARDEN (Stuttgart) Popular park of 276 acres with azaleas and water lilies, fuchsias and camellias. Orchids and cacti well displayed in the glasshouses. See photograph on page 73.

A PICTURE GUIDE TO *Topiary*

The suburban gardener neatly shaping his privet hedge on a Sunday morning probably has no idea that he is practicing an ancient art. Yet topiary (the clipping of trees and shrubs into geometrical or fanciful shapes) dates back to early Rome.

Of course, fruit trees are trimmed to increase their cropping and many flowering shrubs must be cut back to ensure a colourful display the following year. This is the purely practical craft of pruning; topiary is a form of decorative folk art.

Simple topiary was popular throughout the monasteries of mediaeval Europe, and this led to the shaped trees and box-trimmed flower beds of the fifteenth century manor house. But it was not until the French designer Le Nôtre took a ruler to nature that topiary became an international fad. It was a time when man believed that the natural world had to be subdued and the gardens he built were magnificent, if expensive, proof that the green world could be conquered.

The exiled Charles II and his court marvelled at Le Nôtre's skill and on their return the transformation of England's gardens began. When William and Mary came to the throne topiary gained fresh impetus, for they brought the fanciful and fantastic designs from Holland with them. The King built a mock fort of yew and holly at Kensington Gardens, the firm of London and Wise sold vast quantities of clipped trees, and topiary became the national craze by the end of the seventeenth century.

Such artificiality could not last and when fashion took a sudden swing to the natural landscaped look, many of the grand gardens were dug up and remade. This has deprived us of the opportunity to see more than a handful of examples of our ancestors' obsession.

Topiary lived on in Holland and also in the English cottage garden. In France there was much less of a swing to naturalism than in Britain. By the middle of the nineteenth century topiary was back in favour with the British garden designers. The Victorians wanted these symbols of garden maturity and were not prepared to wait ten years for a sizeable tree to be trained. So astute nurserymen turned to Holland for supplies of mature trees. Back came the shears, the secateurs and the training wires, and most of the topiary to be seen in the grand gardens of Britain today is less than 100 years old.

Topiary is not dead, and the production and maintenance of green figures and shapes remains popular in many country gardens. But the work involved in creating extensive topiary gardens must mean that there will never again be another revival. The days when a stately home could employ 80 gardeners have gone forever.

So topiary is an art form and an important one in the story of European gardening. But is it ugly and unnatural or is it a useful element in garden design? The argument began a long time ago – "Images cut in juniper, or garden stuff, they be for children," wrote Francis Bacon in 1624. Only five years later Parkinson described topiary as "the chieftest beauty of gardens."

Visitors to topiary gardens are invariably intrigued by the designer's ingenuity, but probably few would want to have even the traditional peacock on their lawns. However, there is a place in small modern gardens for evergreens in formal shapes. Today's answer to yesterday's passion may lie in the many conifers now available which grow naturally as pillars or pyramids. Design without shears.

TOPIARY SHAPES

ARCH   **SPHERE**   **CONE**   **PYRAMID**

MUSHROOM   **WEDDING CAKE**   **CORKSCREW**   **PILLAR**

BIRD   **ANIMAL**   **FIGURE**   **OBJECT**

INITIAL   **ARBOUR**   **CROSS**   **KISSING RING**

TREE TABLEAUX

Group of clipped trees arranged to form a scene or picture.

Examples:

Sundial	*Ascott, Bucks.*
Playing cards	*Ludstone Hall, Salop.*
Chess set	*Hasely Court, Oxon.*
Bears' picnic	*Dunsborough Park, Surrey*

HEDGE TABLEAUX

Hedgetop trimmed to form a scene or picture.

Examples:

Fox hunt	*Mt. Stewart, N. Ireland*
Castle walls	*Thornbury Castle, Glocs.*
Battle scene	*Airlie Castle, Scotland*
Elephant walk	*Rockingham Castle, Northants.*

PRACTICAL TOPIARY

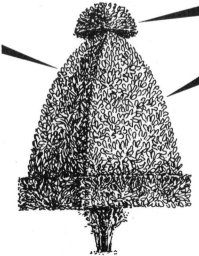

Clip the trained tree in August or September. Use hand or electric shears for yew and box; secateurs for holly and bay. Keep to about 2 inches from the previous year's growth to allow for steady expansion of the specimen.

Do not clip at all for at least 12 months after planting, and throughout the life of the tree never cut off a branch which can be bent into the body of the design.

Choose young plants of yew, about 3 ft. high. Box is the next best planting material. Holly and bay are suitable for simple, geometric shapes.

Finish the design once the desired final height has been reached by shaping the top piece, known as the finial.

Train into the required shape, when the tree is large enough, by taking branches and bending them to form the main framework. Hold in position with tarred string and canes or wire.

Plant in October or May when the soil is moist. Add bone meal to the planting hole and make sure that you plant firmly.

Pick a sunny site which is protected from strong winds. Dig the soil deeply before planting.

EuroTopiary

❶ In **GT. BRITAIN** nearly all early topiary was destroyed during the 18th century back-to-nature revolution. But there are still some outstanding examples, such as

Levens Hall (Westmorland): The most famous topiary garden in Britain, filled with a fantasy of figures, animals, birds and shapes.

Rous Lench Court (Worcestershire): Part of the massive yew topiary is nearly 300 years old.

Packwood House (Warwickshire): Large clipped yews, representing the Sermon on the Mount.

Chastleton House (Oxfordshire): Large topiary garden with a wide variety of figures and animals.

Most topiary in British grand gardens is less than 100 years old. A fine example of this modern work is at Compton Wynyates (Warwickshire). Other examples worth visiting are at Hever Castle (Kent), Nymans (Sussex), Ascott (Buckinghamshire), Gt. Dixter (Sussex), Mt. Stewart (N. Ireland) and Sudeley Castle (Gloucestershire).

There are many more examples of topiary along the roadside than are to be seen in the grand gardens. Look in cottage gardens, churchyards, and around inns and large farmhouses.

If you want to try your hand then yew and box are available at your garden centre or nursery.

The shape will be established after 3 years' careful training and clipping. It is not *quite* as difficult as it looks! Specialist nurseries, selling ready-shaped specimens, include Clifton Nurseries (London) and Robinsons Gardens (Sevenoaks).

❷ **FRANCE** was once a great centre for topiary –evergreens in both grand and humble gardens were trained into geometric shapes; fruit trees and even roses were carefully trained and meticulously clipped. Now topiary is confined to those grand gardens which set out to reproduce the classical French style. Villandry, illustrated below, is a good example.

❸ In **BELGIUM** and **HOLLAND** topiary has generally disappeared from home gardens, but can be found in some villages in northern Holland. It is still to be seen in grand gardens such as Kasteel Twickel (Delden) and Freyr (Namur). Nurseries in Belgium and Holland remain the main suppliers of trained evergreens to Britain and other countries.

❹ **ITALY** ranks with Britain as the home of present-day topiary. There are gardens with fantastic shapes, as at Villa Sciarra (Rome) and Villa la Pietra (Florence). But the strictly geometrical designs of classical times are the general rule–see Villa Lante and Villa Gamberaia. Best of all, perhaps, is the display at Castello Balduino (Montalto di Pavia).

Levens Hall, Westmorland

A PICTURE GUIDE TO Roses

The rose is truly the flower of Europe. Not only is it by far the most popular garden plant, but its roots spread across national boundaries. The British rose grower obtains his rootstocks from Holland or perhaps Denmark and on these he grafts choice varieties which originated in Germany, France, Northern Ireland, Holland, Belgium or Great Britain. The breeders of these varieties will have sought awards at International Trials in countries other than their own, at London, Paris, Rome, The Hague, Madrid, Geneva and the rest. The rose is the complete European hybrid.

Its popularity is obvious to everyone. The British favour Hybrid Teas, most other European countries choose the Floribunda as their favourite, but everywhere it is roses, roses all the way. In Britain there are about 150 million rose bushes in private gardens. The French have lined some of their roads with them; Denmark has lined its railway embankments with the red-flowered Kirsten Poulsen. But it wasn't always so, for after the mediaeval affection for the flower it fell out of favour. Neither the classical garden designers of France nor the landscapers in Britain had any love for our present-day Queen of Flowers.

In 1790 the largest nursery in France only listed 25 kinds. In Britain there was still not a single book devoted to the rose, although the Imperial Library of China had possessed 600 rose books . . . in 500 B.C.

Two events completely transformed the picture and turned the rose into the most popular flower in Europe. The first of these events began with the purchase of Malmaison by Napoleon in 1798. His wife, Josephine Beauharnais, set out to collect every known kind of rose for the grounds of this mansion on the outskirts of Paris. She spent a vast fortune creating the first great rose garden; oceans were crossed in search of rare species and so were battlefields – her nurseryman had a special pass to travel to London in order to buy roses! Here gathered the scientists and the growers of the day to study the flowers which were recorded for all time by the painter she commissioned – Redouté.

The second epoch-making event also took place in France. About a hundred years ago Jean-Baptiste Guillot introduced La France, the first Hybrid Tea rose. At last someone had managed to combine all the vigour and hardiness of the Hybrid Perpetuals with the continuous flowering habit and shapely blooms of the Tea roses. Roses which were in existence before Malmaison are sometimes referred to as *ancient roses*. Those developed between the time of Josephine's collection and the first Hybrid Tea are described as *old-fashioned roses*. La France began the era of *modern roses* and their popularity has never waned.

This is not really surprising for they have all of the requirements for garden success. Planting should be done carefully, but it is a straightforward job, as described on page 90. Once it is done the bush or tree can be expected to flourish for 20 years or more, and upkeep is a simple matter. No staking is required, and only in the colder areas of Europe is it common practice to place straw or bracken between the bushes in winter. In Britain there is no winter treatment and in spring the roses are fed and pruning is completed. From June onwards the reasons for the plants' success are obvious – continuous flowering until the frosts arrive, fragrant blooms, enchanting colours.

Another attraction is the constant promise of something new in the rose world, and the scene is frequently changing. New colours – we now have 'hand-painted' and 'bizarre' varieties. New growth forms – the prostrate variety Nozomi has been introduced from Japan for ground cover or hanging over walls. There is even a new classification, as the proposals of the Royal National Rose Society have recently received international approval. Our Hybrid Teas are to be called *Large Flowered Roses* and the present Floribunda group will be classed as *Cluster Flowered Roses*. The rose first appeared on this earth about 50 million years ago, but still it changes in the search for perfection.

Rose Features

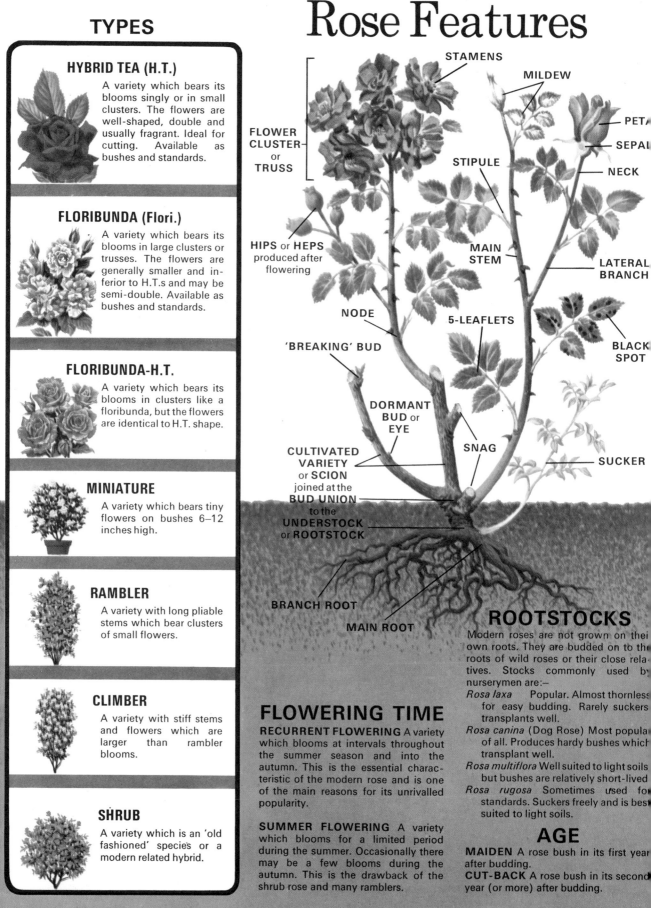

HYBRID TEA (H.T.)

A variety which bears its blooms singly or in small clusters. The flowers are well-shaped, double and usually fragrant. Ideal for cutting. Available as bushes and standards.

FLORIBUNDA (Flori.)

A variety which bears its blooms in large clusters or trusses. The flowers are generally smaller and inferior to H.T.s and may be semi-double. Available as bushes and standards.

FLORIBUNDA-H.T.

A variety which bears its blooms in clusters like a floribunda, but the flowers are identical to H.T. shape.

MINIATURE

A variety which bears tiny flowers on bushes 6–12 inches high.

RAMBLER

A variety with long pliable stems which bear clusters of small flowers.

CLIMBER

A variety with stiff stems and flowers which are larger than rambler blooms.

SHRUB

A variety which is an 'old fashioned' species or a modern related hybrid.

STAMENS

MILDEW

PETA

SEPAL

NECK

FLOWER CLUSTER or TRUSS

STIPULE

HIPS or HEPS produced after flowering

MAIN STEM

LATERAL BRANCH

NODE

5-LEAFLETS

'BREAKING' BUD

BLACK SPOT

DORMANT BUD or EYE

SNAG

SUCKER

CULTIVATED VARIETY or SCION joined at the BUD UNION to the UNDERSTOCK or ROOTSTOCK

BRANCH ROOT

MAIN ROOT

ROOTSTOCKS

Modern roses are not grown on their own roots. They are budded on to the roots of wild roses or their close relatives. Stocks commonly used by nurserymen are:—

Rosa laxa Popular. Almost thornless for easy budding. Rarely suckers transplants well.

Rosa canina (Dog Rose) Most popular of all. Produces hardy bushes which transplant well.

Rosa multiflora Well suited to light soils but bushes are relatively short-lived

Rosa rugosa Sometimes used for standards. Suckers freely and is best suited to light soils.

FLOWERING TIME

RECURRENT FLOWERING A variety which blooms at intervals throughout the summer season and into the autumn. This is the essential characteristic of the modern rose and is one of the main reasons for its unrivalled popularity.

SUMMER FLOWERING A variety which blooms for a limited period during the summer. Occasionally there may be a few blooms during the autumn. This is the drawback of the shrub rose and many ramblers.

AGE

MAIDEN A rose bush in its first year after budding.

CUT-BACK A rose bush in its second year (or more) after budding.

PETALLAGE

SINGLE
5–8 petals
Examples :
Rosa canina
Dortmund

SEMI-DOUBLE
9–15 petals
Examples :
Allgold
Penelope

MODERATELY FULL
16–25 petals
Examples :
Virgo
Queen Elizabeth

FULL
26–40 petals
Examples :
Fragrant Cloud
Rose Gaujard

VERY FULL
over 40 petals
Examples :
Red Planet
Moon Maiden

FOLIAGE

GLOSSY   **SEMI-GLOSSY**   **MATT**   **BRONZE TINTED**

COLOURS

SELF-COLOUR
Petals uniformly
coloured. This colour
may change slightly
with age.
Examples :
Pascali, Super Star

BICOLOUR
Colour of the inner
face of the petal
distinctly different
from the outside.
Examples :
Piccadilly, Pigalle

MULTI-COLOUR
Colour of the petals changes
distinctly with age. Flower
trusses bear several colours
at the same time.
Examples :
Masquerade, Charleston

BLEND
Two or more distinct
colours on the face of
each petal. No clear
dividing lines present.
Examples :
Peace, Dorrit

VARIEGATED
Two or more distinct
colours on the face
of each petal. Clear
dividing lines present.
Examples :
Rosa Mundi, Picasso

TROUBLES

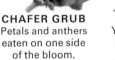

BALLING
Petals cling
together in
wet weather.

THRIPS
Petal edges
blackened.
Blooms distorted.

CHAFER GRUB
Petals and anthers
eaten on one side
of the bloom.

CAPSID
Young buds
brown and
withered.

TORTRIX MOTH
Buds holed;
maggot found
inside.

MILDEW
White powdery
mould on buds.
Very common.

AVERAGE HEIGHTS

Roses vary from tiny miniatures, a few inches high to sturdy climbing varieties reaching the bedroom window. Bush roses are by far the most popular. There is no 'typical' size, so check the expected height before buying. Some rose bushes barely reach 2 ft. Others (Queen Elizabeth and many shrub roses) can easily grow to 7 ft. or more. These taller bushes can be used to make a rose hedge. Ramblers trained along wires are sometimes used for this purpose, but generally they are not as satisfactory as vigorous floribundas or Rugosa hybrids.

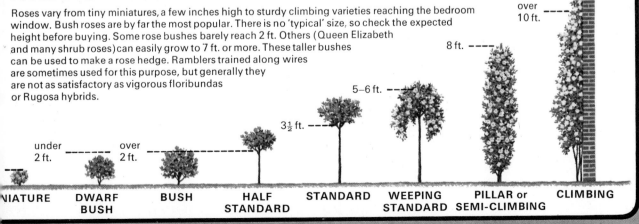

over 10 ft.

8 ft.

5–6 ft.

3½ ft.

under 2 ft.

over 2 ft.

MINIATURE   DWARF BUSH   BUSH   HALF STANDARD   STANDARD   WEEPING STANDARD   PILLAR or SEMI-CLIMBING   CLIMBING

The Great Rose Makers

In 1867 Monsieur Guillot's La France ushered in the era of the modern rose. Lyons became the nineteenth century rose capital of the world and plant breeders everywhere sought new varieties which would make their fortunes. Not all were professionals; two of Britain's most revered varieties, Ena Harkness and Frensham were raised by Mr. Norman in his garden.

Thousands of named varieties have been produced during the past hundred years, and some of the great European rose makers are listed on these pages.

Many countries have been involved, but it is obvious that France, Germany and Northern Ireland have dominated the scene for many years. The pattern may change. Before 1964 the British breeder had no protection for his creation; it could not be patented a in other countries. In that year the Plant Variety Rights Office was founded to "encourage, protect and reward innovation in plant breeding". The first patented rose was Grandpa Dickson.

Now the British rose grower has a real incentive to raise as well as distribute new varieties. In 1960 only 9 per cent of the R.N.R.S. Awards to New Roses went to varieties raised in Gt. Britain. In 1972 the corresponding figure was 59 per cent.

McGREDY
Sam McGredy IV has a family tradition of rose breeding, and since taking over the nursery at Portadown in 1952 has joined the ranks of Europe's great hybridists. His achievements include City of Belfast, Molly McGredy, Elizabeth of Glamis and Mischief – all winners of Britain's top award, the President's International Trophy. No other British breeder can match his record.

DICKSON
The Dickson nurseries in County Down have a long and distinguished history of rose breeding. There were Dickson roses before the beginning of the 20th century, and prewar varieties like Betty Uprichard and Shot Silk still appear in the Rose Society's Selected List. Alexander III and his son Pat now carry on the tradition and have been extremely successful in recent years with Grandpa Dickson, Red Devil, Red Planet and Mala Rubinstein.

SANDAY
Many breeders began their work as children in families already famous in the rose industry. Jim Sanday did not begin until his retirement at 64 from the Caledonian Insurance Company ! His first success was Gavotte (1962). Since then there have been Fred Gibson, City of Bath, City of Gloucester and Bob Woolley.

LE GRICE
Edward le Grice of Norfolk was responsible for one of the best of all the yellow Floribundas – Allgold. His career has been a long one; in 1938 he received a Certificate of Merit for Dainty Maid. In 1970 he was awarded a Gold Medal for News. In between these two milestones were Lilac Charm and Bonnie Maid.

PERNET-DUCHER
Born in 1858, Joseph Pernet-Ducher earned the title "Wizard of Lyons" by transforming the colour range of roses. His early successes included Mme. Caroline Testout, one of the most popular roses ever raised. His greatest achievement, however, was Soleil d'Or, introduced in 1900. This was a cross between Persian Yellow and a Hybrid Tea, and at last the rose world had a repeat-flowering deep yellow variety. From this all of our present-day large flowered deep yellow roses have evolved.

DOT
For nearly 50 years Pedro Dot has been Spain's leading hybridist, and has raised many noteworthy Hybrid Teas. His claim to fame, however, is as the world's leading breeder of miniature roses. Rosina, Pour Toi, Coralina and Baby Gold Star were all raised at the San Feliu nurseries.

GAUJARD
Jean Gaujard took over the great tradition of the Lyons nursery when his father-in-law and employer, the legendary Pernet-Ducher, died in 1928. He has been responsible for many famous varieties, including Opera, Rose Gaujard, Guitare and Femina.

COCKER/HARKNESS

A recent partnership has combined the breeding skills of Alec Cocker of Aberdeen and Jack Harkness of Hitchin. Success has come very quickly, and there have been R.N.R.S. Awards for Alec's Red, Anne Cocker, Escapade, Southampton, Alexander and Yesterday. In 1972 nearly half of the Rose Society's Awards went to this partnership!

POULSEN

The Poulsen family of Denmark have produced many great roses during the past 60 years. Svend Poulsen raised the first Floribundas, and these were launched in 1924 as Else Poulsen and Kirsten Poulsen. He was responsible for many famous varieties (Danish Gold, Sundance, Rumba etc.) and his son Niels has carried on the tradition with Troika, Copenhagen and Chinatown.

KORDES

Wilhelm Kordes and his son Reimer rank alongside Mathias Tantau as the greatest rose hybridists in Germany. From their large nursery in Holstein some of Europe's most famous roses have originated – Perfecta, Ernest H. Morse, Ballet, Iceberg, Peer Gynt and Karl Herbst. This list dates back to 1935 when Crimson Glory was launched. One of their most outstanding achievements was the development of the Kordesii climbers, such as Dortmund and Parkdirektor Riggers.

TANTAU

Super Star and Fragrant Cloud. The Royal National Rose Society premier awards in both 1971 and 1972 with Fountain and Topsi. These are some of the achievements of the father and son partnership of Mathias Tantau and Mathias jun. working in north Germany. Beauty of Holstein was the first of the Tantau roses in 1919. Their successes since then are far too numerous to list in full; examples are Prima Ballerina, Blue Moon, Duke of Windsor, Stella, Dorothy Wheatcroft and Whisky Mac.

DE RUITER

Gijs de Ruiter is the foremost Dutch hybridist. His early success was the introduction of the first orange-scarlet rose. His most famous creation was Europeana, which is grown throughout the world. Recent introductions include Tombola, Michelle and Diorama.

LENS

Louis Lens and his father Victor who died a few years ago have maintained the Lens nurseries as the most successful rose breeding establishment in Belgium for more than 40 years. Pascali remains one of the best of all white Hybrid Teas, and Bel Ange, Percy Thrower and Blue Diamond were all awarded Trial Ground Certificates.

GUILLOT

Jean-Baptiste Guillot was the first of the great rose breeders from Lyons. His creation, La France, was the original Hybrid Tea and caused a sensation. It was planted in rose gardens everywhere and is still in cultivation. In 1877 he introduced another epoch-making variety – Gloire des Polyantha. This was used to develop the Dwarf Polyantha which gave rise to the modern Floribunda.

MEILLAND

François Meilland raised Peace just before World War II and thereby secured a place in Gardening's Hall of Fame. Since then the Meilland and Paolino families have worked together at Antibes and have been responsible for many popular rose varieties such as Belle Blonde, Eden Rose, Grandmère Jenny, Moulin Rouge, Charleston, Concerto and Baccara. The breeding nursery is called Universal Rose Selection and is now one of the most productive units in the world. It is under the direction of François' son, Alain.

ROYAL NATIONAL ROSE SOCIETY

The Royal National Rose Society was founded in 1876 to "encourage, improve and extend the cultivation of the Rose". Support was indifferent in its early years, but it has now grown to be the largest specialist horticultural society in the world with nearly 100,000 members. More than 4,000 members live outside Britain.

Its popularity is due to the many benefits of membership. For the £1.75 annual subscription each member receives *Roses – A Selected List of Varieties* which contains information on 600 reliable roses and is revised every 3 years, *Roses – The Cultivation of the Rose* which is revised every 5 years, the informative *Rose Annual* every spring and the highly entertaining *Rose Bulletin* in the autumn.

Members can use the Society's extensive library and advisory service, and can visit the R.N.R.S. Gardens at St. Albans. The Membership Certificate admits the holder to rose shows throughout the country, and extra tickets are provided for the R.N.R.S. Summer and Autumn Shows. Application forms can be obtained from the Secretary, R.N.R.S., Chiswell Green Lane, St. Albans, Herts.

At the St. Albans Trial Ground about 750 varieties may be seen undergoing merit trials before being introduced into commerce. The President's International Trophy is awarded annually to the best seedling and the Henry Edland Memorial Medal to the most fragrant variety on trial. Over the past 10 years 0.5 per cent of the varieties on trial have been awarded a Gold Medal (G.M.), 2.5 per cent a Certificate of Merit (C. of M.) and 4.5 per cent a Trial Ground Certificate (T.G.C.).

THE STORY OF PEACE

No other variety has ever captured the hearts of gardeners throughout Europe in the same way. Experts and novices, Scandinavians and Spaniards, all were enchanted by the large, yellowy-pink blooms of Peace when it was introduced nearly 30 years ago. Its story epitomises the well-travelled nature of the modern rose.

Seedling No. 3–35–40 was raised by François Meilland at Lyons before the outbreak of World War II and a few plants were sent out on the last plane to America as France fell. He had named the rose Mme. Antoine Meilland after his mother, but his creation was taken to Germany as Gloria Dei and was introduced into Italy as Gioia. When the war ended the U.S. nursery which had raised his stock placed a bunch of the flowers at each place at the Peace Conference – and the rose received its final name. Peace returned once again to Europe and by 1951 over one million bushes had been sold in Britain.

ALEC'S RED

Newer H.T.s . . . . 1st place

ELIZABETH OF GLAMIS

Floribundas . . . . 4th place

Britain's Top Twenty

There is no ideal way to determine Britain's top twenty roses. This year's sales would merely reveal part of the story; an exhaustive survey of gardens throughout the country would provide information on popularity but not on merit.

The Rose Analysis conducted each year by the Royal National Rose Society is the best published guide. Information is obtained from a voting panel consisting of members who grow more than 400 rose trees in thirty or more varieties. These large numbers are needed so that the voters can make proper comparisons, and the final placings arising from their votes are based on both the merits and the popularity of the varieties.

The twenty roses illustrated on these two pages were the top ones in the 1972 Rose Analysis. The complete audit published by the R.N.R.S. is, of course, much more detailed and Northern Counties results are separated from those of the south.

An interesting finding from these audits is the close link between eventual popularity and proven merit in the garden with high honours at the trials stage. Nearly half of these twenty roses were awarded the President's International Trophy for the best new seedling rose of the year, and 65 per cent were Gold Medal winners.

FRED GIBSON

Newer H.T.s . . . . 2nd place

GRANDPA DICKSON

H.T.s for garden use . . . 7th place
H.T.s for exhibition . . . 2nd place

ICEBERG

Floribundas . . . . 1st place

PEER GYNT

Newer H.T.s . . . . 4th place

PINK FAVOURITE

H.T.s for garden use . . . 6th place
H.T.s for exhibition . . . 4th place

PINK PARFAIT

Floribundas . . . . 5th place

ANNE COCKER

Newer Floribundas . . . 2nd place

BONSOIR

Newer H.T.s . . . . 3rd place

CITY OF BELFAST

Newer Floribundas . . . 1st place

ERNEST H. MORSE

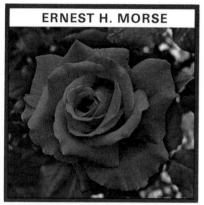

H.T.s for garden use . . 2nd place
H.T.s for exhibition . . . 8th place

EVELYN FISON

Floribundas . . . . 2nd place

FRAGRANT CLOUD

H.T.s for garden use . . . 1st place
H.T.s for exhibition . . 10th place

MOLLY McGREDY

Newer Floribundas . . . 3rd place

QUEEN ELIZABETH

Floribundas . . . . 3rd place

PEACE

H.T.s for garden use . . . 3rd place
H.T.s for exhibition . . 17th place

RED DEVIL

H.T.s for garden use . . 17th place
H.T.s for exhibition . . . . 1st place

SUPER STAR

H.T.s for garden use . . . 5th place

WENDY CUSSONS

H.T.s for garden use . . . 4th place
H.T.s for exhibition . . 12th place

Rose Care

PESTS & DISEASES

There are many pests and diseases which can affect the rose. In general the insects attack in spring and the diseases follow in summer and autumn.

The best plan is to rely on two pesticides. Buy a systemic insecticide such as formothion to keep greenfly, red spider and small caterpillars at bay. Use a systemic fungicide such as benomyl to keep mildew and black spot in check. These systemics go inside the sap and are much more effective than the traditional sprays.

You will undoubtedly see the effects of other pests. There may be tunnelled or tightly rolled leaves and foliage spun together by fine white threads. Pick off the affected parts and burn them.

GETTING READY FOR PLANTING

Leave the packed rose bushes unopened in a cool place until you are ready to start planting. Unpack carefully and prepare the bushes. First cut off all leaves and hips which may still be present. Then cut off decayed and very thin shoots and cut back the roots to about 15 inches. If the roots are dry then plunge them in a bucket of water before planting. If the stems have shrivelled then plunge the whole bush for several hours.

TIMETABLE

Plant between the end of October and the beginning of April when the soil is moist but neither waterlogged nor frozen.

Prune in the spring as soon as the first signs of new growth are seen.

Spray at the first signs of pests or disease.

Hoe each week during the summer months if weeds are a problem. Hoeing has no other benefits, and never push the blade more than an inch below the surface. If annual weeds are the problem, try mulching instead of hoeing.

PLANTING

The commonest mistake is to dig a hole which is deep and narrow. Successful "slit planting" is possible in the hands of the expert, but standard "shallow bowl planting" is much more reliable for the amateur.

The hole should be no deeper than 9 inches and about 12 – 16 inches across. Plant to the soil mark on the stem, which will be about 1 inch above the bud union. Use a planting mixture rather than ordinary soil for filling the hole – 1 part soil, 1 part peat and 4 handfuls of bone meal per barrowload.

Work a little of the mixture around the roots, shaking the plant gently up and down. Firm it down with your fists. Then half-fill the hole and firm down by gentle treading. Add more mixture until the hole is full, tread down and finally lightly rake over the surface.

SOIL & FEEDING

Nearly all soils can be improved to grow fine roses, but chalky gardens are difficult. Roses thrive best in a free-draining medium loam, slightly acid and reasonably rich in humus and plant foods. Dig about a month before planting. Feed established roses when the leaves are beginning to open in spring and again in mid-summer.

MULCHING

A mulch is a layer of peat, well-rotted compost or leaf mould placed around the bushes in mid-May. Water the soil surface before laying down the 2-inch layer of organic matter. Leave the mulch undisturbed until October, when it should be lightly forked into the surface inch of soil. A mulch has many benefits – water retention, weed suppression and soil improvement.

PLANTING DISTANCES

The standard British recommendation is to leave $1\frac{1}{2}$ – 2 ft. between bushes. Extra vigorous varieties such as Peace are planted $2\frac{1}{2}$ ft. apart. Standards are planted at $4\frac{1}{2}$ – 6 ft. intervals.

Roses are planted closer on the Continent. The German recommendation is to leave 1 ft. between bushes.

PRUNING THE NO-FUSS WAY

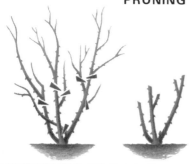

Annual pruning is necessary to get rid of old and unwanted wood and to encourage the development of new stems. Unfortunately a great deal of jargon has crept in . . . low-, hard-, moderate-, long-, light-pruning and so on. Each of these has a place in the vocabulary of the keen rose-grower, but there is a simple no-fuss way for all bushes. First cut out dead and diseased wood. Then remove all very thin stems and those which rub against another. Finally shorten all remaining stems to half their height.

The Great Rose Gardens

The first rose garden has long since passed away, for it was laid out near Paris by King Childebert nearly 1500 years ago. Today there are many great European rose gardens, and a surprisingly high proportion of them are post-war creations. You can see the largest number of plants at Orléans in France. East Germany possesses the garden with the largest number of different varieties, but perhaps the finest of them all is the Parc de la Tête d'Or in Lyons.

QUEEN MARY'S GARDEN London   England
Britain's major rose display is in the circular rose garden at Regent's Park. Climbers and ramblers frame the formal beds, and there are more than 40,000 plants to be seen. Small secluded gardens have been created within the main garden, and there are many mixed borders as well as massed plantings. A popular place for Londoners during the summer months.

PARC FLORAL Orléans – La Source   France
There are 200,000 rose trees in the rose garden of this 35 acre park, and it claims to be the largest in Europe. The summer show is held in June, and in September there is a show of remontant varieties. The top award at the International Rose Trials held there is the Golden Rose of the City of Orléans.

L'HAY LES ROSES Paris   France
This garden owned by the City of Paris has less than 25,000 roses, but it is one of the most comprehensive outdoor rose museums in the world. Here are beds displaying the history and development of the rose, the varieties grown in the Malmaison Gardens, wild roses and even a Theatre of the Rose.

WESTFALENPARK Dortmund   W. Germany
The German National Rosarium was created at Dortmund in 1969. The 1,500 varieties are arranged geographically, and each recognised breeder has his own plot in the area reserved for his country. In these plots the latest introductions are planted each year.

PARQUE DEL OESTE Madrid   Spain
The Rosaleda in the Parque del Oeste provides one of Europe's outstanding rose displays. Climbing roses surround the 270 beds which contain the 30,000 bushes. The Gold Medal of the International Trials held each year is an important honour in the rose world.

PARC DE LA GRANGE Geneva   Switzerland
La Grange is admired for its architecture as well as its roses. It consists of three terraces with pools and floodlighting. There are about 12,000 rose trees in 180 varieties, and each year the Gold Medal of the City of Geneva is awarded to the best new rose at the International Rose Trials held there.

MUNICIPAL ROSE GARDEN Rome   Italy
Perhaps this garden has the finest setting of all – a natural amphitheatre on the slopes of the Aventine Hill. In front of it are the ruins of the Palace of the Caesars. Around its edge runs a gallery of 200 climbing varieties and there are large displays of species roses, early hybrids and popular modern varieties. An important International Rose Competition is held each year.

R.N.R.S. GARDENS St. Albans   England
The Royal National Rose Society's Gardens at Chiswell Green, near St. Albans, are open to members and their friends. The trial ground is planted with new seedlings which have been submitted for an award and around the edge of the trial area are planted the award winners of recent years. In the 7 acre display garden there are nearly 1,000 different varieties, including historical and species roses.

BAGATELLE Paris   France
The Rosaraie at the Bagatelle contains about 2,500 varieties, and one of its attractions is the display of new hybrids. The first International Rose Competition was held there in 1907, and the Gold Medal of the Concours International des Roses Nouvelles is still one of the rose world's top honours.

PARC DE LA TETE D'OR Lyons   France
One of the world's great rose gardens was opened in 1964 at the birthplace of the modern rose. Here you will find 100,000 plants in 14 acres of display garden. Roses of all types are found – miniatures in rockeries, climbers on pergolas, hundreds of old fashioned species and hybrids, and the trial ground for new French seedlings.

GERMAN ROSARIUM Sangerhausen   E. Germany
Founded by the German Rose Society in 1903, Sangerhausen is now the most comprehensive collection of roses in the world, with more than 6,500 different varieties.

CITY OF BELFAST ROSE GARDEN   N. Ireland
The Rose Society of Northern Ireland (membership 300) controls this new display garden and trial ground. It has more than 20,000 rose trees and claims to be one of the finest rose gardens in Europe. The Belfast Gold Medal goes to the best new H.T. and the Golden Thorn is awarded to the winning Floribunda.

WESTBROEKPARK The Hague   Holland
This rose garden is the foremost collection in the Benelux countries, and it houses about 30,000 rose trees in 400 varieties. The judging of the International Rose Trials takes place during the first week of July.

VALBYPARKEN Copenhagen   Denmark
Opened in 1963, this large rose garden is only 10 minutes away from the centre of Copenhagen. There are about 12,000 rose trees in 250 varieties, and Danish rose growers carry out their National Trials in Valbyparken.

The *EuroRose*

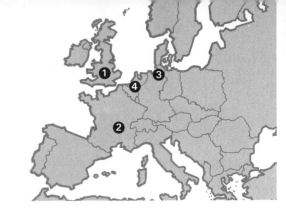

1 In **GT. BRITAIN** there are more gardens with roses than with lawns, and the Hybrid Tea type remains the favourite.

Apart from Queen Mary's Garden and the R.N.R.S. Gardens described on page 91, there are many fine displays throughout the country. At the Syon Park Gardening Centre there is a 6 acre rose garden with 12,000 plants in 400 varieties. Kew has an impressive collection of both rose species and modern varieties, and the R.H.S. Gardens at Wisley have two long rose borders.

There are a number of Provincial Display Gardens where new varieties can be seen growing under local conditions. These are situated in Roath Park, Cardiff; Harlow Car, Harrogate; Saughton Park, Edinburgh; Botanic Gardens, Southport; Vivary Park, Taunton; Pollok Park, Glasgow; Borough Park, Redcar; and the Arboretum, Nottingham. Don't forget that some of the finest and largest displays are to be seen at the larger nurseries – try Wheatcroft, Gregory, McGredy or Harkness.

There are four R.N.R.S. Shows each year – the Spring, Summer, Northern and Autumn. Other shows with good rose sections include Chelsea, Shrewsbury, Nottingham, Newcastle and Southport.

R.N.R.S. Gardens, St. Albans

2 **FRANCE** has undoubtedly the finest display gardens in Europe, and the most famous of these are described on the previous page. Illustrated is the Parc de la Tête d'Or at Lyons, and here each year the title 'La Plus Belle Rose de France' is awarded to the best new seedling raised in France. There are other rose gardens to see at Marseilles, Nancy, Nantes, Nîmes, Provins and Saverne.

The Floral Routes across France are an attractive feature for the tourist with a car, and roses figure prominently. La Route des Roses (R N 19) runs from Paris to Provins.

3 **W. GERMANY** has many rose sights to see. Planten un Blomen in Hamburg has over 60,000 rose trees in 300 varieties. At Mainau there are over 25,000 roses in a fabulous setting and at Kurpark in Baden-Baden the International Rose Trials are conducted each year. This town is the home of the German Rose Society, membership 4,200. Other well known rose gardens are at the Palmengarten in Frankfurt/Main and Nordpark in Dusseldorf.

4 The **BENELUX** countries have few rose gardens in the grand manner. Westbroekpark (see page 91) is the best. There are attractive displays at Zuiderpark in the Hague, Parc de la Citadelle in Ghent and at the Château d'Annevoie, 50 miles S.E. of Brussels.

THE GARDEN SCENE IN ITALY

VILLA BALBIANELLO

Where it all began

We owe an incalculable debt to Ancient Rome, for it was here that European gardening began. The ordinary urban villa had an open courtyard or *atrium* within its walls, and this is where the family sat, walked and dined during the summer months. Plants in pots were a popular feature and many varieties of flowers, vegetables and herbs were grown. Landscapes were sometimes painted on the walls to improve the view.

In the grand estates around Rome and Naples the gardens extended outside as well as within the buildings. There is nothing to see of these gardens today. Tourists are sometimes advised to visit **Villa Adriana** at Tivoli to obtain some idea of the scope of the Roman grand garden but nothing remains except the ruins of this most splendid of all the Imperial Roman villas; the conifers and olives there are less than 250 years old. It is from the writings of Pliny the Younger (62–116 A.D.) that we obtain a picture of the grand villa garden. There were terraces and lawns, fountains and box trees cut into fanciful shapes. There were shaded places to sit and marble-seated outdoor dining rooms. Flowers such as the violet, poppy, iris, lily and pansy were popular, but they could not compete with the rose. Steam-heated hothouses or *specularia* were sometimes maintained to provide all-the-year-round flowers.

The home garden, grand garden and conservatory all began here, and this glory and art faded with the fall of Rome. At the beginning of the fifteenth century there was a rebirth at Florence of these classical ideas and ideals. One of the foundation stones of this new movement was the recreated Ancient Roman garden begun by Cosimo de Medici at Correggio in 1417. Here the philosophers and artists walked and talked, and so the Renaissance was born in a garden.

The first designer of the early Renaissance gardens was Alberti, and his rules dominated the pattern of grand gardening in Florence and the rest of Tuscany for about 200 years. A level site was usually chosen and this was divided up into green squares or rectangles with a central fountain. They were gardens of retreat and contemplation, with a *bosco* (a thickly wooded grove) and a *giardino segreto* (a small hideaway built close to the villa). At the **Villa Capponi** near Florence the *giardino segreto* could only be reached through an underground passage from the house. Today the passage has gone, but Capponi remains one of the most complete examples of the simple Alberti-inspired Renaissance garden once so common in Tuscany.

In the sixteenth century the leadership of the Renaissance passed from Florence to Rome. Pope Julius II, patron of Raphael and Michaelangelo and founder of St. Peter's, was also the man who "changed the whole conception of gardening in Europe." His architect, Bramante, built the *Cortile del Belvedere* at the Vatican. Like Le Nôtre's Vaux-le-Vicomte in France many years later, this creation exploded on the garden scene and became the prototype for everything that followed. The unashamedly ostentatious garden of the High Renaissance had arrived. Hillsides were turned into ornate terraces, connected by grand staircases. There were open-air theatres and water, not plants, provided the great displays. Nowhere in the world is this seen to better effect than at the **Villa d'Este** at Tivoli. The Water Organ towers above the landscape and thunders out its music, the Avenue of the Hundred Fountains (illustrated on page 98) provides a gentler sound and the vast complex of cascades, waterfalls, and water staircases remains an engineering masterpiece. The **Villa Lante** at Bagnaia is considered by many experts to be the most perfect of the Italian Renaissance gardens. It was created for Cardinal Gambara between 1566 and 1570. Some years before the **Villa Medici** had been built on the Pinician Hill at Rome, and at the end of the century the gardens were considerably altered. Today they remain as the only authentic reminder of the sixteenth century Roman garden.

By 1650 the Italian dominance in European garden design had begun to wane and the French star was in the ascendancy. After this date features from the *jardin français* began to appear in some of the Italian grand gardens. **Villa Gamberaia** at Settignano provides a good example. The garden was started in 1610 and its twentieth century restoration has produced a superb example of the Italian Early Renaissance garden. There are four square green parterres with a central fountain, terracotta pots, the *bosco* and elaborate statuary. But early prints show that in the eighteenth century there were elaborate French parterres.

At **Caserta,** near Naples, an era came to an end in the latter half of the eighteenth century. The garden of the Palazzo Reale was the last of the great formal estates to be created in Italy. It was basically French in design, but its main feature, the vast Water Staircase, was inspired by La Granja in Spain.

It all began in Italy 2,000 years ago. The first Botanical Garden was opened in Padua about 430 years ago, and like much of the long history of gardening in Italy it is still to be seen today.

THE ITALIAN HOME GARDEN

It is ironical that present-day Italy should show so little interest in home gardening. The ruins of Pompeii reveal that 2,000 years ago even the humblest home had its garden. Some of these ancient gardens have been restored so that the visitor can see the style and plants which were growing when destruction came in 79 A.D.

During the fourteenth century the number and quality of Italian home gardens were unequalled in Europe. How very different today! There is no generally accepted figure for the proportion of households which own a garden—15 per cent is a generous estimate. The only national society is the *Società Italiana Amici dei Fiori* which has less than 4,000 members. There are horticultural societies in both Lombardy and Piedmont, and the city Flower Clubs provide a social as well as horticultural function. The combined membership of the Flower Clubs of Rome, Florence, Milan, Naples, Turin, Padua, Genoa and Perugia is less than 5,000 . . . in a country with a population of 53 million. The monthly gardening magazine *Il Giardino Fiorito* has increased its circulation to 78,000 copies but this magazine is now Italy's only horticultural publication—*Fiori* closed down in 1969.

Perhaps the brightest spots are the specialist societies. The Camellia Society is the most important body for this shrub in Europe, and it arranges an International Conference and Exhibition each year. The Iris Society holds the major annual International Competition in Europe. Another encouraging point is that more than 300,000 people attended the Euroflora Exhibition held at Genoa in 1971.

Interest is increasing, especially in the gardening strongholds of Lombardy, Tuscany, Liguria and Piedmont, but it lags far behind the enthusiasm found in the countries of northern Europe. The climate is undoubtedly one of the main reasons. In the south the hot, dry summer lasts for about four months and makes garden maintenance a difficult task. Even an ordinary grass lawn is an achievement and the dichondra "lawn" is becoming increasingly popular as in southern U.S.A.

In wealthy homes a full-time or part-time gardener does the work. Elsewhere it is usually the wife's job. The Italian garden is nearly always ornamental; vegetables are rarely grown. There is often a patio or terrace and a survey amongst keen gardeners revealed the most popular plants: Shrubs–rose and magnolia. Climbers–wisteria, honeysuckle and clematis. Perennials–Iris, day lily, carnation and chrysanthemum. Annuals–tagetes, petunia, antirrhinum, begonia, zinnia, viola and calendula.

Gardens may not be common, but balcony gardens and flowers in pots are found everywhere. The geranium is the universal favourite, and the terracotta pot is the traditional container.

Vase

The Terracotta Pot

The terracotta pot has been used for displaying flowers and shrubs around Italian homes for more than 2,000 years. There are a number of basic designs which can still be seen, but their manufacture is a dying art as plastic, fibreglass and concrete pots increase in popularity.

Plant pot (note thickened lip)

Lemon pot

Orange pot

Strawberry pot

Florentine urn

Amphora

Wheat storage pot

Oil jar

THE GRAND SIGHTS

On these two pages and overleaf are some of the grand gardening sights of Italy. There are many more, mainly clustered around the northern lakes, in Tuscany and close to Rome. There are a few modern gardens filled with flowering plants but mostly they are old gardens filled with water, stone and carefully-trimmed trees.

PADUA BOTANICAL GARDEN

Founded in 1545, this is the oldest Botanical Garden in the world. The original form remains, a circular wall surrounding the 4 acres. Every inch is steeped in plant history; from these small plots of ground the potato, cyclamen, lilac, sunflower and rhubarb were introduced to Europe. There is a famous octagonal greenhouse at Padua which protects a single plant, *la Palma di Goethe*.

ISOLA BELLA (Lake Maggiore)

This island garden in Lake Maggiore is one of the great horticultural sights of Europe, like the Island of Mainau in Germany. The layout of Isola Bella is formal, with its 10 terraces rising 100 ft. above the lake. The garden was created in 1670, and the many statues and fountains clearly indicate its Renaissance origin. But it is also a flower-lover's delight, like the modern gardens of Italy. There are many sub-tropical trees, and the white peacocks and green theatre are mentioned in all the guide books.

VILLA BALBIANELLO (Lenno)

One of the many beautiful gardens on Lake Como, considered by some experts to be the most attractive. The terraces overlook the blue waters of the lake, and geranium-filled pots and tubs line the walls and staircases. There are many fine mature trees, for this garden was created nearly 200 years ago.

ISOLA MADRE (Lake Maggiore)

This island garden owned by Prince Borromeo has the best-known tree collection in Italy. It is open to the public during spring and summer, and visitors marvel at the vast size of many of the specimens.

PALAZZO REALE (Caserta)
See page 94

VILLA MONASTERO (Varenna)

A modern flower garden on the shores of Lake Como, well known for its unusual varieties.

VILLA BORGHESE (Rome)

There are two gardens to consider – the Villa Borghese as it was created at the beginning of the 16th century and the garden as it is today. The original estate, 3 miles in circumference, was a superb Renaissance garden. Its strictly formal lines and extensive views inspired the French designers, and the roots of Versailles could well be here. In the 18th century it was changed into an English landscape park, and 70 years ago it was given to the City of Rome as its major public park. There are many fine flower beds and flowering shrubs, and the specimen trees are labelled.

VILLA TARANTO (Pallanza)

The story of this Botanical Garden is the story of a man – Captain Neil McEacharn. He began in 1930 to turn a 100-acre site on the shores of Lake Maggiore into an English-style garden filled with exotic flowers and shrubs. By the time of his death in 1964 Villa Taranto was one of the great gardens of the world and was then taken over by the Italian Government to be run as a major Botanical Garden.

VATICAN GARDENS (Rome)

The experts cannot agree on the merits of the Vatican Gardens. They have been described as "one of the great gardens of the western world" and also as "not particularly interesting." They do have several interesting features – a feeling of tranquility in noisy Rome, an abundance of flowers and angel heads in stone and topiary at every turn.

VILLA CARLOTTA (Cadenabbia)

This garden was built on a steep hillside as a series of terraces in 1745, and is the best known of the Lake Como gardens. It is noted for its *giardini segreti,* lemon-scented terraces and azaleas.

VILLA CICOGNA (Bisuschio)

The place to go if you want to see an original 16th century garden. There are three outstanding features – the large terrace, the water staircase and an underground fern-lined passage.

VILLA GARZONI (Collodi)

This spectacular Baroque garden has been described as the most theatrically magnificent in Italy. The parterres are filled with flowers, and the elaborate 17th century staircase leads upwards past the ornate topiary to the statue of Fame at the summit.

BOBOLI GARDENS (Florence)

The main outline of this Medici garden of the 16th century remains unchanged. Once royal pageants took place in its amphitheatre. Today tourists walk past the fountains and around the terraced gardens.

VILLE D'ESTE (Tivoli)
See page 94

VILLA LANTE (Bagnaia)
See page 94

VILLA MELZI (San Giovanni)

A beautiful informal woodland garden with azaleas, camellias and many exotic shrubs. A Japanese water garden nestles beneath the trees.

VILLA MARLIA (Lucca)

An unusual 17th century garden consisting of a series of outdoor rooms carved out of hedges of yew, laurel and holly. Here Napoleon's sister entertained her guests, and concerts were held in the green theatre cut from yew trees and considered to be one of the finest in the world.

VILLA DORIA PAMPHILJ (Rome)

An enormous park, with a circumference of over 6 miles. There are formal gardens set within the trees, and superb terraces overlooking the city. It is open to the public during October.

LA MORTOLA (Ventimiglia)

The Hanbury Botanical Garden at La Mortola is now administered by the government, but this 70-acre garden was started more than 100 years ago by Sir Thomas Hanbury and maintained by members of his family until after World War II. La Mortola is a promontory jutting into Lake Maggiore and basically it is a beautiful garden which appeals to both the non-gardener and the botanist. There are fountains, pools, cascades, flower-shaded walks and mountain views for everyone; for the serious gardener there are more than 7,000 different varieties to see.

A PICTURE GUIDE TO *Dahlias*

We shall never know on which Mexican hillside the wild dahlia first appeared. But we do know that the first varieties with large, double blooms were bred in Belgium in 1815. Some of Monsieur Donckelaar's novelties were sent to England, and the story of our garden dahlias had begun.

The craze for this new flower spread rapidly throughout Britain, France, Germany and the Low Countries. Within a few years nearly every colour we now admire had been introduced, and catalogues listed hundreds of named varieties.

The nineteenth century favourites were the ball-like double show and fancy dahlias. Today it is the cactus group, with its dazzling plate-like blooms, which captures the popular fancy. Fashions change, but the popularity of this late summer flower remains as strong as ever.

In Britain its disciples have long claimed that only the rose and the chrysanthemum are more popular. A recent survey confirmed this belief; new tubers or rooted cuttings are purchased for about 2 million gardens every year.

The reasons for this devotion to the dahlia are fairly obvious. First of all, the skill of the great breeders in England, Holland, Germany, Australia and America has produced a range of sizes and colours unmatched in the world of garden flowers. Plants taller than a man for the grand garden; dwarf bedding varieties 1 ft. high for the windowbox. Flowers from the size of a twopenny piece to the size of the largest dinner plate. A vast range of flower shapes and almost the whole of the rainbow to choose from.

Equally important is the time of flowering. From the end of July until the first frosts, dahlias provide mass colour when so many garden flowers are past their best.

Above all, the dahlia is an accommodating plant. It likes a good loam soil but will thrive almost anywhere. It relishes sunshine, but can still do well in partial shade. A bed just for dahlias is really the ideal way of growing these flowers, but they are quite at home in the herbaceous border.

And they will put up with the novice. For him growing dahlias is merely a matter of planting the old tubers he dug up last year and stored in the garage, or else planting out pot tubers or rooted cuttings bought from his local shop. Then it's just a matter of a little staking if the plants get too heavy and a little spraying if the blackfly appear. And even with such casual treatment a surprisingly good display can be obtained.

But it need not be an "easy" plant. For the serious enthusiast the growing of dahlias is an exacting but absorbing hobby. There is soil to prepare carefully in winter, cuttings to raise from tubers, fertilizers to mix, growing points to pinch out, side shoots to remove, plants to disbud and show blooms to stage. There are many challenges for the enthusiast: there is the world record 21in. bloom to beat, there is the elusive blue dahlia to raise and there are show awards to win.

But most of the dahlias in our gardens will continue to be grown by the ordinary gardener who knows no favourites. To him the dahlia, with the chrysanthemum, is the answer to the late summer colour gap. He sows seeds for dwarf bedding varieties, and plants tubers or rooted cuttings for his border dahlias. And if ever he should lose a plant, he can take some comfort from one of the names found in books dealing with the history of this fascinating plant. The reason for the ever-lasting fame of the Marchioness of Bute is that in 1798 she received the first dahlia seeds sent to England ... and failed completely in her attempts to grow them!

I
SINGLE-FLOWERED DAHLIAS
One ring of ray florets. Central group of disc florets.

II
ANEMONE-FLOWERED DAHLIAS
One or more rings of flattened ray florets. Central group of tubular florets.

III
COLLERETTE DAHLIAS
One outer ring of flat ray florets inner ring of collar florets and a ce group of disc florets.

IV
PAEONY-FLOWERED DAHLIAS
Two or more rings of flattened ray florets. Central group of disc florets.

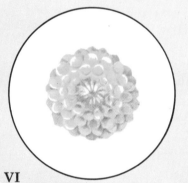

Dahlia blooms are made up of miniature flowers known as florets. The types of floret present are a key to identification.

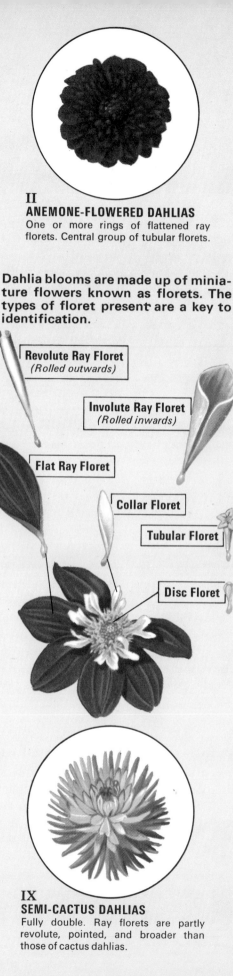

Revolute Ray Floret
(Rolled outwards)

Involute Ray Floret
(Rolled inwards)

Flat Ray Floret

Collar Floret

Tubular Floret

Disc Floret

V
DECORATIVE DAHLIAS
Fully double. Flat ray florets are b and blunt ended

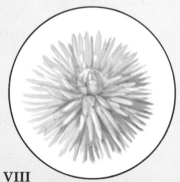

VI
BALL DAHLIAS
Fully double. Ball-shaped, more than 2 in. across. Involute ray florets are blunt (or round) ended.

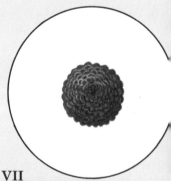

VII
POMPON DAHLIAS
Fully double. Globular, no more t 2 in. across. Involute ray florets blunt (or round) ended

VIII
CACTUS DAHLIAS
Fully double. Revolute ray florets are narrow and pointed.

IX
SEMI-CACTUS DAHLIAS
Fully double. Ray florets are partly revolute, pointed, and broader than those of cactus dahlias.

X
MISCELLANEOUS DAHLIAS
Flower form not belonging to Gr I–IX. Example—orchid-flowering dah

DAHLIA PLANTING MATERIAL

GROUND TUBERS

Usual source: Own garden, dug up in previous autumn and stored over winter.

Every couple of years tubers should be carefully divided. Make sure that each division has a piece of stem with swollen tubers attached.

POT TUBERS

Usual source: Local shop or mail order nursery.

Pot tubers are convenient and easy-to-handle planting material. But it is more economical to use them to provide cuttings which are then rooted for planting out.

ROOTED CUTTINGS

Usual source: Local shop or mail order nursery
or
Home-grown. Tubers are planted in moist compost in March under glass to provide cuttings for potting up and then planting out in late May or early June.

SEEDS

Usual source: Local shop or mail order nursery.

Dwarf bedding varieties (e.g. Coltness hybrids) are raised this way. Sow in gentle heat (60°F) in late March, plant out in late May for flowering in August.

STAKING

Use a 1 in. square oak stake for tall varieties; stout bamboo for smaller types. Insert the stake to a depth of 12–15 in. *before* planting. The height should be about 1 ft. less than that expected for the plant.
Tie the main stem loosely to the stake, using soft string, when growth reaches 9 inches. As the plant grows make additional ties.
For plants with several main stems a few extra stakes may be required.

DEAD-HEADING

The regular removal of faded blooms will prolong the flowering life of the plant.

WATERING & FEEDING

Water thoroughly during dry spells. Feed occasionally from July onwards with a liquid fertilizer which has a higher potash than nitrogen content.

PLANTING TUBERS

Plant dormant tubers in mid April. Wait until early May in cold northern districts.
Dig a hole about 6 in. deep with a spade. Place the tuber in the hole and cover with fine soil. The crown of the tuber should be at least 3 in. below the surface.

PLANTING ROOTED CUTTINGS

Plant in late May in southern districts. Wait until early June in the north.
Water pots about 1 hr. before planting. Use a trowel to dig a hole which is larger than the soil ball of the cutting. Water in after planting.

Treat tubers bearing shoots as rooted cuttings.

MULCHING

Do not hoe as plants are shallow-rooting. Keep weeds out and moisture in by applying a 2 in. layer of grass clippings, straw or compost around the plants.

PLANTING DISTANCES

Tall varieties   — 3 ft. apart
Medium varieties — 2½ ft. apart
Bedding varieties — 1½ ft. apart

PESTS & DISEASES

The worst pests — aphid, capsid, red spider, caterpillar and earwig — are easily controlled by spraying. In wireworm-infested soil rake in bromophos before planting. In a wet summer sprinkle slug pellets around young shoots.
Diseases are rarely serious but the commoner ones (mosaic and spotted wilt) are due to viruses and there is no cure. Lift the plants and burn. Remember to spray against aphids, which are the virus carriers.

SOIL

Pick a spot which gets at least a few hours sunshine during the day. Do not plant under trees nor in soil which gets waterlogged.
Medium loam is ideal, but most soils are satisfactory. In autumn/winter dig in plenty of organic matter such as peat, compost or well-rotted manure. No need to dig deeper than one spade's depth. Rake in 4 oz. bone meal per sq. yd after digging.

STORING TUBERS

When the first frosts have blackened the foliage cut off the stems about 6 in. above the ground. Gently fork out the tubers and discard surplus soil and broken roots.
Stand tubers upside down for a week to drain off excess moisture. Then place them in shallow boxes and cover roots (not crowns) with peat. Store in a cool but frost-free place.

The *EuroDahlia*

❶ GT. BRITAIN boasts the largest National Dahlia Society in the world. Founded in 1881, the N.D.S. now has over 5300 members, scattered from Iceland to Australia. Membership £1.00, Fellowship £1.25. Classified List and Dahlia Annual sent free to members. Write to General Secretary, 26 Burns Road, Leamington Spa, Warwickshire.

Main dahlia shows are the Annual Dahlia Show at the Royal Horticultural Halls, London (last week August) and the N.D.S. Harrogate Show (mid-September). S.E. England is the area of keenest interest, and about 10,000 enthusiasts visit the London Show each year. In other regions there are the Scottish Show in the Kelvin Hall, Glasgow (first week September), the Midland Show at Leamington Spa (last week August) and the West Country Show in the Guildhall, Plymouth (third week August).

To see dahlias growing visit the N.D.S. Show Grounds at The Gardening Centre, Syon Park, Middlesex. Trial Grounds are the places to go if you want a preview of tomorrow's varieties — R.H.S. Gardens (Wisley), Roath Park (Cardiff) and Ward Jackson Park (Hartlepool) are the best.

❷ HOLLAND is the dahlia centre of Europe with its great nurseries, hybridists and annual exports of over 40 million tubers.

Visit Firma Bruidegom at Baarn, near Hilver sum to see the largest dahlia nursery in Europe Or call at the Dahlia Maarse, Utterweg 32 Aalsmeer. A welcome to overseas visitors i: extended by Geerlings Nurseries at Heemstede (14 miles from Amsterdam).

❸ In **BELGIUM** there is a large Display Garden and Trial Ground at the headquarters of the Belgian Dahlia Society at Schoten, near Antwerp.

❹ SWEDEN is not important in the dahlia world, but it was the home of botanist Dr Andreas Dahl (1751-1789) after whom the flower was named. So purists say Dahl-ia, not Day-lia.

❺ In **E. GERMANY** (and Russia) they say *georgine*, not dahlia. This name commemorates Professor Georgi of St Petersburg.

❻ In **W. GERMANY** there is Gruga Park in Essen. The most famous feature here is the huge Dahlia Arena, where hundreds of different varieties are displayed.

THE EXPERT WAY

The expert, with an eye on the next Flower Show, is more interested in quality than quantity of bloom. He needs near-perfect flowers on long stems, and he uses three techniques:

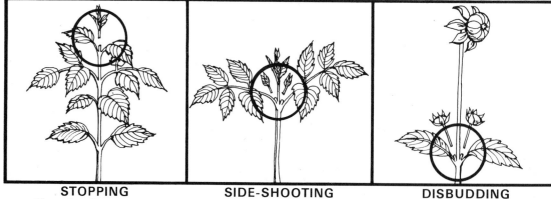

STOPPING
Tips of main stems are pinched out when they are about 10 in. high.

SIDE-SHOOTING
Unwanted laterals are snapped away from the main stem.

DISBUDDING
Side buds are removed, leaving only the terminal bud.

A PICTURE GUIDE TO
Bedding Plants

According to a popular and excellent gardening book "The bedding plant in private gardens has, in general, had its day." Many horticultural writers have over the years put it more strongly. The bedding plant in Britain, they say, is a left-over from yesterday's bad taste, a thing to be used only by the untutored, unimaginative or unfortunate with a tiny garden.

Nurserymen have a different view. Many believe that the bedding plant has certainly not had its day and that its popularity in recent years has gone up, not down. So where does the truth lie?

Before we can answer that question, it is necessary to define a 'bedding plant'. It is an annual (more unusually a biennial or perennial) which is raised under glass or in a nursery bed and then planted out elsewhere as a temporary occupant to provide a colourful display. So the term describes a *use*, not a specific *type* of plant. The calceolaria kept indoors is a 'flowering pot plant'; when planted outdoors it becomes a 'bedding plant'.

We must look to recent surveys to determine how important a role is played by bedding plants in the British garden. About 40 per cent of all people with a garden buy bedding plants each year, and spend about as much as they do on the darling of our garden flowers, the rose. The biggest surprise is that the owner of a large garden is more likely to buy them than the person with a small plot. Many plants are, of course, home-raised and the Royal Horticultural Society Survey (1972) revealed that 71 per cent of its Fellows had bedding plants in their gardens.

The myth that the temporary summer display is only for the public park or poor potterer has been exploded and we must go back into history to see where it started. Several sites have claimed the honour of the first summer bedding scheme – perhaps it was Parc Monçeau in France or Pückler-Muskau Castle in Germany. By 1840 it had firmly taken root in Britain. By 1870 it was a craze. Wealthy homeowners competed with each other to produce the most dazzling, ornate and expensive display. Colours clashed, beds grew more and more bizarre and reaction was inevitable.

Suddenly, bedding out became the symbol of Victorian bad taste. Henceforth, said the gardening giants, bedding plants were not for use by the enlightened gardener. But they have remained – unloved but as yet irreplaceable. The position remains quite stable; popularity has remained practically unchanged during the past few years.

Bedding out takes place at two periods of the year. In September and October the double daisies, wallflowers, forget-me-nots, primroses and other spring bedding plants are set out to bloom from March to May. When they are removed it is time to set out the summer bedding plants – the host of brightly coloured flowers we know so well, which flower from June until the autumn.

Unfortunately little imagination or variety is used in the average garden. The grand displays are in the public parks, at home there are the inevitable begonias and sedums in France, the pansy-based schemes in Germany, and the geranium/alyssum/lobelia scheme so beloved in Britain. Even in Victorian times there were critics – "The common disposition of red, white and blue is better adapted to delight savages than represent the artistic status of a civilised people."

Perhaps the criticism over the years concerns bedding schemes – garish in the 1870s and humdrum in the 1970s. The plants themselves are blameless, for they will provide patches of long lasting colour and enhance the garden when used tastefully. This calls for knowing the right plants, the proper place and the correct way of using them. The pictures and diagrams on the following pages should help you to prove that summer bedding need not be a piece of Victoriana.

EDGING PLANTS

1

2

3

4

5

6

GROUNDWORK PLANTS

11

10

14

20

DOT PLANTS

15

18

19

23

24

29

30

31

27

32

33

34

Summer Bedding Plants

EDGING PLANTS
dwarf plants, up to 8 inches

1 *Ageratum*
2 *Alyssum*
3 Tagetes *(Tagetes signata)*
4 *Lobelia*
5 Pansy *(Viola tricolor)*
6 *Verbena*
7 *Viola*
8 *Mesembryanthemum*
9 *Phlox drummondii*

GROUNDWORK PLANTS
medium-height plants,
reaching 8 inches to 2 feet

10 *Heliotrope*
11 Tobacco Plant *(Nicotiana)*
12 African Marigold *(Tagetes erecta)*
13 French Marigold *(Tagetes patula)*
14 *Calceolaria*
15 *Zinnia*
16 *Petunia*
17 *Salvia*
18 *Begonia semperflorens*
19 Geranium *(Pelargonium)*
20 *Celosia plumosa*
21 *Cineraria maritima* (other name *Senecio cineraria*)
22 Viper's Bugloss *(Echium)*
23 *Gazania*
24 Annual Aster *(Callistephus)*
25 Snapdragon *(Antirrhinum)*
26 *Nemesia*
27 *Coleus*
28 Bedding Dahlia

DOT PLANTS
tall plants, with showy leaves
or flowers, growing singly or in small
groups above the Groundwork Plants

29 Standard *Fuchsia*
30 *Abutilon savitzii*
31 Castor Oil Plant *(Ricinus)*
32 Indian Corn *(Zea mays)*
33 *Kochia*
34 *Grevillea*
35 Indian Shot *(Canna indica)*

Before you start...

It is a mistake to buy boxes of bedding plants or to raise trays of seedlings without first deciding how and where to use them. Start with a pencil and paper and draw your plan; use coloured pencils or felt tip pens to give you an idea of the final colour effect.

Most people adopt a formal multicoloured bedding scheme, but there are many other ways of using bedding plants. Put them amongst the perennials or shrubs to provide midsummer colour; fill window boxes, tubs or hanging baskets; plant drifts of a single variety if your garden is large enough for such a dramatic effect.

Planning the Display

The four types of bedding scheme are described below. Pick the one which appeals to you and then choose the plants to fit in with your scheme.

For spring bedding the choice is rather limited, and bulbs are often used as the framework for the plan. Underplanting can blend in with the tulip colours so that fallen petals are masked. Wallflowers can be used for a Single Genus Bedding Scheme.

For summer bedding there is no shortage of choice. Scores of plants are listed on page 105 and many more appear in the seed catalogue or on display at planting time — penstemon, marguerite, stocks, larkspur, portulaca and so on.

In your bedding scheme try to arrange the plants in large groups. A single line of Edging Plants can be used, but lines and small fussy patches of Groundwork Plants should be avoided. The trend these days is towards large irregularly-shaped blocks of single colours.

The colours, of course, should not clash and many books have lists of do's and don'ts. Don't put orange next to pink, blue next to mauve, scarlet next to crimson . . . do put complementary colours next to each other — yellow and purple, blue and orange etc. But remember that the colour combinations should appeal to *you*, not to the art critic.

On the subject of colour nearly all gardeners think automatically of the flower as the sole source of display. Yet foliage plays a vital role in most successful bedding schemes. The display from colourful and attractive leaves lasts all season long, compared with the more limited life of the floral display.

Most Dot Plants have attractive leaves — the green and red-striped Indian Corn; the white and green foliage of abutilon; the glossy ricinus. Kochia is used for its feathery leaves which turn red in autumn. Some Groundwork Plants have attractive foliage and should feature in your scheme. There is the red-leaved begonia, the silvery cineraria and centaurea, the yellow-leaved matricaria. Coleus provides a multicoloured display.

BEDS & BORDERS

Modern beds have simple shapes — rectangular, oval, circular or informal. Stars and complex outlines are now out of date. Before planting make sure that the ground is weed-free, and rake the earth so that a mound is formed at the centre of the bed.

Make sure that the soil cannot wash into the surrounding lawn or pathway. This calls for having a shallow trench at the edge of the bed (as in the diagram on the right), or a permanent edging of wood, concrete or dwarf trimmed lavender or box.

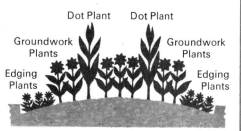

| | SINGLE VARIETY BEDDING SCHEME | A single variety such as 'Cherry Pie' petunia or 'Paul Crampel' geranium is used. Such schemes have been criticised on the grounds of monotony, but the *bedded meadow* effect of a large irregular area treated this way can be spectacular. Increasingly popular in some Continental countries, and perhaps the first real breakaway from the Victorian-based scheme. |

SINGLE VARIETY BEDDING SCHEME — A single variety such as 'Cherry Pie' petunia or 'Paul Crampel' geranium is used. Such schemes have been criticised on the grounds of monotony, but the *bedded meadow* effect of a large irregular area treated this way can be spectacular. Increasingly popular in some Continental countries, and perhaps the first real breakaway from the Victorian-based scheme.

SINGLE GENUS BEDDING SCHEME — An interesting scheme for the specialist gardener, in which a single genus such as antirrhinum, pelargonium or aster is used. The dahlia enthusiast would treat his plants no other way. Varieties of different size, colour and flower form can be chosen to show the full range of the genus.

STANDARD GARDEN BEDDING SCHEME — The almost universally adopted bedding scheme for suburban gardens. Most of the bed is filled with groups or lines of Groundwork Plants; as you will see from page 105 most bedding plants belong to this group. Around these specimens are set the low-growing Edging Plants. Styles and varieties have changed little during the past hundred years, apart from the fall from grace of the once-popular calceolaria.

STANDARD PARK BEDDING SCHEME — The standby of the professional gardener, differing from the Standard Garden scheme by the inclusion of Dot Plants. These tall, colourful bedding plants grow as single, showy specimens above the Groundwork Plants. They give the bed height and colour, as well as providing one or more focal points of interest. The secret of the attractive park display is the Dot Plant. There are many to choose from — those listed on page 105 as well as tall varieties of antirrhinum, standard heliotrope, *Lobelia cardinalis* etc.

Raising Bedding Plants

The usual pattern for raising summer bedding plants is to sow seeds in a greenhouse in March. J. I. Seed Compost or a soilless compost is used, and the seed pans covered with a sheet of glass and paper. It is possible to raise small quantities of bedding plants on the windowsill, using a polythene bag over each seed pan.

Once germination has occurred the tiny seedlings require plenty of light and more air. When large enough to handle they are pricked out into potting compost and then gradually hardened off in a cold frame outdoors until it is time for planting. Most plants are pricked out singly so that each seedling will have enough room to develop into a strong bushy plant. But tiny seedlings like alyssum and lobelia are pricked out as small clumps.

Dot Plants are sometimes raised in small peat pots to ensure that there will be a minimum of root disturbance at planting time. Groundwork Plants with large seeds and long delicate roots, such as zinnia, can be treated in the same way.

Buying Bedding Plants

You cannot expect poor quality plants to produce a worthwhile display. So choose the bedding plants you buy with care, looking for the following points.

Leaves should be firm and a rich green, and must not be spotted or holed. Growth should be bushy; avoid plants that are thin and lanky through lack of light. There should be no roots growing through the bottom of the box or pot, and the plants should not be in flower.

If possible, buy boxes of plants rather than loose ones so as to prevent drying out before planting time. The soil in the box should be moist and the seedlings should not be wilted.

Planting the Display

Nearly all summer bedding schemes contain frost-sensitive plants, so planting out should be delayed until all danger of frost is past. The end of May is the correct time for the south and midlands, the first week in June for the north. Pick a day when the soil is moist.

Water the pots or boxes a few hours before starting work. Use a trowel to take out the planting hole and when handling the seedlings leave as much soil as possible adhering to the roots. Firm the soil around the stems after planting. If the bedding plants are growing in peat pots, plant them intact but make sure you bury the rim of the pot below ground level. When you have finished, water in the newly planted specimens.

Leftover plants should not be thrown away. Set them out in an odd corner of the garden and then use them to fill in any gaps which may occur as a result of insects, disease, cats or children.

Caring for the Plants

The critical time is the first few weeks after planting. During this period regular watering is necessary if there is no rain. Then little attention is required, apart from dead-heading faded blooms if the bed is small and in a prominent position.

All bedding schemes have to be cleared out once flowering has finished. With spring bedding all of the annuals should be put on the compost heap, but save the polyanthus and primroses. Transplant them into a reserve bed and grow them on for next year.

With summer bedding the annuals are again discarded, and the tubers of dahlias and begonias lifted, dried and then stored in a frost-free place. Pot up the geraniums and fuchsias worth saving and keep them in the greenhouse.

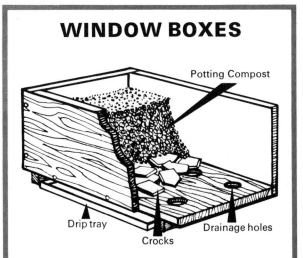

WINDOW BOXES

Potting Compost

Drip tray

Crocks

Drainage holes

Use ½ inch thick teak, cedar or oak to construct window boxes, and use brass screws. Make sure that the boxes are fixed securely to the window frame.

Drainage holes are essential, and a drip tray underneath is useful for collecting water. Compost should be changed every season.

Many of the popular bedding plants listed on page 105 are ideally suited for window boxes. Climbing plants, such as golden-leaved hop, morning glory and nasturtium, are sometimes grown and trailing plants are used to enlarge the display. Choose from the plants described for hanging baskets.

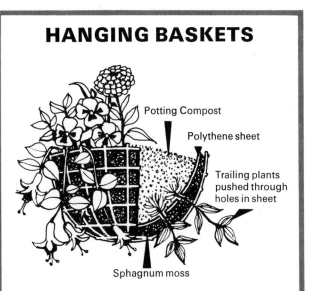

HANGING BASKETS

Potting Compost

Polythene sheet

Trailing plants pushed through holes in sheet

Sphagnum moss

Wire frame about 10–16 in. in diameter, hung from chains. Water by immersing after planting; then water at regular intervals from above.

Trailing plants should be set close to the edge. Suitable examples are Cascade petunias, ivy-leaved geraniums, pendulous begonias, pendulous fuchsias, creeping jenny and trailing lobelia. For the centre of the basket choose from the list on page 105.

EuroBedding

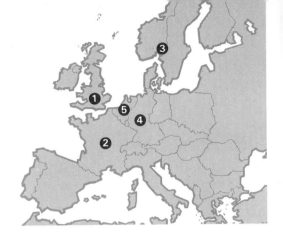

❶ In **GT. BRITAIN** summer bedding plants are extremely popular with both the expert and casual home gardener. Despite pleas for more variety the small suburban garden still relies on allysum, lobelia, tagetes, salvias and geraniums. The beds tend to be rigidly formal in both shape and planting design, and the most lavish examples are found in public parks. Perhaps the largest display in Britain is to be seen at the Italian Gardens in the Trentham Horticultural Centre (Stoke-on-Trent).

Window boxes and plant containers are not a basic feature of the garden scene as they are in Spain, Italy and most other European countries. So the non-garden use of summer bedding plants is quite small.

Once carpet bedding was popular. Dwarf plants with decorative foliage were closely planted in intricate patterns to give a living carpet effect. This called for skill and a great deal of labour, and the craft has now practically disappeared from home gardens. The Floral Clocks and the Coats of Arms carpet-bedded out each summer in holiday towns are a reminder of the style of a bygone age. Edinburgh boasts the finest Floral Clock in Britain.

❷ In **FRANCE** bedding plants are widely used in front gardens, window boxes and plant containers. Petunias, begonias and pansies are much more popular than in Britain, and the French gardener is more likely to raise his plants from seed than to buy them ready-grown.

❸ **SCANDINAVIA** is a place for grass and conifers, but bedding plants are commonly seen in both window boxes and flower beds. Here, as in many European countries, there is a movement

towards the *bedded meadow* effect using a single variety in place of the traditional patterned bed containing varieties of contrasting shapes and colours. Pictured above is a bedded meadow using Scandinavia's favourite, the petunia.

❹ In **W. GERMANY** bedding plants are used everywhere, and they are an important feature in many grand gardens. See the extensive bedded parterres at Herrenhausen (Hanover) and at Schlosspark (Ludwigsburg). The Balcony Gardens of West Berlin, gay with geraniums, are a well-known feature of the city.

❺ In **HOLLAND** and **BELGIUM** window boxes are a common sight on houses near the coast, and here bedding plants which can withstand windy conditions are used. Petunias, violas and geraniums have proved to be the most successful.

THE GARDEN SCENE
IN HOLLAND

KEUKENHOF

Garden supplier to Europe

> 66 A little over 10 years ago Boskoop exporters suddenly discovered
> that people in Montreal, Toronto, London or Birmingham wanting to
> buy Dutch plants had a better chance than Dutch gardeners . . . 99
> C. Verboom, Director of Plant Propaganda Holland

There is much more to the garden scene in Holland than tulips in the Keukenhof Gardens. Flowers and trees in bewildering variety make up a vital part of the everyday life and national economy of this small country, but its claim to be the 'Garden of Europe' overstates its position. Holland has few grand gardens—only Kasteel Twickel and the Keukenhof can be included in the list of Europe's great showplaces. The home garden scene is active but not particularly outstanding. It is on the commercial growing rather than on the domestic display side that Holland shines so brightly. The production and exports of garden plants and flowers cannot be matched, and so Holland can justly claim to be the 'Garden Supplier to Europe'.

The general pattern is one of small nurseries with a strong father to son tradition. Fruit trees were being raised and sold in Boskoop in 1466, and more than a century ago plants were being shipped to Canada and the United States. There has been a spectacular eightfold expansion in exports during the past 20 years:

Exports of Plants, Bulbs & Flowers (1971)

Holland	£111m
Italy	£22m
Denmark	£11m
France	£8m
Belgium	£8m
W. Germany	£5m
U.K.	£½m

PLANT PROPAGANDA HOLLAND

All nurserymen pay a levy on their sales. This money is used by Plant Propaganda Holland to publicise Dutch plants and flowers both overseas and at home.

In Holland it arranges a weekly talk on the radio (1 million listeners). It has published a series of gardening books and has produced millions of pictures and posters.

GRONINGEN

Most of the rootstocks used to raise roses in Britain are grown in this region.

AALSMEER FLOWER AUCTION

Aalsmeer is the largest flower auction in the world, where more than 1,000 million cut blooms and pot plants are sold each year. The new 54 acre complex cost £6 million to build, and there is a tourist gallery giving an uninterrupted view of 3 million roses and a myriad other flowers being sold before noon. Giant auction clocks are linked to a computer. Multilingual guides explain the proceedings; about 500,000 visitors are expected during the tourist season.

THE BULBFIELDS

There are 31,000 acres of bulbs in Holland. One third is devoted to the national flower—the tulip; the next largest area (6,000 acres) is planted with gladioli. Narcissi, hyacinths and iris occupy the rest of the bulbfields.

April and May are the months to see the fields in flower, and the area between Leiden and Haarlem has the most beautiful fields. The 'Floral Route' is signposted at Tulip Time and many bus excursions are available.

THE FLOWER NURSERIES

Aalsmeer is the traditional home of the glasshouses where roses, carnations etc. are grown for cutting. But Westland, with the largest concentration of cultivation under glass in the world, is becoming increasingly important.

Most of the blooms are exported, with West Germany being by far the biggest importer. Some go to the florists of Amsterdam, Rotterdam, etc., and the rest are sold to the many street traders who are an important part of the Dutch flower scene.

BOSKOOP

The largest shrub and tree raising area in the world. There are about 1,000 nurseries, some only an acre or two in size. Holland has captured 45 per cent of the world's trade in trees and shrubs, with Britain and West Germany as its best customers.

Map labels: Groningen, Heerenveen, Lemmer, Alkmaar, Amsterdam, Zwolle, Haarlem, Aalsmeer, Deventer, Apeldoorn, Leiden, Amersfoort, The Hague, Boskoop, Utrecht, Delft, Wageningen, Arnhem, Rotterdam, Breda, Tilburg, Zundert, Eindhoven

THE DUTCH HOME GARDEN

Two in every three households have gardens attached to the house. Holland has the oldest home garden tradition in Europe and it is therefore not surprising that most of these 2 million gardens are carefully tended.

There is a superficial resemblance to the typical British suburban garden. The average front garden is 550 sq. ft., the back garden 1,100 sq. ft. The lawn is considered to be the most important feature with roses and bulbs as the most popular flowering plants.

This could be Rotherham rather than Rotterdam; Amersham instead of Amsterdam. But there are a number of important national differences, the main one being the stronger architectural basis of the Dutch home garden. Here the garden is a place to be lived in; much more of an outdoor living room than the English suburban garden. Fifty per cent of households receive and entertain visitors outside—there is a terrace or patio attached to 70 per cent of the homes in Holland. Large multicoloured murals are becoming popular, a throwback to those early days when the Dutch had pictures painted on their garden walls and statues were coloured in life-like tones. In a recent survey 9 out of 10 gardeners felt that it was the garden's job to make the house look prosperous.

Linked with this feature is another difference from the British scene—vegetables are rarely grown. Flower borders feature in only 45 per cent of Dutch gardens, with dahlias, begonias and pelargoniums being more popular than chrysanthemums.

The homeowner takes a great deal of interest in his garden, as he does in his home or car. Both husband and wife want a plot of which they can be proud, and are willing to invest both time and money. Unlike Britain, gardening actually ousts watching TV as the most time-consuming leisure activity. Half the households spend more than £14 each year on horticultural supplies. But the practical Dutch see no great merit in doing all the work if you can afford to engage outside help—with the richer families about 40 per cent employ a full-time or part-time gardener.

Window boxes are an important but by no means universal feature. One in every 5 homes has them, and the colourful show of geraniums, petunias and violas is a welcome sight. On window sills everywhere are the living curtains of house plants which, with cut flowers, are so much more popular than in Britain. Flower colour and greenery are part of the home with the favourite indoor plants of Holland—ivy, ferns, croton, bromeliads, azalea, cyclamen, chrysanthemum and vases of cut roses, carnations and tulips.

An important trend is the purchase of a second home for holidays or weekends. There are 100,000 of these dwellings, and their gardens tend to have a more natural or wilder look than the suburban plot.

LIVING HISTORY

In the Middle Ages Holland had no special part to play in the garden scene of Europe. Home gardens were undeveloped, the gardens of the grand houses were standard European models. A reconstruction of a mediaeval garden can be seen at **Pieterburen**.

In the sixteenth century Holland moved to the forefront of horticultural science. The scientific study and collection of plants was still in its infancy when a professor at Leiden, Charles de l'Ecluse or Clusius (1526–1609) became one of the great early botanists. He introduced the lilac, popularised the tulip and provided details of 600 plants which had never been described before. Visit the **Leiden Botanical Garden,** founded in 1587. Here they have reconstructed the garden of Clusius, laid out and planted according to his records.

Tulip fever gripped Holland. In 1636 a single bulb fetched 13,000 florins. Vast fortunes were made and lost, and onions were no longer eaten so as to avoid insulting the spirit which dwelt within bulbs. The **Hortus Bulborum** at **Limmen** is the world's finest bulb museum and much of this story can be seen there. There are a thousand types of tulips on view including the ancestors of the present-day varieties.

The seventeenth century saw the rise of Holland as a great colonial power. Plants from S. Africa, China, America and many other areas were sent home to Holland. For the first time the pelargonium, the chrysanthemum and many other plants entered Europe.

With its colonial wealth Holland developed a unique social level—a large and comfortable middle class. These burgers with their houses on the outskirts of town had the national love of flowers and so the first suburban garden style in Europe was developed. Clipped box hedges formed complex patterns and the enclosed beds were filled with flowers or coloured stones. Tulips were popular, of course, and so were ornaments, ponds and statuary. The village of **Zaanse Schans** at **Zaandam** affords a unique opportunity to see this early Dutch style. The gardens around all of the eighteenth century wooden houses have been faithfully reconstructed.

Zaanse Schans, Zaandam

THE GRAND SIGHTS

Holland has few grand gardens surrounding stately homes for the visitor to enjoy. Instead it offers some excellent botanical gardens and there are several fine collections of conifers to be seen. In April and May there is a flower explosion with tulip parades, petal mosaics, rainbow-coloured flower beds and bulb-filled boxes everywhere.

KEUKENHOF GARDENS (Lisse)

Six million bulbs—crocuses, narcissi, hyacinths and tulips in 65 acres, open to the public from the end of March to the middle of May. Nearly a million people come to this showpiece of Holland, which is also a showcase for the bulb growers who display their new varieties at the Keukenhof each year. In the glasshouse area new and delicate varieties are grown and displayed. Beautiful lakes mirror the multicoloured display, there are fountains, flower arranging demonstrations and flamingos, yet Keukenhof means "kitchen garden".

FLORAL PARADES

The high spots in the Dutch floral calendar are the *Bloemencorsos* (Flower Parades). The Spring Parades take place at the end of April in the bulb regions, but the largest number occur in August and September when roses, dahlias, begonias and other plants are used.

The Lisse Spring Bulb Parade is the most spectacular of all. Flower decorated floats assemble at Lisse on a Friday at the end of April. The next day they drive through the blooming bulb fields for 16 miles from Haarlem to Sassenheim. Bands accompany them, flower mosaics are laid out along the route and motorists bedeck their cars with garlands of flowers.

Bloemencorsos Calendar

late April	Haarlem – Sassenheim
early August	Rijnsburg – Leiden
mid August	Katwijk aan Zee
late August	Leersum Winterswijk Eelde – Paterswolde Lippenhuizen
early September	Aalsmeer – Amsterdam Zundert
mid September	Frederiksoord Tiel Winkel Valkenswaard

HERB GARDENS

A feature of some Dutch gardens is a reconstruction of the mediaeval monastery garden with small plots of medicinal, aromatic and culinary herbs divided by stone pathways. The best is the Muiderslot Herb Garden at Muiden, with over 2,000 herbs on display. There are others at Arnhem and Buitenpost.

BOTANICAL GARDENS & TREE COLLECTIONS

Gardens for study, with plants properly classified and carefully labelled, are popular in Holland. This is to be expected in a country with such a distinguished record in horticultural science.

AMSTERDAM BOTANICAL GARDEN Established 1682. Interesting greenhouses. 3 acres.

GIMBORN ARBORETUM (Doorn) Large collection of trees, shrubs and heathers. 57 acres.

CANTONSPARK (Baarn) Large rock garden. Greenhouses with over 1,000 orchid varieties. Well worth a visit. 12½ acres.

DE WOLF GARDEN (Groningen) European wild flowers growing under natural conditions. 74 acres.

BLIJDENSTEIN PINETUM (Hilversum) Only small (2½ acres) but still one of the best collections of conifers in Europe.

LEIDEN BOTANICAL GARDEN See page 111.

DE DENNENHORST PINETUM (Lunteren) Good conifer display. About 25 acres.

LANDGOED SCHOVENHORST (Putten) Private collection; dwarf conifers a speciality. 82 acres.

TROMPENBURG ARBORETUM (Rotterdam) Private collection; more than 1,000 varieties of trees and shrubs. 12½ acres.

BOERHAAVE GARDEN (Voorhout) Created in honour of a famous Dutch botanist. It is planted with specimens of the plants Boerhaave collected.

WAGENINGEN BOTANICAL GARDEN Part of the University School of Agriculture. It houses a large and important collection of ornamental garden plants. 70 acres.

PARKS

The public park has an important part to play in the Dutch garden scene. The new Het Bos in Amsterdam covers 2,200 acres and is the most ambitious creation in Europe for many years. But this was not designed as a horticultural showpiece, and we need to look at much smaller examples for floral displays.

SONSBEEKPARK (Arnhem) One of the most attractive parks in Holland, with waterfalls, fountains, lakes and lakeside flora.

VONDELPARK (Amsterdam) Created in the centre of town, Vondelpark has lakes and lawns with many attractive trees.

WESTBROEKPARK (The Hague) On the outskirts of town, this park is generally considered to be the finest in Holland. It has a world-renowned rose garden, and there are also mixed borders, lakes and a rockery.

ZUIDERPARK (The Hague) A popular park with two noteworthy features—a fine rose garden and a large collection of unusual trees.

PRIVATE GARDENS

Some of Holland's most attractive grand gardens are not open to the public, but permission to visit can be obtained by writing to the owner. Gardens of this type are POORT ZUYLENSTEIN (Leersum), RAAPHORST (Wassenaar) and DE HARTEKAMP (Bennebroek).

KASTEEL TWICKEL (Delden)

The most beautiful garden in Holland. It was originally created in the 18th century and still maintains the intricate flower beds, topiary and orange trees associated with that period. The 20th century owner, Baroness van Heeckeren, constructed additional features—a rose garden, a rock garden and a large mixed border. A gardener gives a guided tour on Wednesdays and Fridays.

JAPANESE GARDEN (The Hague)

In the Clingendael there is a fine Japanese Garden with winding paths, magnolias, willows, stone bridges and a tea house.

KASTEEL MIDDACHTEN (De Steeg)

The garden was restored in the French style by Hugo Poortman. The original open air theatre and orangery remain.

HEIDENTUIN (Driebergen)

A comprehensive heather collection with about 300 different varieties.

KASTEEL WELDAM (Goor)

A Poortman reconstruction of an old Dutch garden. There are elaborate box flower beds, treillage and a maze. Open to the public on Tuesdays and Fridays.

THIJSEE'S HOF (Bloemendaal)

A comprehensive collection of local flowers and plants in a 5 acre garden.

ROYAL DUTCH HORTICULTURAL SOCIETY

The Royal Dutch Horticultural Society (*Koninklijke Nederlandse Maatschappij voor Tuinbouw en Plantkunde*) was founded in 1872 and now has 28,500 members. Its monthly magazine *groei en bloei* goes to all members and it is the leading gardening paper in Holland. The Society helped to organise the 1972 Floriade at Amsterdam and it has a monthly television programme on plant care.

THE SUPPLIERS

Until recently most gardeners obtained their plants and sundries from specialised garden shops, florists or hardware shops. In Amsterdam the horticultural shopping district is along the Singel.

The flower stall and open-air market have always been a favourite place to buy flowers, and research has shown that these sales do not decrease the standard florist trade.

It is the job of most nurseries to supply the wholesale trade and not the public, but a few of the larger growers have sought to interest the gardener, especially the tourist from overseas, in their produce. The 'Tulipshow' of Frans Roozen· is famous, and signposts lead to the show gardens and 100 acres of bulbfields at the Vogelenzang nursery.

The development of garden centres has occurred as rapidly in Holland as anywhere in Europe. Already there are over 100 and new ones appear regularly. The garden centre is expected to dominate the garden supply scene of the future.

THE FLOWER SHOWS

late February	WEST FRIESIAN SHOW Exhibition of forced bulbs held at Bovenkarspel
early July	LELIADE Flower show, mainly lilies, held at Akersloot
early October	HERFSTFLORA Show of autumn flowers held at Laren
mid November	INTERNATIONAL FLOWER TRADE SHOW Very popular exhibition, open to the public as well as to the trade, held at Aalsmeer. 30,000 attended in 1971.
late December	CHRISTMAS HOTHOUSE EXHIBITION Pot plant show, open to the public as well as to the trade, held at Aalsmeer.

VOLKSTUINEN

Volkstuinen (allotments) first appeared about 100 years ago as small pieces of land lent free of charge to the poor for food production. In the rural districts of Holland, as in the whole of Britain, most allotments are still used as vegetable gardens.

About 40 years ago the first chalets appeared on the Dutch town sites. The movement away from production and towards relaxation had started. Today most of the country's urban *volkstuinen* are chalet gardens. Each plot, about 250 sq. yds. in size, houses a chalet. These can cost up to £800 and loans are available from the local authority. Tenants are allowed to sleep in them during spring and summer, and outside there are roses, trees, lawns and flower beds. Vegetables can be grown but the garden must be kept tidy, otherwise the occupier is fined or evicted.

The local association can take this strong line as there are long waiting lists at all sites. In some areas a fee must be paid in order to stay on the waiting list. Many of these people join the association even though they do not have a chalet garden, all of which is so different from the depressed state of the allotment movement in Britain.

The General Association of Allotment Holders Societies in Holland represents about 170 local associations, or 25,000 individual allotments. There are about 50 sites which do not belong to the General Association.

A major problem facing the General Association is the difficulty in finding more plots in a country with a chronic land shortage. Allotments are scarcer in the Netherlands than in other European countries involved in the chalet garden movement. In the latest survey Rotterdam and Amsterdam had about 8 allotments per 1,000 people. In Malmo there were 10 allotments, in Hamburg 16 and in Copenhagen 24. Even in Britain where interest in allotments is declining there are still 10 – 20 allotments per 1,000 people in the larger towns.

A PICTURE GUIDE TO

In every corner of Britain you will find small pots of spiny, green cacti adorning windowsills and glasshouses. The popularity of these plants continues to grow each year. In Germany there is even more interest in cacti, and massed displays of these fascinating and easy-to-grow plants are a common sight in flats and offices. The cactus grower's bible 'Die Cactaceae' was written and published in Germany.

So cacti are an important and established part of the indoor Eurogarden scene, and yet they are relatively recent immigrants. The first cactus to be described by a European was *Cereus peruvianus*, and the date was 1547. The simple truth is that all cacti originated on the American continent, and when Linnaeus got down to giving latin names to the plant kingdom in the mid-eighteenth century he had to deal with only 24 species of cacti.

The hobby of collecting these succulents has had its ups and downs over the years. Some large collections were established in the nineteenth century, but these were mainly in the mansions of the nobility of France and Germany. Cactus collecting in ordinary homes became fairly popular at the turn of the century, but the interest waned as the Victorian age passed away.

Suddenly, in the 1930s, there was a cactus boom. There were new varieties, new cultural ideas, new books, new enthusiasts. The Cactus and Succulent Society of Great Britain was founded. Vera Higgins wrote the first popular English handbook on the subject. The cactus had at last arrived as a popular plant.

Today there must be very few gardeners in this country who have not had at least one specimen to care for, and there are now several thousand species to choose from. This popularity is easy to understand when you remember that hardly any other indoor living thing can be expected to put up with so much neglect and yet outlive its owner!

But the hobby remains one of cactus *collecting* rather than cactus growing. In most cases they are kept as semi-alive, green ornaments which hardly alter throughout their stay. The joy appears to be in collecting different types, as one might collect stamps.

It all stems from the fallacy that cacti *enjoy* neglect, and that they only flower once every seven years. After all, they are desert plants so sand and drought is what they need . . .

But too much fine sand in the soil can kill them. Drought in summer will put them to sleep. Cacti will actively grow *and* flower on the windowsill in your living room, but you will have to follow the few simple rules described on the next page. If given lots of sunshine, repotted every year when young, kept cool and dry in winter and provided with plenty of water and fresh air in summertime, then your dusty cacti will come alive and flower as regularly as daffodils in the spring.

For the enthusiast a greenhouse is essential and ideally this should be used solely for cacti. They do not like moist air which is so vital for many non-succulent greenhouse plants.

Pests are rarely a problem. Scale and Mealy Bug can occur, but they are easily picked off with a pointed matchstick. Rot is the main disease and this is caused by overwatering or potting into too large a container.

Most cacti are easy to propagate from cuttings. In the spring cut off side branches or small offsets growing near the base. The secret here is to allow these cuttings to dry out for a day or two before planting in seed compost.

New plants from old. Spectacular flowers from your half-asleep specimens. It's all so easy if you remember that cacti are living things.

HOW TO RECOGNISE A CACTUS

ALL cacti (except *Pereskia* and young *Opuntia*) are leafless. The 'leaflets' of the forest cacti are really stems.

ALL cacti have areoles (woolly or bristly tufts on the stem surface). With many cacti the flowers appear at these points.

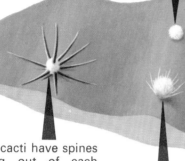

MOST cacti have spines growing out of each areole. These spines are modified leaves or shoots. They may resemble wool (e.g. *Cephalocereus senilis*) fish-hooks (e.g. *Ferocactus wislizenii*) needles (e.g. *Opuntia subulata*)

SOME cacti (*Opuntia* species) have small hooked hairs called glochids growing out of each areole. Handle with care!

DESERT CACTI

Come from the warm semi-desert regions of America. Nearly all cacti belong in this group.
Examples:
Cereus
Mammillaria
Opuntia
Rebutia

Need very little or no water between October and March.

Require as much sunshine as possible, especially for flowering. Suitable for south and west facing windowsills.

FOREST CACTI

Come from the forest regions of Brazil, where they grow on trees. Used to be known as Phyllocacti.
Examples:
Epiphyllum
Schlumbergera
Rhipsalis
Zygocactus

Need some water and feeding during winter months.

Require some shade during hottest months of the year. Suitable for north and east facing windowsills.

Pendant

Aporocactus flagelliformis
Rhipsalidopsis rosea
Rhipsalis cassutha
Schlumbergera gaertneri
Zygocactus truncatus

Globular

Epithelantha micromeris
Mammillaria prolifera
Notocactus concinnus
Parodia aureispina
Rebutia minuscula

Columnar

Cleistocactus strausii
Opuntia cylindrica
Mammillaria elongata
Notocactus leninghausii
Wilcoxia poselgeri

Strongly Ribbed

Astrophytum myriostigma
Cereus chalybaeus
Echinopsis eyriesii
Ferocactus melocactiformis
Trichocereus macrogonus

Strongly Tubercle

Ariocarpus fissuratus
Copiapoa montana
Dolichothele sphaerica
Leuchtenbergia principis
Mammillaria zeilmanniana

Hairy

Cephalocereus senilis
Espostoa lanata
Mammillaria hahniana
Oreocereus trollii

Flattened

Opuntia bergeriana
Opuntia compressa
Opuntia microdasys
Opuntia rufida

CARING FOR DESERT CACTI

SUNSHINE is vital all the year round. Keep your plants in the sunniest spot available, especially in winter. Make sure greenhouse glass is clean, except during the hottest months when shading may be necessary.

WARMTH is required once growth has started in the spring, but cool conditions are needed in winter. During this dormant period a minimum temperature of about 40–45°F (4–7°C) is required, but a temperature of more than 50°F (10°C) throughout the winter is too warm.

SPRAYING the plants with a fine mist of water is beneficial between May and July. Do not spray when the sun is shining.

FEEDING can be carried out in moderation if the plants have not been repotted for some time. But desert cacti, unlike the forest cacti, do not benefit from regular feeding.

FRESH AIR is important. Ventilate freely except when the weather is cold or foggy. If possible stand the pots outdoors in a sunny spot from mid-June to mid-September.

WATER is essential, but more cacti die from overwatering than from any other single cause. If plants are kept at 40–45°F (4–7°C) during winter then no water at all will be required for most species. Under ordinary room conditions watering at monthly intervals may be necessary to prevent shrivelling.

Once growth has started in the spring, water at weekly intervals. In summer water every few days, but at no time should you water when the surface soil is moist. Reduce watering to once a week when September arrives.

Use rainwater if available. Always give the pots a good soaking and then let the pots drain freely.

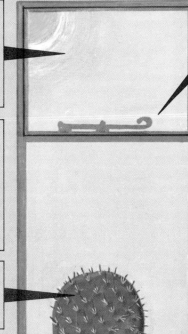

HOW TO MAKE YOUR CACTI BLOOM

Many cacti, especially the ones illustrated, will bloom when the plants are quite young and will continue to flower each year. Spring is the usual flowering season, but even a modest collection can be selected to provide a few flowers during every month of the year.

The secret lies in the fact that most cacti will only flower on new growth, and with desert cacti a period of winter rest is essential. This calls for summer care and winter "neglect", as described above.

Some cacti, like *Opuntia* and *Cereus*, are grown for their shape alone as they cannot be expected to flower under ordinary room conditions.

Rebutia

Gymnocalycium

Zygocactus

Parodia

Chamaecereus

Mammillaria

Notocactus

Echinopsis

Lobivia

Aporocactus

The *EuroCactus*

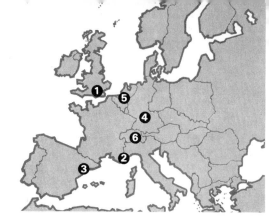

1 In **GT. BRITAIN** cacti are indoor plants. They can be grown outdoors in the milder south-west districts, but even here there is some risk during a severe winter.

For the enthusiast there are several outstanding collections to be seen. Visit the Holly Gate Collection, Spear Hill, Ashington, Sussex, where there are many thousands of cactus species on display (25p entrance fee). The Exotic Collection, 16 Franklin Road, Worthing, Sussex, houses about 9000 species which can be viewed by members (subscription £2.00 per annum). The Royal Botanic Gardens, Kew, has an attractively landscaped display of cacti and succulents in the Sherman Hoyt House.

There are two societies, both of which welcome new members. The National Cactus and Succulent Society (Hon. Secretary, 19 Crabtree Road, Botley, Oxford) has about 6000 members and associates, and the Cactus and Succulent Society of Great Britain (Hon. Secretary, 5 Wilbury Av. Cheam, Surrey) has a membership of 1100.

2 On the south coast of **FRANCE** cacti can be seen growing wild. At Monaco there is the Jardin Exotique, considered by many to be the finest exhibition of cacti in Europe.

3 **SPAIN** has areas where *Opuntia* and *Cereus* have become naturalised. Worth visiting is the display at the Pinya de Rosa at Blanes on the Costa Brava.

4 **GERMANY** is the home of many great cactus nurseries; outstanding is the Uhlig Nursery at Romelhausen, near Stuttgart.

5 The **BENELUX** countries, together with Switzerland, Germany, Austria, Gt. Britain and Czechoslovakia are the main centres for growing cacti in Europe. There are a number of important nurseries in Holland and Belgium, and there are good collections to be seen at the University Botanical Gardens at Leiden and Antwerp.

6 **SWITZERLAND** has one outstanding collection – the Städtische Sukkulentensammlung at Zurich. The 7 greenhouses and 13 outdoor displays are sponsored by the International Succulent Society.

POTTING CACTI

Your collection should be repotted every other year to ensure active growth. Use clay or plastic pots and a compost of 1 part very coarse sand plus 5 parts John Innes Potting Compost No. 1. Alternatively, use one of the modern soilless potting composts recommended for cacti. Choose a pot which is only slightly larger than the existing one. Spring is the best time for this work and do not water for several days after repotting.

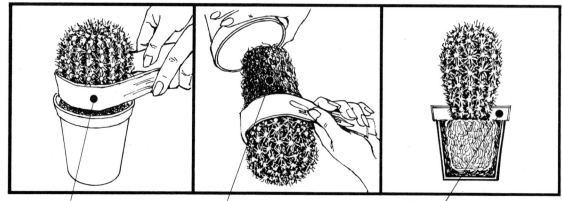

Collar of folded newspaper

Remove broken roots and some of the old soil

At least ½ inch watering space

International Exhibitions

The great International Horticultural Exhibitions held in Europe are fascinating . . . and confusing. Various names are used to describe them – Floriade, I.G.A., etc. and it seems difficult to predict the venue of the next show. Sometimes more than one occur in a season, and they can last from several days to several months. Despite this apparent lack of pattern the timetable and overall organisation of the International Horticultural Exhibitions are carefully and efficiently controlled by two official bodies – A.I.P.H. (Association Internationale des Producteurs de l'Horticulture) based in Holland and B.I.E. (Bureau International des Expositions) based in France.

A few definitions will help to clear the confusion. The *Grandes Expositions Internationales d'Horticulture* (Category A.1) last between 3 weeks and 6 months, and cover every aspect of gardening. Only one such major show can be held each year and cannot be held in the same country more than once every 5 years. Other International Horticultural Exhibitions (Category A.2) last for 3 weeks or less, and more than one can be held during the year.

There are some National Horticultural Exhibitions with international participation (Category B). To be accepted in this category the organisers must make at least 10 per cent of the total area available to other countries.

The name of each International Exhibition depends on the country which acts as host. In Holland it is the **Floriade,** in France and Belgium the **Floralies,** in Germany the **I.G.A.** (Internationale Gartenbau-Ausstellung) and in Austria the **W.I.G.** (Wiener Internationale Gartenshau).

Some major exhibitions have fallen into a regular pattern. The first Hamburg I.G.A. was held in 1869, and has adopted a regular 10-year cycle (1953, 1963, 1973) in recent years. The 1973 I.G.A. attracted exhibitors from 48 nations to its 138 acre showground. The Ghent Floralies are held every 5 years (1965, 1970, 1975) and the Austrian W.I.G. every 10 years (1964, 1974). Holland's first Floriade was held in 1960; the 1972 exhibition was a success and the next one is planned for 1982.

YEAR	TOWN	COUNTRY	NAME OF EXHIBITION	CATEGORY	DURATION
1966	Genoa	Italy	Euroflora	A.2	9 days
1967	–	–	–	–	–
1968	San Remo	Italy	E.I.F.R.	A.2	9 days
1969	Paris	France	Floralies	A.1	5½ months
	Dortmund	W. Germany	Bundes Gartenschau	B	5¾ months
1970	Ghent	Belgium	Floralies	A.2	11 days
1971	Nantes	France	Floralies	A.2	2 weeks
	Genoa	Italy	Euroflora	A.2	9 days
	Cologne	W. Germany	Bundes Gartenschau	B	7 months
1972	Amsterdam	Holland	Floriade	A.1	6 months
1973	Hamburg	W. Germany	I.G.A.	A.1	5¼ months
1974	Vienna	Austria	W.I.G.	A.1	6 months
	Valencia	Spain	Iberflora	A.2	1 week
1975	Ghent	Belgium	Floralies	A.2	10 days
	Karlsruhe	W. Germany	Bundes Gartenschau	B	7 months
1976	Genoa	Italy	Euroflora	A.2	9 days

1869 Internationale Gartenbau-Ausstellung, Hamburg

1973 Internationale Gartenbau-Ausstellung, Hamburg

A PICTURE GUIDE TO *Climate*

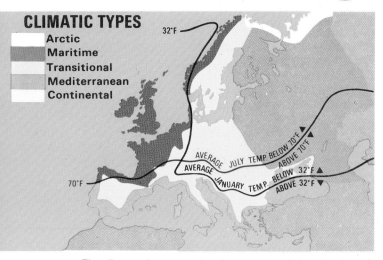

AVERAGE JULY TEMP. BELOW 70°F / ABOVE 70°F

AVERAGE JANUARY TEMP. BELOW 32°F / ABOVE 32°F

32°F

70°F

Between the extremes of the Maritime and Continental climates lies the Transitional region of Central Europe. Moving from west to east through this region the annual temperature range increases and the amount of rainfall decreases. To the far north lies the Arctic region – intensely cold, dry and desolate. In the extreme south the Mediterranean type of climate is found, with mild wet winters and warm dry summers.

This simple picture explains many of the differences between the garden plants and practices in the countries of Europe. For example, the position of the January temperature line on the map explains why the gardener in South Germany has to protect his roses with straw and bracken during the winter whereas the English gardener has no need to take such measures.

Yet this purely meteorological approach leaves much unexplained, and from the gardening standpoint it is more useful to classify climate according to the number of **Growing Months** per year. A Growing Month is defined as a month during which the average temperature is above 43°F. At this temperature plant growth outdoors is sustained provided that moisture is available and daylight is intense enough and long enough for the plant in question. The map below illustrates that the number of Growing Months per year in Europe varies between 3 and 12.

The climate of a country is, of course, one of the prime factors determining the species of garden plants which succeed outdoors. The experts cannot agree on the best way to classify the widely varying climatic conditions found in Europe, and one of several well-established schemes is shown above.

The Maritime areas of western Europe are greatly influenced by the warm North Atlantic Drift, and the basic characteristic is that the winters of a locality in this zone are milder than you would expect from the position on the map. For instance in January the Shetland Islands are warmer than Odessa, 1,000 miles to the south.

At the other end of the scale is the zone of Continental climate which starts at the Russian border. Winters are intensely cold and summers hotter than on the Atlantic coast. Rainfall is seasonal and fairly small compared with the round-the-year rains of the Maritime areas.

The main body of the Continent has 6–11 Growing Months and this vast area is the Cool Temperate Zone. It also represents the Standard European Garden – ferns but not tree ferns, roses but not reindeer moss.

Where the number of Growing Months is less than 6 there is a profound effect on the vegetation. This is the Cold Zone, and a number of well-known garden plants can no longer be grown (see page 127).

At the other end of the scale there are parts of Europe that have Growing Months throughout the year, and in this Warm Temperate Zone the sub-tropical plants are able to flourish. This explains the link between S.W. Ireland, the Scilly Isles, part of the Brest Peninsula and Portugal.

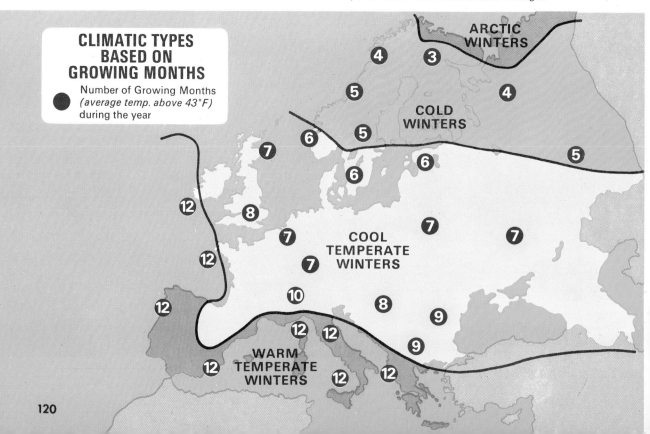

CLIMATIC TYPES BASED ON GROWING MONTHS

Number of Growing Months *(average temp. above 43°F)* during the year

ARCTIC WINTERS

COLD WINTERS

COOL TEMPERATE WINTERS

WARM TEMPERATE WINTERS

THE GARDEN SCENE IN SPAIN

PARQUE ALAMEDA,
MALAGA

The Oldest Gardens in Europe

If you want to see the oldest living gardens in Europe, then you must travel to Andalusia in southern Spain. The Moors, that odd collection of arabs, jews and greeks from North Africa, had overrun most of the Spanish Peninsula by 718 A.D. During the ninth century they created their gardens at Seville, Cordoba and elsewhere in Andalusia.

These gardens were completely enclosed by buildings and high walls to provide both shade and privacy. Like the Persian models on which they were based, they were designed for outdoor living within the confines of the house. Unlike the later French grand gardens they were not vast areas for lavish entertaining.

The Moorish gardens consisted of several courtyard gardens or *patios*, with water as the connecting link. Each *patio* contained a long canal or a basin with a central fountain, and the tiled walls, pillars and floors were sumptuously ornate. Gardens of water, high walls and ornate tiles . . . with plants used in moderation and for a definite purpose. Cypress or orange trees were planted in sunken beds and usually lined the inside of the walls to provide extra shade. Aromatic shrubs and flowers were grown in pots set along the water's edge to scent the air. There were no lawns, and statues in human form were strictly forbidden by the Koran.

Most of these Moorish gardens fell into decay following the reconquest of Spain, but two outstanding examples in Granada remain today— The Alhambra and Generalife. The **Alhambra** was started in the eleventh century and finished in 1369. Several of the original patios remain, including the *Patio de los Arrayanes* with its long pool lined by clipped myrtle hedges and the *Patio de los Leonos* with its famous statue of lions. Even more fascinating are the gardens of the nearby **Generalife,** the white-walled summer palace of the rulers of Granada. Here you will find the *Patio de la Riadh* (Courtyard of the Pool) which is nearly fifty yards long with curving jets of water falling into the flower-edged central canal. This, say the garden historians, is the true spirit of Moorish Spain.

The Hapsburgs and later the Bourbon rulers brought the Italian and French formal gardens to Spain. **La Granja** is the finest existing example, created by Philip V during the eighteenth century. This 350-acre *jardin français* stands high in the hills near Segovia, and water is its most famous feature. There are long cascades, tall fountains and attractive pools and lakes. Another grand Bourbon garden surrounds the Royal Palace at **Aranjuez.** Once again there are many fountains, cascades and elaborately planted parterres.

The modern grand gardens of Spain are a mixture of types and styles. There are beautiful parks and Botanical Gardens (almost all of which are open to the public) and the gardens around the homes of the nobility (almost none of which are open). There is one garden which is a living museum of Spanish garden history. At the **Alcázar** in Seville there are the Moorish *Galera* and *Gruta* gardens. Next to them are the Renaissance *Naranjal* and *Grande* gardens created after the reconquest, and to complete the picture there are modern flower gardens.

1350 Moorish Garden—the Courtyard of the Myrtles at the Alhambra.

1973 Ultra-Modern Rose Garden—the Seville Rosaleda opened in March 1973.

THE SPANISH HOME GARDEN

The tourist returning from his eight days on the Costa Brava brings back the impression that the Spaniard is not a keen gardener. Most of the homes are gardenless, and in the smart coastal villas it is a gardener and not the owner who is seen doing the work.

The few garden statistics available for Spain seem to support the tourist's instant impression. In the 1969 survey only about 7 per cent of households owned a garden, and 70 per cent were maintained by a full-time or part-time gardener.

The position until a few years ago was quite static and clearly defined. It was the wealthy families who owned the homes with gardens, and the largest of these were in the northern coastal area. The rest of the population generally lived in apartments or houses without gardens.

What the tourist would not have detected is that the garden scene is changing quite dramatically. Housing estates with gardens are being created on the outskirts of the larger towns, and both foreigners and middle-class Spaniards are building second homes near the coast. The number of Spanish gardens is now increasing at the rate of 20 per cent per annum, and obviously the owner-maintained plot will become much more common.

There are other signs of this upsurge in interest. A bimonthly magazine *Jardin y Paisaje* was launched in 1972. A weekly TV gardening programme was started in 1973 and there are now several regional societies. The most dramatic change in the past 10 years has been the emergence of the landscape architect. Today about 60 per cent of new gardens are professionally designed at the time the houses are erected.

Spanish home gardens vary widely with size and locality, but there are a few typical features. The style is nearly always purely ornamental—only 5 per cent have vegetables. The patio or paved courtyard is very common, and the favourite flowers are carnations, roses and geraniums. Trees are regarded as indispensable for the shade and privacy they provide; the provision of a cool oasis within the garden has always been a factor in garden design in this country. From earliest times the *glorieta* (a small arbour covered with tiles or climbing plants) has been a feature in Spain. Some of the more popular trees and shrubs are yucca, cypress, cycad, cedar, poplar, eucalyptus, oleander, myrtle and catalpa. Lawns appear in about half the gardens, and are generally studded with concrete stepping stones to protect the grass.

The sales of plants and seeds (£24 million per annum) is still very small compared to most other large European countries, but the figure is increasing rapidly. Garden centres have begun

to appear during the past few years and some, such as *Jardin de San Valero* at Barcelona, run a landscape design service.

Gardens as we know them are appearing in Spain at an unprecedented rate, but flowers around the home are nothing new. Large pots filled with greenery, fragrant plants or brightly-coloured flowers were standing in the courtyards, along the steps or on the white-painted walls of Spanish homes when gardening in England was strictly for the monks and lords of the manor. These pots can still be seen everywhere, and our tourist must not confuse a disinterest in gardening with a lack of affection for flowers. To dispel any doubts, watch the loving care with which flowers are arranged on crosses or spread as street carpets on the Feast of Corpus Christi.

In October 1972 the first National Horticultural Exhibition *iberflora 72* was held at Valencia. There was a wide variety of stands; the one illustrated above displayed the traditional garden collection of southern Spain – water, palms, succulents and large ornamental pot. The showground of 7 acres was small by Continental standards and the exhibition lasted for only 10 days, but there were 500,000 visitors. *Iberflora 74* is to be recognised as an International Exhibition.

MARIA LOUISA PARK
(Seville)

This large park is considered to be one of the most attractive in Spain, following its redesign by Forestier in 1928. It was formerly an English landscape park, but it was transformed into a truly Spanish garden. There is a series of green enclosures, each with its own pool and tiled fountain, its own palms and water lilies. The small rose garden attracts many visitors.

GENERALIFE (Granada)
Courtyard of the Pool
See page 122

MADRID PARKS

The public parks in Madrid and other large Spanish cities are of great importance to the residents, for they provide a refuge from the oppressive heat of the summer and also greenery for a gardenless population.

Buen Retiro Park (see below) is the largest of the city parks in Madrid, but the forest park of **Casa de Campo** is even more extensive. At the **Parque del Oeste** there is one of the finest rose gardens in Europe with about 30,000 bushes in an outstanding garden setting of pools and fountains. This is a sight not to be missed if you are in Madrid. Another unique attraction is the **Madrid Botanical Garden** situated next to the Prado. In all other Botanical Gardens it is strictly forbidden for you to take home "free samples", but here anyone asking for medicinal herbs between 11.00 a.m. and noon must be provided with them free of charge. More than 30,000 different species from all over the world are grown in this 20-acre Botanical Garden.

There are several gardens near the Royal Palace, such as the formal **Sabatini Gardens** with clipped hedges, topiary and statues and the **Campo del Moro** with its informally planted shrubs and trees.

EL PALMERAL (Elche)

The Palm Grove of Elche is reputed to have been founded by the Phoenicians nearly 3,000 years ago. Today it is Europe's finest collection of palms. There are many thousands of date palms, but it is the *Palmera Imperial* which the tourists come to see. This mighty tree, more than 200 years old, has 7 trunks and a strange candelabra-like appearance.

ALHAMBRA (Granada)
Gardens of the Partal
See page 122

BUEN RETIRO PARK
(Madrid)

The *Retiro* is the largest and finest of the many parks in Madrid. Imposing avenues lined with tall trees and statues of Spanish rulers cross its 325 acres, and the large lake, small zoo and free evening concerts are popular features. The rose garden with its flower-covered pergolas and attractive small pools is the main attraction for the flower lover.

MAR Y MURTRA (Blanes)

This 11-acre Botanical Garden was opened in 1921 and is now maintained by the Karl Faust Foundation. There are more than 3,000 different species to be seen along the paths, and the routes are clearly marked to provide a sub-tropical nature trail. You will find cacti, agaves, palms, conifers and exotic flowers everywhere.

Nearby is **Pinya de Rosa**, a 250-acre Botanical Garden with a vast collection of cacti and succulents. It is private, so ring or write before you call.

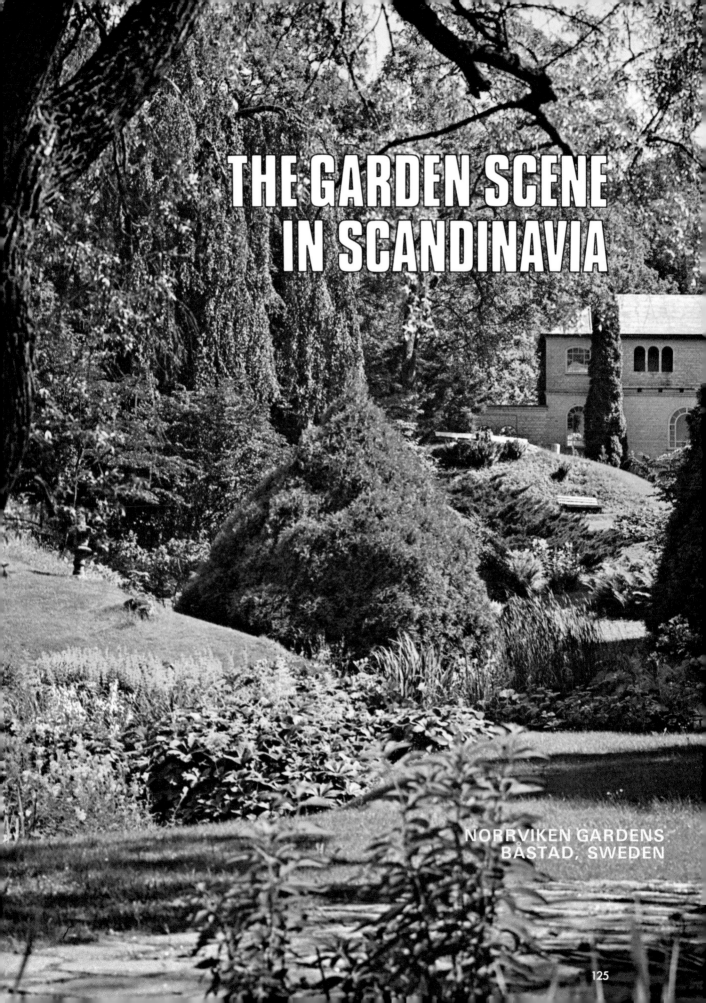

THE GARDEN SCENE
IN SCANDINAVIA

NORRVIKEN GARDENS
BÅSTAD, SWEDEN

Spruce, Silver Birch and Snow

Much of Scandinavia is covered with spruce, silver birch and snow during the winter months, and this can give the impression that these countries with their conifer forests and long hard winters have added little or nothing to the garden scene of Europe.

This is not so. In their grand gardens, home gardens and especially indoors the Scandinavian countries have made a significant contribution. Beginning with the grand garden, both Sweden and Norway have perfected the Modern Sculpture Garden, with fine contemporary statues in a floral setting. They have modernised an age-old tradition of ornamental stone in the garden, begun in Italy and popularised in France.

Scandinavia has updated and perfected another type of once-popular attraction – the Pleasure Garden. This type of park is attractively planted and provides a pleasant place to stroll or sit during the day. As such it is similar to any other type of park, but there is the special feature that it comes alive at night – illuminations, dining, music, dancing and so on. Once there were famous (later notorious) Pleasure Gardens in London, such as Vauxhall and Ranelagh, but they disappeared during the nineteenth century. Battersea Festival Gardens were opened in 1951 in a brave attempt to revive the tradition, but nothing in Europe can compare with the Tivoli Gardens in Denmark.

The home garden style which is characteristic of Scandinavia is the Natural Garden. The gardens of new houses, summer homes and housing estates are *slipped into* the surroundings rather than being *carved out* of the countryside as generally happens elsewhere.

This must not be confused with the English landscape style of the eighteenth century, where an apparently natural landscape was created by artificial means. In Scandinavia the contours of the land, the native grass and the trees of the forest are maintained wherever possible and garden trees, shrubs and some flowers are fitted into this scheme of things. One of the most spectacular examples is the new town of Tapiola in Finland. The guiding principle has been that "the connection between man and nature was not to be broken." Landscape architects from many lands go there to see how natural forest, artificial stone and gardens can be merged into one harmonious whole.

Many reasons have been put forward to account for the Scandinavians' love of natural gardens. The growing season is too short for year-round gardening . . . a desire not to spoil a beautiful countryside . . . an unwillingness to spend much time in the garden, so that nature must do part of the work! There is some truth in all of the theories.

The position is totally different indoors, for the people of these northern countries spend more time and skill on creating house gardens than almost anyone else in Europe. Not for them the occasional pot on a window sill – here you will find planted troughs running the length of the room and specially adapted windows filled with exotic flowers. The Victorian conservatory has been updated—the Danish *vinterhave* (winter garden) inside which plants are landscaped, often with hardly a pot in sight.

Linnaeus AND HIS GARDEN

Carl von Linné was born in South Sweden in 1707. He was a rather dull child but worked hard and eventually became Professor of Medicine and Botany at the University of Uppsala. Today he is remembered neither as von Linné nor as a doctor – he has been immortalised under his latin name, Carolus Linnaeus.

This is appropriate, because he evolved the modern system of plant classification, whereby each plant has basically two latin names, the first one (the genus) is like a person's surname and the second one (the species) is similar to a christian name. A simple idea, but before it there was great confusion and afterwards the door was opened for scientific plant breeding and the advance of botanical science. "God created the plants and animals, and Linnaeus put them in order."

The ideas of Linnaeus live on, and so does his garden. The Linnaeus Garden and Museum at Uppsala are open to the public, and only those varieties which were known and described by Linnaeus are found there. He began the garden in 1741 and his original plan was faithfully restored about sixty years ago. Annuals are on one side of the path, perennials on the other and all in neat separate rows according to his revolutionary system of classification.

THE SCANDINAVIAN HOME GARDEN

It is 1,200 miles from the top of Norway to southern Denmark. This land mass covers a wide range of climatic conditions, and yet there are a basic group of features which are frequently found in Denmark, Sweden, Norway and Finland which together make up the Scandinavian Garden.

The typical boundary is curved and irregular, and trees are virtually always present. There are silver birch and conifers, of course, and also fruit trees. It is the stone fruits which dominate here— plums are more popular than apples. Found even more frequently are soft fruit bushes, with currants easily topping the popularity poll. More redcurrants and blackcurrants are home-grown than shop-bought in Scandinavia, but only a small minority bother to grow vegetables.

The terrace or patio is an important area, and the materials used for construction depend on the country. In Norway planks of treated spruce are widely used; stone and concrete are preferred in Denmark and Sweden. The long-lasting blanket of snow makes the cultivation of good turf difficult, and *Fusarium* disease is a problem. Bulbs are the heralds of the long-awaited spring, and are as popular as in most other European countries. Bedding plants have less appeal, except in urban gardens, pots and window boxes.

The prime garden plants are trees, shrubs and roses and choice is dictated by the climate. Sweden is divided into eight zones based on climatic conditions, and all catalogues show the zones in which the listed plants can be grown. Nearly all of the first four zones lie below a line from Stockholm to Oslo, and here the climate is only a little more severe than in Britain. Further north in zones V—VIII a much more restricted range of plants can be grown. Many universal favourites of temperate regions are unsuitable, such as rhododendrons, pears and berberis.

Over much of Scandinavia the home owner wants a garden with a semi-natural look and one which does not require constant attention. There are other more important calls on the family's time, with sport and active outdoor pursuits as the major hobbies. One out of every four Danes is a member of a sports club. Another reason why it is undesirable to have a garden which requires weekly attention is the cult of the summer home. Nearly 20 per cent of the households of Scandinavia have a second home near lake, sea, mountain or forest where the family can spend weekends or summer vacations. This means that the garden at home must be capable of being left without attention for fairly long periods. But it also means that the total number of gardens is increased, as these summer homes each have their own small natural garden with grass, trees, shrubs and a few roses.

DENMARK

There are one million home gardens, owned by 63 per cent of the households in Denmark. The average size of the plots around older houses is about 9,000 sq. ft., mostly back garden and filled with grass, trees, flower beds and fruit. Houses built since 1950 have an average plot of 5,500 sq. ft. Garden illumination is a popular feature.

Window boxes, flower-filled balconies and plants in tubs and pots are to be seen everywhere, and especially in Copenhagen. Near to the coast there are 175,000 summer homes.

SWEDEN

Only 42 per cent of Swedish households have a garden around the main residence. This results in the remarkable situation that there are one million home gardens and no less than 500,000 summer homes. The average size of the home garden is 5,500 – 9,000 sq. ft., and the keen gardener follows his sporting instinct by trying to grow some plants which are classed as too tender for his locality.

Potted plants are moved outdoors during the summer months, and the balcony gardens of Sweden are most attractive.

NORWAY

Sixty-one per cent of the households in Norway have a garden around the home, and the average size of these 700,000 gardens is about 8,000 sq. ft. Roses are grown in the south and west; the choice of plants in North Norway is very limited.

The cultivation of indoor plants is a major home activity. Fourteen million house plants were sold in Norway in 1972, which represents more than 10 per household.

THE GRAND SIGHTS

Southern Scandinavia abounds with Grand Gardens which are open to the public. Some are in foreign styles, such as English landscaped parks or French formal gardens. But there are many in true Scandinavian style, like the conifer garden, modern sculpture garden or pleasure garden.

MILLES GARDEN (Lidingo)

A famous sculpture garden designed by Carl Milles. It consists of a series of terraces built on the cliffs near Stockholm. Amongst the trees, shrubs and flower borders stand the Milles statues.

DROTTNINGHOLM PALACE (Stockholm)

An excellent example of the Grand French style in Scandinavia. Rigidly formal, with large parterres, avenues of pleached limes, box-edged lawns, classical statues and fountains.

ROTTNEROS PARK (Värmland)

A Swedish industrialist, Dr. Pählson, created this world-famous garden during and after World War II. Its fame centres around the unique collection of statues set throughout the formal gardens, the work of modern Scandinavian sculptors. Here you can find bronzes and granite figures by Hasselberg, Eriksson, Eldh, Milles and Grate. This 100 acre park, with its natural areas and classical gardens, attracts several hundred thousand visitors each year.

NORRVIKEN GARDENS (Båstad)

One of the finest living museums of horticultural styles in Europe. A series of individual gardens have been created — there are Mediaeval, Renaissance, Baroque, Japanese and Scandinavian examples.

SOFIERO CASTLE (Skane)

The gardens of the summer Royal Palace are open to the public each afternoon, and they are noted for their rarities and new varieties. Rhododendrons and roses are the most famous features.

GOTLAND

This island off the east coast of Sweden is a flower-lover's paradise. The Alvena Lindang Wildflower Reserve contains many orchids; Visby, the main port, is known as the "City of Ruins and Roses".

TRÄDGÅRDSFÖRENINGEN (Gothenburg)

The popularity of this park in South Sweden arises from its lavish flower displays, fountains and palm house. There is a restaurant in these idyllic surroundings.

GISSELFELD (Have)

An 18 acre landscape park, laid out at the end of the 19th century. There are 5 lakes with rhododendron and rose islands, and many rare trees have been planted. Tropical plants are grown in the glasshouses.

KNUTHENBORG (Bandholm)

This is the largest *jardin anglais* in Scandinavia — 1,500 acres of woods, parkland and lakes with more than 500 species of trees and shrubs.

FREDERIKSBORG (Hillerød)

One of the finest French style gardens in Scandinavia. All the ingredients are there — magnificent vistas, long avenues, terraces and parterres.

VALLØ (Køge)

Reputedly the largest bulb park in the whole of Scandinavia. Other Grand Gardens nearby are around the castles of Bregentved and Vemmetofte.

SOCIETIES

SWEDEN

There are several societies, the leading one being the *Riksförbundet Svensk Trädgård* (National Association of Swedish Gardening). It was founded in 1900 and has 20,000 members, who are entitled to purchase the Society Handbooks at a reduced price. It publishes a quarterly magazine *hem trädgården.*

DENMARK

Denmark does not have a single national society. Instead there are 3 regional bodies which co-operate to produce a monthly magazine *Haven* (circulation 75,000) which is distributed through local societies to the members.

Society	Membership
Det KGL Danske Haveselskab (Copenhagen)	1,900
Det Jydske Haveselskab (Jutland)	32,000
Østifternes Haveselskab (Islands)	34,000

The Jutland Society is the leading one, and its centenary was commemorated in 1973 by a special stamp issue (see illustration above). The strength of the societies lies in their excellent advisory services, and there are 26 full-time advisers, supported in part by a state subsidy.

Free detailed advice is given to members, and a landscape design service is offered. Short courses are arranged for gardeners and in Jutland in 1972 about 46,000 people attended.

NORWAY

Det Norske Hageselskap is the Norwegian Horticultural Society, and was founded in 1884. It is still very active, and its 30,000 members pay an annual subscription of 35 N Kroner, for which they receive the monthly journal *Norsk Hagitend* and other benefits.

The Society is deeply concerned with the proper landscaping of new homes and housing estates, and it circulates its booklet of gardening plans and landscaping advice (*Tomt og Hus*) to all the local councils throughout the country. These plans underline the need to maintain the natural contours and vegetation as much as possible.

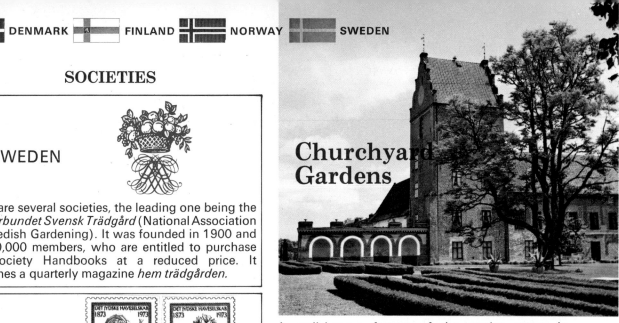

Churchyard Gardens

A well-known feature of the garden scene in Denmark is the unique churchyard garden. The cemeteries here are not open checker-boards of gravestones; the stones which are present are screened by attractive plantings of box and conifers. In this way the mourners have privacy at the graveside and the local population has a small and pleasant park in which to sit or stroll.

ALLOTMENTS

The old-style allotment gardens have rapidly declined in Scandinavia, mainly due to the high standard of living removing the need for cheap home-grown vegetables. These plots have been replaced by chalet gardens with lawns, flower beds and small statues.

The popularity of these colonies of away-from-home gardens varies widely from country to country. Norway has a mere 2,500 chalet gardens and they are of little importance on the national scene. The Swedish *Koloniträdgård* (chalet garden) is usually part of a town park and it is only in the large built-up areas that these play a significant role. The vegetable allotment has virtually disappeared from Sweden.

Denmark is one of the leading nations in the European chalet garden movement. It has some of the best laid-out colonies in Europe, with oval shaped gardens (*Kolonihaver*), paddling pools, shops, community centres and even representatives on the local councils. There are 20,000 chalet gardens in Copenhagen alone, and each tenant pays about £10 per year for his plot. Larger chalets than in most other European cities are permitted, and unusual designs are allowed. The *Kolonihaveforbund* (National Allotments Association) has about 50,000 members and a monthly magazine is circulated.

MAGAZINES

The only important regular magazines are the journals of the Horticultural Societies. These are colourful and well-produced. A group of Swedish garden centres, the *Gröna Ringen,* publishes the gardening annual *mästare i trädgård* which is distributed free of charge to 600,000 homes in the urban areas. The annual catalogue of the *Gröna Ringen* is sold for 3 S Kroner in garden centres and about $\frac{1}{4}$ million copies are bought each year.

Pleasure gardens

TIVOLI (Copenhagen)

Over 4 million people visit this 20 acre Danish showpiece every year, equivalent to almost the total population of the country. Every day between May and September many thousands of Danes and tourists stroll through the pleasant gardens to admire the 200,000 flowering plants. In the evening the lakes and flowers are floodlit and they serve as a background to the entertainment side of Tivoli — theatres, 18 orchestras and bands, 20 restaurants, a concert hall and firework displays.

LISEBERG (Gothenburg)

Nearly twice the size of Tivoli and with outstanding landscaped gardens — pools, lawns and flower beds. The variety of entertainment is, of course, much more limited than in the illustrious Copenhagen Pleasure Garden.

GRÖNA-LUND TIVOLI (Stockholm)

A miniature version of the Tivoli Gardens close to the SKANSEN PARK. At Skansen there is a herb and rose garden, and other attractions include an outdoor buildings museum, zoo, concerts, country crafts exhibitions and playgrounds.

GAVNØ (Naestved)

A large park planted with 100,000 tulips, narcissi and hyacinths. There is a rock garden and a rose garden.

EGESKOV (Kvaerndrup)

The grounds around the 16th century castle contain several gardens in different styles. The *jardin français* and rose garden are the best known.

FROGNER PARK (Oslo)

A post-war garden in which bold blocks of a single species (pink petunias, yellow tagetes, red begonias, etc.) are set in abstract patterns amidst the lawns. This modernistic setting houses hundreds of stone and bronze statues, the work of Gustav Vigeland.

GRIEG GARDEN (Bergen)

The lakeside home of the late Edvard Grieg is open to the public, and is a good example of the Scandinavian woodland garden. There is an assortment of garden plants set in a forest of silver birch and spruce, and a winding path leads to the cabin where Grieg composed his music.

BOTANICAL GARDENS & TREE COLLECTIONS

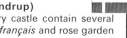 NORWAY

BERGEN BOTANICAL GARDEN One of Norway's best known public parks. There are 4 acres of gardens with various displays — the rhododendrons, heathers, lilies and primulas are outstanding.

OSLO BOTANICAL GARDEN Large garden — famous for its extensive collection of Norwegian alpine flowers. Included in the grounds are tropical houses and an arboretum. 35 acres.

KONGSVOLL ALPINE GARDEN Nearly 2,000 ft. above sea-level in the Dovre Mountains. Varied collection of alpine flowers, including many rarities.

FINLAND

ARBORETUM MUSTILA (Elimäki) Privately-owned collection of conifers and rhododendrons. 300 acres.

HELSINKI BOTANICAL GARDEN Fine 12½ acre park containing 9 display glasshouses.

OULU BOTANICAL GARDEN Noted for its collection of arctic as well as alpine plants. 22½ acres.

TURKU BOTANICAL GARDEN More than 3,000 different plants, including 700 kinds of orchids, are on display in the glasshouses. 19 acres.

SWEDEN

GOTHENBURG BOTANICAL GARDEN One of Scandinavia's finest Botanical Gardens, covering 375 acres. Notable features are the rockery (3,000 species), conifers, roses, rhododendrons, bamboos, orchids and nature reserve.

HALSINGBORG BOTANICAL GARDEN Interesting ecological garden, demonstrating the effect of exposure and soil type on the growth of plants. 14½ acres.

LUND BOTANICAL GARDEN Flowers from various regions have been planted here — South Sweden, Aegean Islands and South Africa. 17 acres.

BERGIANSKA BOTANICAL GARDEN (Stockholm) Noted for its glasshouse displays and trees, shrubs and flowers from the Far East. Unusual feature — plants are available for sale. 19 acres.

UPPSALA BOTANICAL GARDEN One of the oldest Botanical Gardens in Europe. There is a comprehensive range of garden annuals and perennials grown here, and native plants have been collected from all over Scandinavia. 46 acres.

DENMARK

CHARLOTTENLUND ARBORETUM A 10 acre collection of conifers.

COPENHAGEN BOTANICAL GARDEN There are many things to see in this 24 acre garden — alpines, begonias, cacti, orchids, fruit trees and conifers.

HVEDDE DESERT ARBORETUM An interesting collection of trees capable of surviving desert conditions. 46 acres.

AGRICULTURAL COLLEGE BOTANICAL GARDEN (Copenhagen) Large collection of hardy shrubs; 5 display greenhouses are open to the public. 20 acres.

JUTLAND GARDEN OF TREES In this area of Rold Skov (Denmark's largest forest) all the trees native to Denmark have been planted.

A PICTURE GUIDE TO
Chrysanthemums

Unless you are a gardening expert or a chrysanthemum enthusiast, prepare to be confused. The myriad varieties are arranged in a profusion of groups, classes, sections and subsections, and around them has grown a long list of technical terms. Despite this complexity, or because of it, the chrysanthemum is surpassed only by the rose as Britain's top hobby flower. Size and perfection of each bloom rather than the overall appearance of each plant are the aims of the enthusiast, yet the chrysanthemum is a fine garden plant.

It comes in many forms. The annual chrysanthemum is a hardy plant raised quite easily from seed, and the perennial chrysanthemums include the popular herbaceous border plant *C. maximum* (shasta daisy). But these are merely unimportant relatives of the late summer- and autumn-flowering plants with dark green, lobed leaves which we all know as the chrysanthemum.

Technically it is the Florists' Chrysanthemum and there are two basic groups – the outdoor varieties and the greenhouse ones. The outdoor (or early flowering) group contains a large number of sections but the major choice is between two types of display. First of all there are the smaller-flowering types which are grown for the massed effect of their blooms rather than the quality of each individual flower. The single-flowered, anemone-flowered, pompon, sprays and korean chrysanthemums belong here, and they are all very easy to grow. There is no stopping or disbudding to worry about, and staking is usually not necessary.

The second type, the decoratives, are a little more difficult because staking is essential to support their large flower heads. For garden display the shorter-growing varieties are usually chosen. The plants are *stopped,* which means that the growing tip of each stem is removed shortly after planting. The purpose of this is to make the plant flower earlier and to give it a better shape, and this technique does not deserve its reputation for being difficult for the ordinary gardener.

Things are not so easy for the enthusiast with his eye on the show bench. He has to time the first stopping and sometimes a second stopping with great care in order to make sure that the blooms will be at their best on the day of the show. The varieties chosen for cut flower production are often taller than the ones used for garden display and the practice here is to *disbud,* which means the removal of every unwanted lateral shoot and flower bud on a stem so as to allow the selected one to grow to its fullest extent. This single bloom at the top of each stem is sometimes covered by plastic sheeting or enclosed in a paper bag to protect it from rain and grime.

So much for the outdoor group; simple or skilful depending upon your reason for growing them. The greenhouse group come into flower as the outdoor ones fade in October, and once again the choice is between general display and cut flower production.

For cut flowers the exhibition and decorative varieties are usually chosen, and the ritual of stopping and disbudding is essential. Large exhibition varieties produce blooms which are at least 10 inches across. Spray varieties are grown to provide attractive heads of smallish flowers which are widely used in flower arranging, and such varieties are not disbudded.

Many greenhouse chrysanthemums are grown for general display as flowering pot plants. Dwarf varieties are chosen, although in recent years commercial growers have been able to use chemicals which have a stunting effect on non-dwarf varieties. Flowering season as well as height can be altered. By altering the day length A.Y.R. (All the Year Round) chrysanthemums are produced for sale. New techniques for a flower which was being cultivated for the gardens of the Far East more than 2,000 years ago.

Despite its long history in China and Japan, the chrysanthemum is a relatively recent arrival in Europe. The first imports into Britain did not begin until the 1830s, and until the First World War the blooms were only a few inches across. Nearly all the spectacular facets of this plant are twentieth century creations. The charm chrysanthemum is an example, which was introduced in 1947. It is easily grown from seed, and produces an attractive pot plant covered with hundreds of blooms.

CLASSIFICATION

Each floret is really a miniature flower with fused petals, and the shape and type of florets which are present provide the key to identification. They may be small, club-like and on a central disc (**disc florets**) or in a similar position but larger and tube-like (**tubular florets**). The 'petals' are **ray florets** and these may be flat or rolled. The direction in which the ray florets are curled to make up the bloom is an important recognition point.

   These flower types may be found on outdoor or greenhouse varieties, and both of these types can be subdivided according to the purpose for which the plant is grown.

SINGLE-FLOWERED
Not more than 5 rings of ray floret
Central group of disc florets.

INCURVED
Florets are turned in towards the centre.
Bloom forms a tight ball.

INTERMEDIATE
Florets are loosely and irregularly incurved or partly reflexed.

REFLEXED
Florets are turned outwards and dow wards from the centre of the bloom.

ANEMONE-FLOWERED
Not more than 5 rings of ray florets.
Central group of tubular florets.

POMPON
Florets are tightly packed, not curled, forming a small globular bloom.

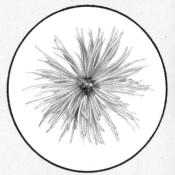

SPIDERY-FLOWERED
Florets are thread-like (Rayonnant varieties) or spoon-shaped.

OUTDOOR VARIETIES
Other names : Early-flowering chrysanthemums
           Border chrysanthemums
Includes all varieties which bloom in a normal season in the open ground before 1st October without any protection.

Small-flowered varieties for garden display

No stopping or disbudding required.

Large-flowered varieties for garden display

One stopping only. Little or no disbudding.

Large-flowered varieties for cut flowers

Stopping and disbudding as required.

GREENHOUSE VARIETIES
Other name : Late-flowering chrysanthemums

Includes all varieties which normally bloom between October and late December under glass.

Flowering pot plants

Dwarf varieties of standard types. Also Charm varieties.

Large-flowered varieties for cut flowers

Stopping and disbudding as required.

Cascade varieties

Pendulous stems have to be trained.

CHRYSANTHEMUM PLANTING MATERIAL

ROOT DIVISIONS
In spring the outer portions of last year's stools can be detached, each bearing new shoots and roots. These clumps can be used to propagate all chrysanthemums, but in practice they are used only for koreans and a few other outdoor varieties. Cuttings are more successful.

ROOTED CUTTINGS
Last season's stools are kept in a cold frame or brought into the greenhouse in January. Cuttings 2–3 in. long are taken in February – April from the new shoots at the base (not side) of the stems. These are rooted at 50–60°F and then transferred into 3 in. pots.

SEEDS
Seeds are not used to propagate chrysanthemums because the plants produced are rarely true to type. The charm and cascade varieties are exceptions — these are often raised from seed sown in February.

STAKING
Insert a stout bamboo cane to a depth of 12–15 inches *before* planting large-flowered or tall-growing varieties. Tie the stem fairly loosely to the stake, using soft string. As the plant grows make additional ties. Extra staking in August-September might be necessary.

STOPPING
When the plant is about 8 in. tall the soft growing tip should be pinched out or *stopped.* This will stimulate the early growth of flower-bearing side shoots instead of a useless break bud.

PLANTING
Plant out rooted cuttings in early May. Water pots thoroughly the day before and use a trowel to dig a hole which is wider but only slightly deeper than the soil ball of the cutting. Never plant chrysanthemums too deeply. Fill the hole with fine soil and press down firmly.

GROWING GREENHOUSE VARIETIES
In April transfer the rooted cuttings from 3 in. to 5 in. pots. In mid-May move into 8 in. pots and insert one or more stout canes to support the stems. Stopping is necessary as with outdoor varieties.

In early June move the pots outdoors on to a standing ground of ashes, tiles or concrete. Secure the plants to wires stretched between stout posts. Water regularly, but do not keep the compost constantly moist.

At the end of September bring the pots back indoors. Disbud as necessary. Feed regularly until the buds show colour.

MULCHING
Do not hoe after the middle of June. Keep the soil cool and moist by applying a 2 in. layer of peat or compost around the plants.

WATERING AND FEEDING
Water thoroughly during dry spells, but do not keep the ground constantly soaked. Overhead spraying of the foliage is beneficial. Feed every fortnight with liquid fertilizer until the buds begin to swell.

SOIL
Pick a spot which gets at least a few hours sunshine during the day. Never plant under trees. Most soils are satisfactory and liming is not usually necessary. Chrysanthemums prefer slightly acid conditions.

In winter dig in plenty of organic matter. No need to dig deeper than one spade's depth. Rake in 4 oz. bone meal per sq. yd. after digging.

PLANTING DISTANCES
Garden display
Koreans, pompons – 2 ft. apart
Others – 1½ ft. apart
Cut flower production
– 3 ft. rows,
plants 1½ ft. apart

PESTS & DISEASES
Slugs and birds are serious early pests — young plants can be stripped. Both aphids and capsids can become troublesome, but they are easily controlled by spraying with a systemic insecticide. Use lindane to destroy leaf miner and earwigs.

Mildew and grey mould can be prevented by proper management; spray with a systemic fungicide such as benomyl if spots appear. The worst headache is chrysanthemum eelworm, revealed by the blackening of the lower leaves. Plants have to be destroyed and the land is unfit for growing chrysanthemums in future.

STORING STOOLS
In November cut back the stems to about 6 inches. Lift the roots carefully and shake off the soil. Trim off any stem leaves and tie a label on each stem. These prepared roots or *stools* should be closely packed into boxes and surrounded by compost. Store the boxes in a cold frame and begin watering when new growth appears.

The *EuroChrysanthemum*

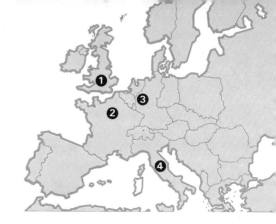

❶ GT. BRITAIN is the European home of the chrysanthemum, and there are 13,000 members of the National Chrysanthemum Society to prove it. Only the Royal National Rose Society tops this figure amongst specialist societies, and this flower is popular in Britain in all its forms for growing, exhibiting, arranging and giving as a present.

The annual subscription for Fellows of the N.C.S. is £1.50, and privileges include a Year Book, a review of new introductions, regular bulletins and passes to the National Shows held in London during September and November. Provincial Shows are held at Harrogate, Birmingham, Edinburgh, Cardiff and Paignton. Write to the Secretary, National Chrysanthemum Society, 65 St. Margaret's Avenue, Whetstone, London N.20 for an application form. Join if you are keen on this challenging flower – the Society offers a number of textbooks; the *Chrysanthemum Manual* has sold over 30,000 copies.

To see the new varieties go to the joint N.C.S. and R.H.S. trial grounds at Wisley or visit Rouken Glen, Glasgow. For the northern enthusiast trials are held at Greenhead Park, Huddersfield.

❷ In **FRANCE** the chrysanthemum is *la fleur des morts* – the funeral flower. In its white cut flower form it is shunned by the gardener except for dressing graves. There are 1,200 members of the *Société Française des Chrysanthemistes*, and an annual exhibition is held.

❸ W. GERMANY shares the Continental dislike of the large-flowered Chrysanthemum as a cut flower because of its association with death – there is no Chrysanthemum Society. This attitude is changing and more than 11 million pot chrysanthemums are raised each year.

❹ In **ITALY** spray chrysanthemums are sold in large numbers in early November for decorating cemeteries. The general European stigma is less marked in Italy than in neighbouring countries and younger Italians use these flowers for indoor display. A large exhibition is held each year at the Villa Doria Pamphilj in Rome.

THE EXPERT WAY

Exhibitors seek to produce large and perfect blooms which will be gently 'dressed' just before the show. Three special techniques are often used during cultivation:

SECOND STOPPING
Early stopping will have prevented the useless central bud from forming (A in the diagram). First crown buds will develop on the side shoots and these are generally the best. The exhibitor sometimes prefers second crown buds, and so he carries out a *second stopping*.

DISBUDDING
When growing large varieties for cut flowers the aim is to produce one superb bloom per stem. Disbudding is therefore carried out, which means the removal of every unwanted lateral shoot and bud on the stem. This is referred to as *securing the bud*.

BAGGING
Many exhibitors use bags or plastic sheets to protect their outdoor show blooms. Bagging is a popular technique for white or yellow varieties; a greaseproof paper bag is placed over the opening flower bud as soon as the petal colour can be seen.

A PICTURE GUIDE TO Begonias

For the majority of gardeners the begonia comes in just three types. First of all there is the showy double begonia (*B. tuberhybrida*) with its rose-like blooms which can reach the size of a saucer. These plants are raised from tubers in the spring, and can be grown in pots to decorate the greenhouse or add colour to the living room. But it is much more likely that they will be planted out in the garden when the danger of frosts has passed, to provide a non-stop floral display from July until October. The tubers are then carefully lifted and stored until the following year, when they will start the cycle again.

The second type frequently found in gardens is *B. semperflorens*, which will usually be bought as a summer bedding plant along with the tagetes, lobelia and ageratum. Many varieties are available, and the masses of white, pink or red flowers they produce are at the heart of many bedding schemes. An added attraction is their glossy green, bronze or red foliage.

For the third popular type of begonia it is necessary to go indoors – to the pot of *B. rex* standing on the sideboard or on a north-facing windowsill. Its large multicoloured leaves are known to everyone.

The adventurous gardener can find much more in the *Begonia* genus than just these three everyday species. You can buy *B. multiflora maxima* tubers in the spring to provide compact bedding plants bearing abundant rose-like double blooms. There are *B. corallina* and *B. coccinea* which grow taller than a man. *B. glaucophylla* will climb for many feet up a moss-covered pole for indoor display, and the flower-covered stems of *B. pendula* weep gracefully from hanging baskets. Just a few of the interesting species from the thousand which make up the genus *Begonia*.

In some European countries the popularity of begonias has steadily increased over the years, whereas in Britain this group of plants has never quite recaptured its late Victorian glory. Once with the calceolaria it dominated the flower beds of the suburban villa, the winter-flowering 'Gloire de Lorraine' hybrid was a favourite Christmas present and *B. weltoniensis* was to be seen in cottage windows everywhere.

There has been a begonia revival in recent years, but the membership of its society is still less than 1 per cent of the Royal National Rose Society. Perhaps part of the problem is that the begonia still lacks an important ingredient — fragrance. Perfumed tuberous varieties were available in the nineteenth century, but today's big blooms have no smell. Hybridists are looking for the answer, and it may be a keen amateur who finds it. If you want to learn more about growing these plants or how hybrids are produced, then join the National Begonia Society, annual subscription 75p. Write to the Secretary, 50 Woodlands Farm Road, Erdington, Birmingham B24 0PG.

One large marquee at the Birmingham City Show is devoted entirely to the annual exhibition of the society, but it is to Belgium you must go if you wish to see these plants in variety and quantity. To Ghent, the begonia capital of the world. Here there are 950 acres devoted to this flower, and they produce 80 million tubers each year. In summer many thousands of tourists flock to the rainbow-coloured fields and to the Annual Festival of the Begonia at Lochristi.

It is often assumed that Belgium must have been the birthplace of the garden begonia, but it is in England where the story began with the importation and sale of the first tubers in 1865 by James Veitch & Son of Chelsea. This British firm also raised and sold the first hybrids, but it was a Frenchman, M. Lemoine, who raised the first outstanding double begonia. Other hybridists were also at work, and Louis van Houtte imported some of the Veitch tubers into Belgium. He persuaded growers in the Ghent area to specialise in this new garden flower, and so one of Europe's industries was born.

Tuberous rooted

Begonia tuberhybrida

Green leaves; large rose-like flowers 3 – 6 in. across. This is the most popular type of garden begonia and is grown for both indoor display and outdoor summer bedding. There are several flower forms of these 'doubles'.

Marmorata
Standard
Camellia
Fimbriata
Picotee

Plants grow about 1 ft. high, and many varieties are available in white, yellow, pink, orange and red. Tubers are large, ranging from $1\frac{1}{4} - 2\frac{1}{2}$ inches in diameter.

Begonia pendula

Stems are slender and drooping, bearing numerous 2 – 3 in. flowers throughout the summer. These plants are ideal for hanging baskets and window boxes. Sometimes called 'basket begonias'. Red Cascade is a popular variety.

Begonia multiflora

Hybrids developed in the late 19th century which combine the attractive flower form of tuberous begonias with the free-flowering nature of B. semperflorens. These plants are therefore excellent for bedding out —growing 6 in. high and bearing abundant blooms until the first frosts.

Begonia multiflora maxima

A recent improvement on B. multiflora, and perhaps the best of all begonias for bedding out. The compact and free flowering habit of ordinary multifloras is maintained, but the double blooms are twice the size.

CLASSIFICATION

Begonias defy simple classification, and even the textbooks disagree on how to group the multitude of varieties and hybrids. Perhaps the simplest way to sort them out is to recognise two major sections: the *tuberous rooted* begonias which are raised each spring from tubers and the *fibrous rooted* begonias which are raised from seed or cuttings. Both sections are grown mainly for their flowers, and between them lies the smaller *decorative leaved* section containing those begonias which are grown as foliage house plants.

Decorative leaved

Begonia rex

Most popular species in the group. Leaves are multicoloured and the patterns are highly varied.

Begonia masoniana

The Iron Cross begonia, introduced into Britain in 1952 from the Far East.

Begonia boweri

Characteristic chocolate-brown edging to the small leaves. Easy to grow.

Begonia maculata

Leaves are silver-spotted on the upper surface and purplish below.

Fibrous rooted

Begonia semperflorens

A popular summer bedding plant, also known as the 'wax begonia'. Leaves are usually green, and the flowers are about $\frac{3}{4}$ in. across and are white tinged with pink. Many hybrids are available with red or bronze leaves and pink, white or red flowers. A new hybrid from Denmark, *B. semperflorens grandiflora*, bears flowers $2\frac{1}{2}$ inches in diameter.

'Lorraine' Begonias

Popular indoor plants for the Christmas season, bearing masses of pink blooms about 1 in. across from November to January.
Popular varieties include Gloire de Lorraine, Mrs. Lionel de Rothschild and Turnford Hall.
'Hiemalis' begonias are a similar group of winter-flowering hybrids, but the blooms are larger and there is a wider colour range.

Begonia haageana

Shrub-like; hairy leaves are green above and red below. The flowers are white tinged with pink. It is one of the hardiest of all indoor begonias.

Begonia fuchsioides

Shrub-like; glossy green, oval leaves. The flowers are pink or red and appear between October and March.

Begonia albo-picta

Shrub-like; narrow green leaves with silvery spots. Small whitish flowers appear throughout the summer.

Begonia coccinea

Height 6 ft. or more. The leaves are kidney-shaped and reddish underneath. The 1 in. red flowers are borne throughout the summer. President Carnot is a popular variety.

Tuberous rooted

Start the tubers into growth in March or April by pressing them hollow side uppermost into boxes of moist peat. Leave some space between the tubers to avoid root damage later, and keep them at 60° – 70° F. Belgian experts recommend that shoots should be showing before tubers are planted in this way, and some British authorities believe that the crowns of the tubers should be covered over with peat to reduce the risk of rotting.

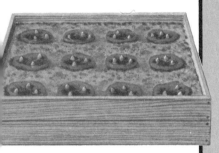

Keep the peat moist but not wet. When the shoots are about 2 in. tall carefully transplant each tuber, taking care to break as few roots as possible. Use 5 in. pots and Potting Compost. Transfer into 8 in. pots about a month later.

If the begonias are to be planted outdoors then gradually harden them off in May for planting out in June. During the flowering period stake if necessary and apply a liquid fertiliser. With *B. tuberhybrida* disbud as shown below if you want maximum size blooms.

Male bloom

Female bloom single and insignificant. Pinch off whilst still small.

Lift the tubers carefully in mid October. Keep indoors and remove the stems after the foliage has died. Store the tubers in dry peat in a frost-free place over winter.
B. tuberhybrida can be grown as a specimen greenhouse plant. It requires a temperature of at least 55° F. and the air must be kept moist. Summer shading is essential.

CULTIVATION

Most begonias prefer soil or compost which is rich in organic matter with little or no lime present. Outdoors in summer they thrive in a cool and moist situation, but indoors they do need to be kept fairly warm during the winter months as they are not hardy. Their three great enemies when grown as pot plants are cold winter nights, dry air and gas fumes. They are not sun lovers and nearly all of them prefer some shade.

Apart from these few points it is not possible to generalise about begonias. Precise details of care and propagation depend on the section to which the variety in question belongs. Some begonias, like Gloire de Lorraine, are too demanding to be kept as permanent house plants; others such as *Begonia boweri* are easy to maintain indoors throughout the year.

Decorative leaved

The decorative-leaved begonias are not the easiest of house plants. The compost must be kept moist during the growing season and rather dry during the winter months. They need moist air but moist leaves are to be avoided, so surround the pots with damp peat. Feed throughout the growing season, and keep them out of direct sunlight. In winter a minimum temperature of 50° – 55° F. is required. One final cultural point – keep them slightly pot bound.

The large-leaved members of this section are propagated by leaf cuttings in May or June. Use mature but not old leaves and nick the main veins. Lay the leaf on moist Cutting Compost and use pebbles to hold the leaf in close contact with the surface. Keep the container covered with glass or polythene and maintain a temperature of 65° – 70° F. New plants will develop at the cuts and can be potted up as soon as they have developed 2 or 3 leaves.

Fibrous rooted

B. semperflorens are usually bought as bedding plants at the end of May or in early June. Remove flowers and flower buds before planting. To raise your own plants sow the dust-like seed on Seed Compost in February or March. Don't cover the seed – merely water the surface with a light sprinkling. Cover the seed pan or pot with a polythene bag and keep at about 60° – 70° F. Remove the polythene cover as soon as germination takes place. Prick off the seedlings when the first true leaves show.

Many varieties of fibrous-rooted begonias are grown indoors as evergreens, and specimens up to 10 ft. high can be found. These established plants are repotted each year in April. Liquid feeding is necessary during the growing season. A minimum winter temperature of 50° – 55° F. is required, and frequent syringing of the foliage is necessary. During the summer keep the plants in a well lit spot, but out of direct sunlight. With shrubby varieties occasionally pinch out the growing tips to prevent the plant from becoming leggy.

Most fibrous-rooted begonias can be propagated by stem cuttings during the summer months. Use non-flowering shoots, about 3 in. long, and insert several in a suitable Cutting Compost. Cover the container with a polythene bag until rooting has taken place, and then pot up the rooted cuttings in the usual way.

A PICTURE GUIDE TO

Concrete

For many years concrete has played a part in the making of the garden. Paths, drives and garage floors are made of this material – grey, durable and uninteresting. In recent years its use has been stimulated by the advent of ready-mixed concrete. Most suppliers will deliver to homes within a 15 mile radius, provided that the order is large enough. If you need more than 3 cubic yards for your new path or driveway, then this is usually the best way to buy the material.

But the surface is still grey and uninteresting. The present keen interest in concrete has been mainly due to three major developments in precast concrete manufacture. First of all, pure white concrete is now available which is attractive for many purposes or can be dyed to produce a wide range of pastel shades. Next, there is a wide selection of surfaces now available, ranging from smooth, polished faces to deeply sculptured textures. Finally, there is a vast range of shapes to choose from – hexagonal or circular slabs, pierced blocks for screen walling and so on.

Colour, texture, shapes. With these new facets to work with architects in many countries have produced interesting and exciting surrounds to public buildings, housing estates and pedestrian precincts. Britain is well up with the leaders in this respect. But in the home garden the use of new style concrete to produce decorative effects has not caught on to the same extent. The use of concrete by the amateur to produce attractive features around the home is increasing but we lag behind Scandinavia, Germany and Switzerland.

The reason is not hard to find. There is always a distrust in this country of any innovation which threatens to reduce the area available for our two loves – the lawn and the flowers. Some critics scorn the trend towards "stone gardens" as advocated by the high priests of modern garden design.

This is not really fair to the new wave of designers. Professor Gerd Däumel, perhaps the world's leading authority on the garden use of concrete, stated that blocks or slabs "provide a good background for plants, which should always be the principal building material in a garden." In this country Nicolette Franck of the Cement and Concrete Association has made it quite clear that "concrete can provide, easily and economically, all the framework for which planting will be the flesh." Nobody wants stone gardens, least of all the experts.

There is one real danger in this present trend towards the architectural garden. Bad workmanship or poor taste in lawn laying or planting is often hidden or soon overgrown. But the effects of indifferent skill or a lack of colour sense when building a decorative wall or patio can be shockingly obvious and permanent.

So avoid the temptation to rush out and lay some of the attractive slabs or blocks now available. Think about your project and prepare for it. Before you start, look through the colourful catalogues of the precast concrete companies. Then look at the examples at your local garden centre or other supplier. Remember the advice of the experts to avoid bright or strong colours; try to use white, creams, buffs or greys rather than greens and reds. Above all, send off for two free books which will tell you more about the subject than many costly manuals. Their titles are 'Concrete in garden-making' and 'Concrete round the house'. Write to:

Publication Sales,
Cement and Concrete Association,
Wexham Springs, Slough SL3 6PL.

No payment is necessary if you live in the U.K. Enclose 25p if you are resident overseas.

Concrete is returning to the garden, with which it has a most surprising historical connection. In the 1860s a French gardener, Joseph Monier, decided to put iron mesh with the concrete when making his plant tubs. He produced much stronger containers and in the process founded the whole of the modern construction industry with his reinforced concrete.

SCREEN WALLING

The screen wall is an increasingly popular form of decorative boundary. It extends the view, which is important in small gardens. Laying the wall is not a job for the amateur unless he has some experience in construction work. Minor defects can show.

SOLID WALLING

A wall can *divide* one piece of land from another, and here both faces are exposed. Or it can *retain* land, with only the front face exposed. This exposed face may have an imitation stone texture, but there is no reason why it should not be unashamedly concrete.

PRECAST CONCRETE

A wide variety of concrete blocks, slabs, tiles and ornaments are available for installing as ready-made units. Avoid using too many colours and surface types if the area is small. The advantages compared with in-situ concrete are the vast range of design possibilities and the consistently high quality of the finished product.

PATIO

The word *patio* is now frequently used in leaflets on paving and books on garden design, but nobody gives a definition. This relatively new term is generally used for a paved area attached to the house on which one can walk about or sit. Ideally it is screened in some way to divide it from the rest of the garden. The older term *terrace* is still widely used for such areas.

Pier cap
Coping
Pierced block
Pier block
Walling block
Walling tile
Jumper block

Paving slab
U block
Built-in plant container
Movable plant container

RECONSTITUTED STONE

For garden ornaments and plant containers a material known as *reconstituted stone* is sometimes used. This is a special type of concrete in which crushed and graded stone is used in place of sand and gravel. After manufacture the surface is treated to produce a natural stone effect.

The process dates back to Roman times and these artificial stone ornaments have been used in English gardens for hundreds of years. Such ornaments are not cheap, and are usually copies of notable objects from the past. A fountain or large urn can cost several hundred pounds.

PAVING

Paving provides the main skeletons of the garden, and pathways, drives and terraces are the main uses for concrete. Precast concrete is becoming increasingly popular. There is the *paving slab* made in open moulds and available in many shapes and sizes from 9 in. x 9 in. to 2 ft. x 3 ft. Slabs more than 2 ft. x 2 ft. are difficult to handle and lay. There is also a range of thicknesses from $1\frac{1}{2}$ in. to $2\frac{1}{2}$ in. Choose the thicker slabs for garage driveways, and hydraulically-pressed slabs (known as *flags*) if you expect heavy traffic.

When ordering remember that textured surfaces (see below) are generally non-slip and always ask for a few extra slabs to allow for breakages on site.

IN-SITU CONCRETE

Much of our garden concrete is poured and cast on site, using a containing mould known as *framework* or *shuttering*. The starting point can be a bagged dry-mix to which water is added, or you can buy the three ingredients (cement, sand and gravel) and mix them yourself. A range of coloured cements is available.

For large jobs ready-mixed concrete is usually more convenient. Remember to arrange for people to help you; mixed concrete must be placed within an hour. The advantages compared with precast concrete are speed and economy. But large plain areas can look dull.

SURFACES & SHAPES

'Faced' or 'fair-faced' surfaces are specially prepared so as to look attractive. This fair-faced surface may be *smooth* or *textured*. There are several types of textured surface – the exposed aggregate type is becoming popular.

SMOOTH

BRUSHED

EXPOSED AGGREGATE

IMITATION STONE

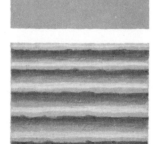
RIBBED

MODELLED

SCULPTURED

EuroConcrete

① In **GT. BRITAIN** small areas of decorative concrete are now becoming a feature in many gardens. The range of precast concrete units which is available can be seen at the larger garden centres and in the illustrated catalogues of the manufacturers. Many types of paving, walling and ornaments are on show at the major Flower Shows.

Undoubtedly the best way to learn how concrete can be used in the garden is to visit Wexham Springs, near Slough. This 70 acre estate, owned by the Cement and Concrete Association, is open occasionally under the National Gardens Scheme and Gardeners' Sunday Scheme (see page 24). Here you will see small gardens and features designed by well-known landscape architects, together with examples of almost every type of walling block and paving slab. Large display panels contain examples of the various types of textures and shapes which are available.

About 3000 visitors go to Wexham Springs on the open days each year to see the raised beds, patios, walkways, plant containers, seats, fountains and so on. Below is part of the Town Garden with its three raised concrete pools designed by Sylvia Crowe in 1966.

② **W. GERMANY** is probably the leading country in Europe in the use of garden concrete. Throughout the country there are fine examples of the skilful blending of different materials—

precast with in-situ concrete, smooth slabs with cobblestones, rough exposed aggregate blocks with still water. At the Federal Garden Shows impressive displays have been built, and these remain as permanent showpieces.

In the garden of Professor Däumel illustrated above, many of the features advocated by this famous landscape architect can be seen – modelled blocks, cantilevered steps and planting pockets in the wall.

③ For one use of concrete **SWITZERLAND** is the master. There are superb terraces and balcony gardens constructed on the hillsides. Halen (near Berne) is famous, but the most spectacular of all is the Muhlehalde terrace colony where each garden is constructed inside a vast concrete basin suspended from the side of the house.

④ **SCANDINAVIA** is a trendsetter in the modern approach to garden design. The architect Arne Jacobsen designed the houses and their internal paved courtyards as single units when he created the Albertslund suburb of Copenhagen. Designing house and garden as an integrated whole is a feature of much of modern Scandinavian architecture, and can be seen at Tapiola in Finland and Ammerud in Norway.

THE GARDEN SCENE IN BELGIUM

Begonias by the million

Belgium's pride is not in her grand showpieces nor in the quality of her two million home gardens. Instead it centres on the production of a few special plants for the gardens of the world.

Begonias by the million. Postage stamps, flower festivals and leaflets in various languages all proclaim Belgium's pre-eminence in begonias, but *Azalea indica* is even more important to the country's economy.

An old inn called Frascati's still stands in Ghent. It was here that a few gardeners founded the Agricultural and Botanical Society of Ghent in 1808, and from this tiny seed many important aspects of European horticulture have grown.

The first exhibition of this small Society was held in one of the rooms of the inn in 1809, and it was based on the flower shows that one of the members had seen in the industrial areas of Britain. From this one-room show and its 50 varieties of plants has evolved the Ghent Floralies, one of the great horticultural exhibitions of Europe. In 1819 a plant new to the western world was put on display at the show at Frascati's – *Azalea indica* or the Indian azalea, which has become one of Europe's favourite flowering pot plants for Christmas decoration. Not all the early members were professional gardeners – a Ghent baker, M. Montier, bred the first deciduous azalea hybrids which now grace our gardens with their vivid blooms in springtime. These are still called Ghent azaleas.

A flourishing horticultural industry grew up around Ghent, and to this area in the latter half of the nineteenth century Louis van Houtte brought the idea of growing tuberous begonias. Before the end of the century the Ghent region had won international fame as the begonia centre of Europe.

Van Houtte helped to found the *Syndicale Kamer der Belgische Tuinbouwkundigen* in 1880, and it remains the powerful voice of the Belgian growers.

THE FLOWER FIELDS OF BELGIUM

The flower and pot plant growing area lies in the north west corner of the country, and the greatest concentration is around Ghent. Begonias and azaleas have made this region world-famous, but there are other important ornamentals grown in this area. Each year millions of gloxinias and foliage house plants are exported and their value exceeds that of begonias and azaleas combined.

BEGONIAS

Every year between the end of July and mid September scores of thousands of tourists flock to the Ghent region to see the begonia fields in bloom. There are nearly 1,000 acres, and they produce about 80 million tubers annually. The area is a patchwork of 700 begonia nurseries, and the main concentrations are around Melle and Lochristi. Nearly all of the nurseries are small, family-run businesses with generations of tradition and accumulated knowledge. About 80 per cent of the tubers are exported, and the main customers are France, U.S.A., W. Germany, Holland and Britain. Belgium, not surprisingly, claims the garden with the greatest variety of begonias in Europe – Jardins Ankaert, avenue Reine Astrid, Spa.

AZALEAS

The Indian azalea is a favourite winter pot plant in many countries. Belgium produces about 20 million plants a year, and the main growing area of 650 acres is around Lochristi. About 85 per cent of these plants are exported; France and W. Germany are the biggest customers followed by Holland, Britain, Italy, Sweden and Switzerland. The average grower has about $2\frac{1}{2}$ acres with one fifth of his land under glass. Most of his plants are the early varieties which go on sale at Christmas time; others are sold in February and the late varieties are on sale in April.

CUT FLOWERS

There is a thriving cut flower industry, with roses and carnations as the most popular plants. Orchids are grown with the export market in mind, and Belgium claims to be the largest producer of these exotic blooms in Europe. But nearly all of the other cut blooms are grown for home consumption, and they are sold at the gay flower stalls in the open air markets which are a feature of the Belgian scene.

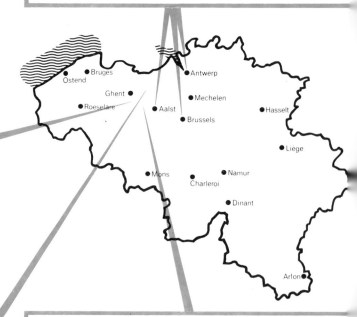

FOLIAGE HOUSE PLANTS

There are nearly 300 acres of glasshouses in Belgium devoted to raising foliage house plants, and a wide variety are grown. Exports are important, especially to France and Germany, but the majority of the plants are still sold on the home market. The Belgians, as noted on the next page, have a passion for greenery in their homes.

THE BELGIAN HOME GARDEN

There is no shortage of gardens in Belgium — about 64 per cent of all households have a garden of their own. These are generally laid down to lawns, trees, shrubs and flowers in the urban areas, and the plots in the rural districts are used as mixed ornamental/vegetable gardens. The average plot is about the size of the typical French garden and it is generally the husband's job to keep it in order.

Two million gardens, traditionally regarded as the poor relations of northern Europe. There is little of the national gardening pride found in Holland and Germany, there is no large annual Summer Flower Show at which the keen gardener can select plants for his own plot, and there is no old-established National Horticultural Society with its journal, advisory service etc.

Things seem to be changing. The gardens of new houses tend to be smaller than the average, and the new generation of young householders are much keener than their parents to have an attractive garden. Readership of garden magazines per head of population is now higher than in Britain, and the newly-formed Club des Jardiniers already has 17,000 members, most of whom are women. Each week 'Monsieur Jardinier' answers listeners' queries on radio.

Belgium's leading supermarket chain, GB Enterprises, has opened Super Bazaar Garden Centres in the suburbs of Brussels, Antwerp, Ghent and Bruges. Undoubtedly there is an awakening of gardening interest in Belgium, but the interest in allotments continues to decline. There has been no attempt to actively promote the idea of chalet gardens, and in some areas potato growing is not permitted. The working-class image of the allotment lingers on, and undoubtedly the advancement of Belgian domestic horticulture will have to be in the home garden. "With no trees there will be no man" proclaims the Club des Jardiniers. Whether the Belgian householder will really take up this call only time will tell.

THE FLOWER SHOWS

The main annual show for gardeners is the *Salon du Jardin* at the Centre International Rogier in Brussels. It is held for about one week at the beginning of March, which would be unthinkably early for a British horticultural show for the general public! Another show held in March is the Flanders Spring Fair in the Floralia Palace at Ghent, where home and garden exhibits can be seen. Every other year the International Exhibition of Horticultural Techniques is held at this site.

The Ghent Floralies take place every 5 years at the Parc de la Citadelle and dwarf all other Belgian shows. The Floralia Palace was built in the park for the 1950 show, and more than one million visitors came to see the plants and flowers in their new home.

THE MAGAZINES

Belgian gardening journals are plain and intensely practical with none of the glossy image of the leading French, German and Dutch magazines.

Jardins & Logis
    Monthly.   Circulation 6,000
l'Ami des Fleurs
    Monthly.   Circulation 52,000
Bloemen Vriend
    Monthly.   Circulation 27,500
Le Club des Jardiniers
    Monthly.   Circulation 17,000

INDOOR PLANTS

A visitor to Belgium could easily feel that the national plant must be *Sansevieria trifasciata* and not the begonia. The tall upright stems of the Mother-in-law's Tongue (called Lawyer's Tongue in Belgium) are to be seen on window sills everywhere. The Belgians spend less than most Europeans on cut flowers, but foliage house plants are immensely popular. *Sansevieria* leads the field, followed by *Ficus decora*, *Monstera deliciosa*, ivies, ferns and bromeliads.

PARKS

PLACE DU PETIT SABLON (Brussels) A small but popular park in the Capital, noted for its statues and decorative railings.

BOIS DE LA CAMBRE (Brussels) About 100 years ago this 275 acre landscape park was created on the edge of the Forest of Soignes. Lakes, woods and restaurants make this a favourite place for relaxation.

PARC DE LA CITADELLE (Ghent) One of the finest public parks in the country. Both the rose garden and rockery have international reputations.

ZOOLOGICAL GARDEN (Antwerp) Plants are as interesting as the animals. Fine displays of succulents, water plants and bedding plants.

BOTANICAL GARDENS & TREE COLLECTIONS

GHENT BOTANICAL GARDEN Famous for its *Victoria regia* and blue lotus flowers. 9 acres.

LIEGE BOTANICAL GARDEN Good collection of begonias and bromeliads at the 10 acre city site. New gardens have been built outside Liège.

KALMOUTH ARBORETUM Extensive collection of trees and shrubs, perhaps the best arboretum in Belgium.

GROENENDAAL ARBORETUM Wide variety of forest trees, especially conifers. 33 acres.

TERVUREN ARBORETUM (Brussels) Nearly 250 acres containing hundreds of different trees and shrubs native to N. Europe.

THE GRAND SIGHTS

The grand gardening sights of Belgium include a Botanical Garden and several parks, but most of the showpieces are around the châteaux. Until recently only a few, such as Beloeil and Annevoie, were on view. In 1971 the 'Year of the Châteaux' was held and proved to be immensely popular, and now about 60 estates are open to the public.

BELOEIL

This is the most popular grand garden in Belgium and is visited by more than 100,000 people each year. There are 240 acres of French style garden and English parkland, with a permanent floral display in the Orangery. Look out for the rose garden with many interesting old varieties, the 15 acre Neptune Pool and the topiary arches.

ANNEVOIE

The most outstanding garden in Belgium, combining a classical *jardin français* with the statuary and water of an Italian garden and the informality of an English park. The feature which makes Annevoie unique is the natural spring water which unendingly issues from fountains and cascades, and fills the pools and lakes.

NATIONAL BOTANICAL GARDEN (Meise)

An extensive collection of plants from all over the world. In this 230 acre garden there are 13 display houses in which tropical plants are arranged geographically.

LEEUWERGEN (Oombergen)

A French style garden in the grand manner. The 5 acre canal is a fine feature, but the most famous part of the garden is the *Théâtre de Verdure* (Garden Theatre) with stage, auditorium and even the boxes composed of trimmed ash trees.

ATTRE (Ath)

An 18th century garden with two distinct parts. There is a standard French garden and also a park containing a grotto, temple and other "follies".

ROYAL BELGIAN GARDENS (Laeken)

This vast 500 acre park was created by Leopold I near the Royal Palace at Laeken, and along its miles of pathways are countless flower beds, rhododendrons and lakes. The great showpiece, the 5 acre Royal Greenhouse complex, is only open to the public for a few weeks each year. So if you are in Belgium during early May you should not miss seeing one of the finest glasshouse displays in Europe.

FREYR (Dinant)

An historic garden, reputedly designed by Le Nôtre and with some of the old orange trees still edging the lake each summer. Noted for its arbours, pavilion and avenue of lime trees.

RUBENS' HOUSE (Antwerp)

Pay close attention to the garden when you visit Rubens' House. This famous painter designed his own garden in about 1630, and the flower-filled formal layout has been carefully preserved.

PARC DE BRUXELLES

The largest park in Brussels, created in the formal French style during the 18th century. It has a large circular pool and a theatre nearby, and its long straight avenues are thronged with tourists and residents during the summer months. It has served as a battlefield and in 1830 the Belgians won their independence here.

GAASBEEK (near Brussels)

A 100 acre garden surrounds the old castle at Gaasbeek. It is French in style, and the flower-filled parterres are perhaps the best in Belgium.

BEGONIA CARPETS

During the last weekend in August the Begonia Festival is held in the streets of Lochristi. Hundreds of thousands of begonia blooms are used to produce multicoloured floral carpets and displays. In 1971 a begonia carpet was laid out in the Grand Place, Brussels. This vast mosaic, illustrated below, contained a million blooms and was the largest single carpet of begonias ever created.

BELGIE·BELGIQUE

2F

THE GARDEN SCENE IN SWITZERLAND

HOME GARDEN, ZURICH

Alpines and Architecture

Nobody claims that gardening is the most popular hobby in Switzerland. The gardener in Britain, Holland or Germany knows that he is taking part in his country's favourite pastime, but he does not have to face the problems of his counterpart in Switzerland.

Everything seems to be against the Swiss gardener. The climate is difficult – sometimes spring is very late and June is usually the wettest month. The laws are stringent – lawn mowers can only be used at certain times of the day . . . permission has to be sought from the local council before planting a tree or shrub which your neighbour might find objectionable. Finally the land itself, often sloping at an angle which makes traditionally simple garden jobs quite difficult.

So the Swiss look to the mountains for their main leisure pursuits. Here they find large drifts of mountain flowers, and these are regarded as part of *their* garden. Both State and local authorities regard the provision and preservation of green space as matters of vital importance.

Nothing, however, can stop the keen gardener. About 30 per cent of Switzerland's 2 million households have a garden, and these are increasing at the rate of about 10,000 new gardens a year. The average garden is large – 5,000 sq. ft. in urban areas and 10,000 sq. ft. in country districts. Town gardens are similar to the German pattern – lawns in 70 – 80 per cent of them, vegetables in virtually none of them, paved areas, pools and stepping stones are much more frequent than in Britain and flowers are grown everywhere.

Roses are popular and 4 million bushes are bought each year. Shrubs, conifers and bulbs are gaining in popularity; bedding plants are losing favour. Glasshouses and sheds are surprisingly rare.

The rural garden is not used as a vegetable patch as in some European countries. It is often skilfully planned with ornamental and vegetable sections. This reflects the strong sense of design which is the most important feature of the Swiss garden scene. Some of Europe's most beautiful home gardens can be found around Zurich and Geneva. If Switzerland has not produced many ordinary gardeners it has produced some great garden architects. The School for Garden Architecture was founded at Oeschberg-Koppigen in 1925. It is significant that Switzerland's first (and last!) national horticultural show was the First Swiss Exhibition of Garden Architecture held in Zurich in 1959. Today Swiss landscape architects work throughout Europe.

The main Society for gardeners is the *Verband deutschschweizerischer Gartenbauvereine* founded in 1880. There are 10,000 members and each one receives the Society magazine *Schweizer Garten*. There are only 1,000 members of the 'Swiss Friends of the Rose' Society but then Switzerland is the country of alpines and garden architecture.

ROOF GARDENS

Window boxes and balcony gardens are seen everywhere, and the geranium is the favourite flower. A spectacular extension of the balcony garden can be seen in some of the modern terraced housing estates where the roof of one apartment forms the large balcony garden of the one above. The most spectacular roof garden in Switzerland is at the *Grosse Schanze* in Berne. Here a garden complete with pine, lawn and a pond has been created on top of the railway station, with the peaks of the Alps in the background.

INDOOR PLANTS

The degree of interest in cut flowers depends on the locality. In the German-speaking area there is the custom of taking flowers when visiting, so the sales of roses, carnations, tulips and even orchids are very high. In the French and Italian-speaking areas the interest is much less. The Migros chain of supermarkets is the outstanding flower-selling organisation in Europe. Nearly 400 stores sell pre-packed cut flowers and pot plants; sales have reached £1 million which is equal to Britain's sales of roses.

Interest in house plants is steadily increasing and both cacti and *Clivia* are as popular as ivies and rubber plants. *Monstera* is popular in Switzerland and large foliage plants are widely used in office landscaping.

ALLOTMENTS

There are about 25,000 allotments in Switzerland and the number has continued to fall since the peak in 1944. The concept of 'leisure gardens' has not taken firm root here, and the *familiengarten* is generally used for growing vegetables and soft fruit. The average plot is 250 sq. yds. and costs about £1 per year. The major appeal is to people in the lower income bracket and as the standard of living rises the need for allotments declines.

An active Association, the *Schweizer Familiengärtner-Verbandes* looks after their interests, and the monthly magazine *Garten freund* is circulated to the members. Its circulation of over 20,000 makes it one of Switzerland's most widely read gardening magazines, only beaten by *Mehr Freude am Garten* published by the Seed Dealers Association (circulation 40,000).

THE FLOWER SHOWS

National horticultural shows are surprisingly absent in a country with such a strong sense of display and design. There are no amateur competitions and no prizes. Some specialist exhibitions are held – these include an Orchid Show, Camellia Show, Dahlia Show and Rose Show. Most shows are arranged by growers.

Grand gardens are not an important feature of the garden scene in Switzerland. Some castles have opened their gates to the public; you can visit the gardens at Jegenstorf and Utzenstorf (near Berne), Oberhofen, Schadau and Gerzensee (Thun), Andreas (Cham), Brestenberg (Zurich) and Heidegg (Gelfingen).

These castle gardens are often quite small, and the public parks are generally much simpler than the German showpieces. There are one or two exceptions, such as the Parc de la Grange in Geneva with its superb rose garden, but it is the Botanic Gardens of Switzerland which are outstanding.

BOTANICAL GARDENS

BASLE BOTANICAL GARDEN Orchid, succulent and alpine collections in a 3 acre garden. New Botanical Garden at Münchenstein will be opened in 1974.

BERNE BOTANICAL GARDEN Alpines are the speciality here, and the collection is divided geographically. 5½ acres.

FRIBOURG BOTANICAL GARDEN Interesting displays of medicinal plants and Swiss alpines. 4 acres.

BRISSAGO BOTANICAL GARDEN A boat from Locarno or Stresa takes you to this sub-tropical garden on the Island of Brissago in Lake Maggiore. The exotic plants in this 8 acre collection are from the Mediterranean, S. America, S. Africa and the Far East.

GENEVA BOTANICAL GARDEN One of the most interesting of all the Swiss Botanical Gardens. The alpines are grouped in geographical sections. There is an orchid collection, unusual water plants and an arboretum. 25 acres.

LAUSANNE BOTANICAL GARDEN Medicinal and alpine plants. 5 acres; illustrated above.

PORRENTRUY BOTANICAL GARDEN The plants from the Jura mountains are displayed here. 2½ acres.

ST. GALLEN BOTANICAL GARDEN Many small clearly-labelled collections. Good orchid and succulent houses. 5 acres. Guided tours take place on the first Sunday of each month.

ZURICH BOTANICAL GARDEN The first Botanical Garden created outside Italy was at Zurich (1560). The present garden is only 4 acres, but houses about 18,000 different varieties. Good display of Mediterranean flora.

STÄDTISCHE SUKKULENTENSAMMLUNG (Zurich) About 4,000 cacti and succulents are on display. One of Europe's leading collections.

Alpine Gardens

An alpinetum is a carefully selected and comprehensive collection of alpine plants. It can be constructed far away from the mountains — there are fine ones at Cambridge and Edinburgh in Britain and at Ghent in Belgium. But to see these plants as nature intended then you must go to the *Alpengärten* or Alpine Gardens of Switzerland between May and July. Set in the mountains and beautifully landscaped, there can be no better way of seeing alpines than in one of these spectacular gardens.

SCHYNIGE PLATTE In the photograph above, the Jungfrau towers over this 2 acre Alpine Garden which is 6,000 ft. above sea level. A mountain railway takes you from Wilderswil (near Interlaken) to this garden where about 600 different Swiss alpine varieties have been planted.

RAMBERTIA (Rochers-de-Naye) This privately-owned Alpine Garden is open to the public between June and October, and is a short walk from the mountain railway terminus from Montreux. It is the highest Alpine Garden in Europe (altitude 6,700 ft.) and in its 8 acres are more than a thousand alpine varieties from Switzerland and other countries.

LA THOMASIA (Pont-de-Nant sur Bex) An extensive garden covering more than 11 acres. It is about 4,000 ft. above sea level and contains more than 2,000 different varieties.

LAC CHAMPEX This Alpine Garden is 4,500 ft. high on the slopes of Mont Blanc. It covers only 2½ acres, but is considered by some authorities to be the most comprehensive collection of alpines in Europe. More than 4,000 different varieties have been gathered from all over the world.

LA LINNAEA (Bourg St. Pierre) An Alpine Garden, 5,700 ft. above sea level, for the use of students of the University of Geneva but also open to the public.

ALP GRÜN One of the highest Alpine Gardens in Switzerland. 6.270 ft. above sea level.

A PICTURE GUIDE TO

Bulbs

Even a modest beginner feels that he knows all about the popular spring-flowering bulbs. There are no mysteries here; from childhood he will have learnt that daffodils, tulips, hyacinths and crocuses are planted in the autumn. Each one is put in a hole with a depth two or three times the width of the bulb, and there is then nothing to do until the floral display is over. When the foliage on the tulips has died down they are lifted and the bulbs stored for autumn planting. The daffodils are left in the soil unless the ground is needed for summer bedding, and the foliage is knotted to hasten ripening of the bulbs.

This child's guide to bulb growing is quite satisfactory. There are a few points of detail which are not covered – botanical or species tulips should be left in the ground whereas delicate narcissus varieties such as *N. tazetta* should be lifted each year. Perhaps the only important error is the knotting of the foliage of narcissi. It takes about one month's active growth after flowering for the bulbs to swell satisfactorily, so leave the foliage alone.

The reason why successful bulb planting is so easy is that very little can go wrong provided that the soil is not waterlogged. The purchased bulb, if healthy and sufficiently large, will have its flowering quality already laid down, and the skill of the gardener can have little effect. With proper care and cultivation these bulbs will improve and multiply over the years; with poor handling the stock will quite rapidly deteriorate.

So there are new lessons to learn. Make sure that the soil is well-drained and fairly rich in humus. Bone meal is the best fertiliser, and fresh manure should never be used. If the ground tends to be damp, daffodils will do better than tulips.

Always try to use top quality bulbs; there is no point in planting tiny daughter bulbs unless you are prepared to leave them to grow on for a few years. Hyacinths are an exception; second-size bulbs are generally more satisfactory for outside use than the larger and more expensive bulbs sold for growing in bowls.

When flowering is over, the leaves must be allowed to produce the food for next year's bulbs.

If the bed has to be cleared then remove the plants and transplant them elsewhere in a shallow trench.

Blindness in daffodils generally means that the bulbs are too close to the surface or have become overcrowded. In either case the answer is to lift the bulbs at the end of June, divide the clumps and replant immediately at the recommended depth.

So far only the popular spring-flowering bulbs have been mentioned, and for many gardeners this group is their only involvement with the vast range of bulbous plants. This is a pity, for there are so many other varieties which could add individuality or novelty to any garden. The modern hybrids of narcissus, tulip and crocus have 'wild' ancestors known as species, and are catalogued by their latin names – *Narcissus bulbocodium*, *Tulipa fosteriana*, *Crocus aureus*, etc. These species bulbs deserve to be more widely grown, especially in the rockery. There are also many other bulbs, and even the brief list on the next page indicates that you can have flowers from bulbs all the year round. Your best guide is a good catalogue; in such a booklet and in this chapter the term *bulb* has no botanical meaning – it includes true bulbs, corms and a few tubers and rhizomes.

The story of bulbs in Europe is a fascinating one, and it began with the lily. From ancient times it has rivalled the rose as the flower of royalty, and was the symbol of Imperial France although the *fleur-de-lis* was really an iris.

The Tulip Story has been told many times, and began with Ambassador Busbecq carrying a small package of bulbs from Istanbul to Vienna in the mid-sixteenth century. He grew some in his garden, he gave some to the great botanists of the day, and some were stolen. By 1630 Holland was in the grip of tulipomania, and fortunes were made and lost. The madness soon passed, but the fascination for tulip novelties remains. In 1960 a grower paid more than £200 per lb. for a green-flowering variety, and in 1973 the stocks of tulips treated to bloom three weeks after planting were very rapidly sold out.

LILIES

Lilium martagon
(Martagon Lily)

Lilium candidum
(Madonna Lily)

Lilium canadense
(Canadian Lily)

Lilium regale
(Regal Lily)

Lilium hansonii

Lilium tigrinum
(Tiger Lily)

Lilium auratum
(Golden-rayed Lily)

Lilium Hybrid
'Enchantment'

TULIPS

Early Single Tulips
6–15 inches • mid April

Early Double Tulips
12–15 inches • mid April

Darwin Tulips
2–2½ ft. • May

Lily-flowered Tulips
18–24 inches • late April

Cottage Tulips
up to 2½ ft. • late April

Rembrandt Tulips
2–2½ ft. • May

Parrot Tulips
18–24 inches • late April

Triumph Tulips
up to 20 inches • late April

NARCISSI

Trumpet Narcissi ('Daffodils')
Cup at least as long as petals.

Large-cupped Narcissi
Cup more than ⅓rd length of petals.

Small-cupped Narcissi
Cup less than ⅓rd length of petals.

Double Narcissi
More than one ring of outer petals.

Triandrus Narcissi
Several blooms on stem; drooping
flowers and slightly reflexed petals.

Cyclamineus Narcissi
Drooping flowers, long trumpets and
reflexed petals.

Jonquilla Narcissi ('Jonquils')
Small central cup; scented.

Tazetta Narcissi
Several blooms on stem; scented.
Some vars. not hardy.

Poeticus Narcissi
White petals; frilled red-edged cup.

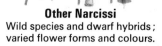

Other Narcissi
Wild species and dwarf hybrids;
varied flower forms and colours.

THE POPULAR GARDEN BULBS

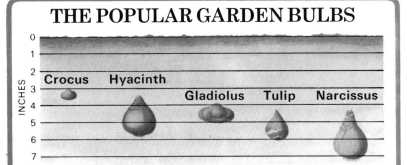

CROCUS HYBRIDS

Plant in September,
  4 inches apart.
Height 3-6 inches,
in bloom March-April.
Do not dig up corms each
year; lift and divide only
when overcrowded.

GLADIOLUS

Plant in March-mid May,
  6 inches apart.
Height 2-5 feet,
in bloom July-September.
Do not remove too much
leaf when cutting blooms.
Dig up corms each year
when leaves die down.

NARCISSUS

Plant in August-September,
  6-9 inches apart.
Height 4-24 inches,
in bloom late March-May.
Do not dig up bulbs
each year; lift and divide
clumps after several years.

HYACINTH

Plant in September-
  November, 8 inches apart.
Height 8-16 inches,
in bloom April-May.
Cut off dead flower heads.
Dig up bulbs each year
when leaves turn yellow.

TULIP

Plant in October-November
  4-8 inches apart.
Height 6-30 inches,
in bloom late March-May.
Cut off dead flower heads.
Dig up bulbs each year
when leaves turn yellow.
Replant in autumn.

CAUTION

When planting a large bulb
make sure that you avoid an
air pocket, as shown above.
Always set the
bulb on a flat,
soft base.

OTHER BULBS

Name	When to plant	Planting depth	Height	Flowering season
ACIDANTHERA	May	3 in.	2-3 ft.	July-Oct.
ALLIUM	October	4 in.	1-4 ft.	May-July
ANEMONE	Oct.-Feb.	3 in.	3-12 in.	April-July
CAMASSIA	September	4 in.	1½-4 ft.	July-Aug.
CHIONODOXA	October	2 in.	3-6 in.	March-April
COLCHICUM	August	3 in.	6-8 in.	Sept.-Oct.
CONVALLARIA	Nov.-March	1 in.	6 in.	April-May
CYCLAMEN	July-Sept.	2 in.	3-6 in.	April or Sept.
ERANTHIS	Aug.-Oct.	2 in.	2 in.	Jan.-Feb.
GALANTHUS	Sept.-Nov.	4 in.	4-8 in.	Jan.-Feb.
IRIS (bulbous)	October	3 in.	½-2½ ft.	Jan.-July
LEUCOJUM	Aug.-Sept.	3 in.	4-18 in.	Jan.-May
MONTBRETIA	March-April	3 in.	1-2 ft.	July-Sept.
MUSCARI	September	3 in.	4-8 in.	April
RANUNCULUS	Nov.-March	2 in.	8-12 in.	May-June
SCILLA	October	4 in.	4-16 in.	Feb.-May

LILIES

Lilies do not have the universal popularity of the spring-flowering bulbs; they are much more expensive to buy and they are generally considered to be rather difficult.

There is some truth in this belief because you cannot guess what to do with a lily bulb; you must read and follow the instructions. First of all, treat the bulb with respect as it has no outer protective cover. So plant it immediately and don't store it; if planting has to be delayed then keep the bulb covered with peat.

Pick the right spot, in sun or partial shade, and make sure that the drainage is good. If it isn't, then don't bother to attempt to grow lilies. Plant the bulb on a layer of coarse sand and the planting depth will depend on the group to which it belongs. Stem-rooting varieties need 6 inches of soil on top of the bulb; base-rooting types need only 3 inches of soil over them and both *L. candidum* and *L. giganteum* need to be set with the bulb tips just below the surface. Be guided by the catalogue or supplier.

The plants will need little attention during the growing season. Keep slugs and greenfly under control and use a mulch instead of a hoe around the plants. Stake if necessary and pick off the dead blooms after flowering. Cut down the dead stems in autumn.

Don't be disappointed if only a few flowers appear in the first season. Leave the bulbs undisturbed and there will be a fine display in the years to come. The bulb clusters can be divided every 5 years. Plant some of the new bulbs in the garden; grow the remainder in plant tubs. In this way your initial outlay will be more than repaid.

The *EuroBulb*

❶ Come to **GT. BRITAIN**, daffodil capital of the world! Surprising but true – half the world's commercial narcissus acreage is found in England, with more of these bulbs grown in the Holland area of Lincolnshire than in the whole of the Netherlands!

Most of these bulbs are sold for home use, as the demand in Britain continues to expand. About £12 million is spent each year on tulips, hyacinths and narcissi – more than on roses or any other group of outdoor plants.

The showplace is Springfields, about one mile east of Spalding. This 20-acre display garden of the British Bulb Industry is open from early April until mid-May, and here you will find bulbs of all types, both outdoors and under glass. The climax is the Spalding Flower Parade, held on a Saturday in mid-May, when a mile of floats, decorated with more than 6 million tulip heads, follow a four-mile route past Springfields.

In parks and grand gardens throughout Britain you will find superb displays of spring-flowering bulbs. Look for species tulips and unusual bulbs in the Botanic Gardens.

Springfields, Lincs.

❷ The tulip is the national flower of **HOLLAND**. The 1972 export of bulbs was commemorated by the issue of 30 million stamps, each portraying 40 tulip blooms. A bloom for each bulb exported – 1,200 million.

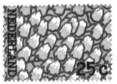

One quarter of Holland's tulip fields are devoted to just 3 varieties – Apeldoorn, Merry Widow and Prominence. If you want to see a wonderland of spring-flowering bulbs then visit the greatest display in the world at the Keukenhof (see page 112). If your interest is more academic and you wish to learn about the history of bulbs and bulb growing, go to the Hortus Bulborum at Limmen.

In spring the bulb fields are one of the great floral sights of Europe. The tulip gardens of Frans Roozen and John van Grieken at Vogelenzang are popular tourist attractions in mid-May.

❸ **W. GERMANY** grows few of the bulbs which are planted in her gardens – there are less than 1,000 acres devoted to commercial production. There are large imports from Holland each year as tulips, narcissi and hyacinths are extremely popular. The best displays are in the parks; you will see 250,000 bulbs in bloom at the Planten un Blomen in Hamburg. The largest German display is at Mainau, which boasts a spring display of more than 1 million bulbs.

❹ In **FRANCE** more than 70 per cent of the bulb acreage is devoted to gladioli, and these stately flowers are an important part of the French gardening scene. Spring-flowering bulbs are not as popular as in Britain, Holland or Germany, but there are fine displays in the parks of Paris each year, and especially in the Parc Floral at Orléans – La Source.

151

THE GARDEN SCENE
IN THE REST OF EUROPE

MOUNT USHER GARDENS,
REPUBLIC OF IRELAND

Palms under Grey Skies

In horticultural terms the gulf between Britain and Ireland is much wider than the Irish Sea. In both countries about 4 in every 5 households have a garden, but the average size is quite different. The 10,000 sq. ft. Irish plot is several times larger than the typical garden in land-hungry Britain. Another difference is that gardening is usually regarded as woman's work in Ireland; nowhere else in Europe are gardeners so predominently female.

But the major difference is a climatic one. Both eastern and western coasts of Ireland are blessed with mild winters, and in these 'oceanic' regions most of the major grand gardens are congregated. It is the West Coast Phenomenon which makes part of this country a garden-lover's paradise. The winters in the west and south are practically frost-free, so that the growing season lasts 12 months in the year as in Spain and Italy. Unlike most Mediterranean regions there is no dry season, so a unique collection of lush semi-tropical plants can be grown. Clare, Kerry and Cork can seem like Capri or Crete — tree ferns, strawberry trees, acacias, palms and tender azaleas. Here greenhouse fuchsias grow as hedges, dahlias stay in the ground and geraniums grow as perennials.

Some of Ireland's grand gardens are shown on this page and overleaf. Other famous ones are Annesgrove (Co. Cork), Mt. Congreve (Co. Waterford) and Dereen (Co. Kerry). A fine tradition in grand gardening, but the ornamental side of home gardening was neglected until recently. The cottage garden was used to grow potatoes; the suburban garden grew vegetables, fruit, grass and some flowers. Now the trend is towards smaller gardens, and the layout is quite similar to the standard English model. Vegetables have rapidly shrunk in importance, and allotments have almost disappeared since the war.

The imports of garden stock, mainly from Holland, have quadrupled in the past 6 years. Home production nearly doubled in the same period. The magazine *Irish Householder & Gardener* was founded in 1972 and now has a circulation of 23,000. Obviously interest is growing but it lags behind the fanaticism found in England. The Royal Horticultural Society of Ireland has less than a thousand members; *An Faisce* (The National Trust of Ireland) has about 4,000. There is still no national flower show, although the flower and plant section of the Royal Dublin Horse Show in August is very popular. Whether the Irish will ever become as keen as the English is debatable, but if this does happen then perhaps a unique semi-tropical style will be evolved in the milder areas.

POWERSCOURT (Co. Wicklow)
The much-photographed view from the high terrace to the Sugar Loaf Mountain is one of Ireland's great showpieces. Six terraces with black and white pebble mosaics lead down to the Triton Pool with its 70 ft. fountain. The statues, flower beds, urns and wrought ironwork are superb, but it is not all formal — delightful woodland paths and a Japanese garden lead to the highest waterfall in the British Isles. There is a strange twist to the tale — the designer of this most stylish and stately of gardens worked only when drunk and had to be moved round the site on a wheelbarrow . . .

TULLY (Co. Kildare)
Devised by Lord Wavertree and landscaped by his Japanese gardener Eida in 1906–1910, this symbolic garden represents the Life of Man. From the Cave of Birth the visitor moves past the ups and downs of the Hill of Ambition, the quiet lawns of Peace and Contentment and the weeping trees around the Hall of Mourning. Beautiful plants and hidden meanings are everywhere.

BIRR CASTLE (Co. Offaly)

A plantsman's garden, which is what you would expect from its owner, Countess Rosse, who grew up at the famous English flower garden of Nymans. Birr Castle is noted for its spring colours – daffodils, tulips, magnolias etc. and also its autumn tints from the Japanese maples and drifts of colchicums. The remains of the Rosse Telescope, once the largest in the world, are still there and the giant clipped box hedges are the tallest in Europe.

HOWTH CASTLE (Co. Dublin)

Plant historians like to stare at a 400-year-old English elm in this garden, the oldest foreign tree planted in Ireland. But the two most popular features are the Beech Hedge Walk (30 ft. high, $\frac{1}{2}$ mile long) and the Rhododendron Walk (2,000 specimens, many rare and undoubtedly the finest collection in the country.) Surprisingly, both the soil as well as the shrubs were brought into the garden from outside.

GARINISH ISLAND (Co. Cork)

Garinish (or Ilnacullin) is an island garden reached by ferry-boat from Glengarriff. It was started at the beginning of this century, and the work of its designer, Harold Peto, is clearly seen in the Italian garden. There is a long lily pool, tall cypresses, Mediterranean-style buildings and a surrounding stone terrace. The walled garden at Garinish contains fine herbaceous borders, but it is the informal wooded areas which are so spectacular. Here exotic trees, shrubs and flowers provide a jungle-like lushness.

MT. USHER (Co. Wicklow)

This world-famous 20 acre garden is a paradise for the amateur plant hunter. Despite its natural appearance, it abounds with rare plants from all parts of the world and each one is clearly labelled. Take the Riviera Walk, Azalea Walk, Palm Walk, etc. Eucalyptus trees and Montezuma pines soar 100 ft. into the sky; unusual delicate ferns cling to the rocks in their shadow.

MUCKROSS GARDENS (Co. Kerry)

These gardens are part of the 11,000 acre Vincent Memorial Park at the foot of the Killarney Mountains. There is a rock garden and sunken garden, but visitors travel to Muckross for the nature trails amid sub-tropical plants. Woodland walks meander between magnolias, strawberry trees, camellias and rhododendrons.

GLASNEVIN BOTANIC GARDEN (Dublin)

This 47 acre garden is one of the most famous botanical collections in Europe, with 25,000 different plants on display. Botanists go to see the collections of tree ferns, filmy ferns, tropical palms, orchids and plants set out in their scientific order. For the gardener there are herbaceous borders, rock garden, cactus house, rose garden and a vast tree and shrub collection.

The Land of Contrasts

Portugal is a land of great contrasts. The inland areas close to the Spanish border have baking summers and freezing winters, whereas the 'Atlantic' zone has mild summers and frost-free winters. Some of the towns in this zone have a higher annual rainfall than Manchester.

These maritime parts of Portugal have the lush greenness of a gardener's paradise, and nowhere else in Europe can support such a fantastic range of exotic vegetation without winter protection or summer irrigation. But this is not for everyone, for Portugal's contrasts result in some beautiful flower-filled gardens around the fine homes of the wealthy and yet only 6 per cent of Portuguese households have a private garden. Poverty and a paucity of gardens go hand in hand.

There has been no increase in grand gardens during this century; in fact many of the royal estates have disappeared since the republican revolution of 1910. Some show gardens remain and Fronteira is the best of them. Look for the decorative coloured tiles (azulejos) covering walls and lining pools—a feature of the traditional grand garden of Portugal.

The Botanical Gardens and the large parks are the real showpieces, for here you can see the full range of plant life that can grow in this corner of Europe. Visit the Botanical Garden at Coimbra, the Forest of Bussaco and the Monserrate Subtropical Park at Sintra.

ROYAL PALACE GARDEN (Queluz)

The garden of the former Royal Palace near Lisbon (illustrated above) is open to the public and represents a fine example of the formal 18th century grand garden in its Portuguese form. As in France, Britain and Germany there are fine parterres, clipped box hedges, white statues, carved fountains and planted urns. But this is Portugal, and the long canal is lined with decorative tiles.

ESTUFA FRIA (Lisbon)

The *Estufa Fria* (Cool Oven) in Lisbon has been a popular tourist attraction since its opening in 1930. A vast jungle of tropical plants live in an open-air garden, the temperature and ventilation being controlled by a system of movable slats.

Paths wind between the palms, tree-ferns, banana trees, hibiscus and water-lily ponds. Concerts and ballets are held within the Estufa Fria during the spring and summer, and on such occasions the gardens are floodlit.

FRONTEIRA (Benfica)

In the Lisbon suburb of Benfica you can see a 17th century garden. Here, as at Villandry in France, there are intricate 'compartments' within a vast parterre. But this is no modern reconstruction; some of the clipped box hedges making up the 16 beautifully-maintained green squares are several hundred years old. The statues and topiary are noteworthy, but the most famous part of the garden is the great rectangular pool with its surrounds of blue and white *azulejos* portraying knights on horseback and other figures.

Parks for the People

There is an age-old tradition of gardening on the grand scale in Austria. Five hundred years ago Vienna was described as "one vast delectable garden" and the royal Hapsburg family which ruled Austria for over 600 years was mainly responsible. One of them, Emperor Maximilian I, wrote a book on horticulture and another, Archduke Ferdinand I, created the estate at Ambas which was famous as one of Europe's finest sixteenth century gardens.

Ambas is gone, but the gardens of some of the former royal palaces remain. These are now state-owned and have been converted into public parks, where no admittance fee is charged. Parks for the people.

This tradition of converting royal estates into public parks began a surprisingly long time ago in Austria, when such a step was unheard-of in the rest of Europe. The largest park (5.3 sq. miles) is the Prater in Vienna, and this former royal hunting estate was opened to the public in 1766 by Emperor Josef II. The same king opened Augarten as a public park in 1755 and it remains a popular place for the Viennese.

There are more than 750 parks in Vienna and these are regarded as extensions to the city-dweller's home. The other important feature of the Austrian scene is the Alpine Garden, and several superb collections are maintained.

On the domestic scene about 44 per cent of households have a garden. These are usually similar to the standard German model, with the leisure side being of prime importance. Nearly all have a lawn and about one third have a paved play or dining area and small pool. The trend is towards roses and trees and away from time-consuming bedding plants and herbaceous borders. The popularity of fruit- and vegetable-growing has been declining for many years. The national interest in home gardening is not very high; there are only 5,000 members of the *Österreichische Gartenbau-Gesellschaft* (Austrian Horticultural Society) which was founded in 1837. The attractive monthly magazine *garten magazin für alle* produced by the Society has a circulation of less than 10,000. There are many flower shops in the larger towns, but there is a mere handful of garden centres in Austria.

A National Garden Show is held each spring, and a different venue is chosen each time. About 100,000 people attend but the major horticultural event is the W.I.G. (International Horticultural Exhibition of Vienna) held every 10 years.

House plants, cut flowers and flowering pot plants are extremely popular. About 7 pots per head are purchased each year and in the alpine regions geranium-filled window-boxes and balcony gardens are part of the landscape.

SCHÖNBRUNN (Vienna)

Schönbrunn Palace was the summer residence of the Hapsburgs. Its Baroque garden was created during the 18th century in the Classical French style, and it remains the grandest of all the Imperial Austrian gardens. With its enormous parterres fountains and wide pathways around the palace the *jardin français* image remains, but there have been additions in other styles. Today it is a 500-acre public park and an important botanical collection of over 1 million plants. The display greenhouses cover ½ acre and the exotic plants grown here are this Botanic Garden's most noteworthy feature.

MUNICIPAL PARKS

DONAUPARK (Vienna)
This 250-acre park was created on a former rubbish dump near the Danube for the 1964 International Horticultural Exhibition. It is now Vienna's most popular park with miniature gardens, roses, alpines, dahlias, heather and rhododendron gardens and also the Tower Greenhouse where the plants are on a moving belt. The 830 ft. high *Donauturm* has a rotating restaurant near the top.

WERTHEIMSTEINPARK (Vienna)
The most famous feature of this park is the Viennese Garden for the Blind, created in 1959 and unique in Europe. There are plants to smell and touch, Braille labels to inform and hand-rails to guide the blind visitors around the garden. There is a singing cymbal fountain and a large rock garden.

VOLKSGARTEN (Vienna)
Johann Strauss played in the park restaurant and generations of Viennese have admired the famous fountain and rose garden.

TÜRKENSCHANZ (Vienna)
An old *Englischer Garten,* with beautiful trees and a lake. It also contains a small zoo.

RATHAUSPARK (Vienna)
A popular park in the centre of the city, filled with interesting trees, statues and monuments.

STADTPARK (Vienna)
A pleasant park stretching for 17 acres on both sides of the River Wien. Concerts are held here, and there are statues commemorating Austria's famous composers.

LUSTSCHLOSS HELLBRUNN (Salzburg)

This bishop's pleasure palace is famous for its *wasserspiele* or water jokes. Surprise fountains are one of the oldest of all garden features, started in the early Italian Renaissance gardens and still found today in many parts of Europe, including Chatsworth in Britain. At Hellbrunn there is a wide variety of waterworks – keeping balls in the air, making figures move and drenching unsuspecting seated guests, as illustrated above. Rather heavy-handed humour from a bygone age.

BELVEDERE (Vienna)

The Belvedere is a 50-acre estate surrounding the summer palace built by Prince Eugene of Savoy. The garden was created at the beginning of the 18th century and its design was basically French, but there was strong Italian influence – cascades, terracing and simple parterres. There are two levels; the lower section is a terraced Baroque garden and above it is the *Alpengarten im Belvedere,* the oldest and one of the finest collections of alpines in Europe.

BOTANICAL & ALPINE GARDENS

FROHNLEITEN ALPINE GARDEN One of the largest alpine collections in Europe (6,000 varieties).

GRAZ BOTANICAL GARDEN Contains a wide selection of plants – alpines, flowers, tropical trees. 5 acres.

INNSBRUCK ALPINE GARDEN On Patscherkofel Mountain, reached by cable car.

INNSBRUCK BOTANICAL GARDEN Fine collection of alpines and Mediterranean plants. 5 acres.

LINZ BOTANICAL GARDEN One of Austria's most attractive Botanical Gardens, with a large rock garden and many floral displays. Collections of bog plants, orchids, cacti and wild flowers.

RANNACH ALPINE GARDEN (St. Veit) Comprehensive display of plants from the eastern and western Alps. 10 acres.

VIENNA BOTANICAL GARDEN This 20-acre Botanical Garden controlled by the University of Vienna is noted for its orchids and succulents.

The Rock Garden

GIBRALTAR

Aristolochia (Pipe vine)

Gibraltar has several beautiful gardens, filled with sub-tropical plants to fascinate the visitor from colder climes. In the Alameda Gardens there are specimens of Europe's only native palm tree – the fan palm. Between the winding pathways are orange and lemon trees, hibiscus, *Bougainvillea,* dragon trees, *Strelitzia* and date palms.

This is not really a country with gardens – it *is* a garden. It is not even a particularly vast one; it could be fitted quite easily into half of Windsor Great Park. But it is extremely rich in its variety of wild flowering plants and ferns; nearly 600 species have been recorded and if you walked over every inch of the British Isles you would only find three times that number.

It is a rock garden in which limestone predominates. This is no place for the acid-loving plants such as rhododendrons and heathers, but plants from many lands which thrive in neutral or alkaline soil grow on the Rock. At Christmas there are enormous drifts of paper-white narcissi in bloom and many strange flowers are commonly found, such as the pipe vine, friar's cowl and squirting cucumber. Undoubtedly the best floral walk is the Mediterranean Steps, which takes you past olives, orchids and flowers extraordinary.

The Mixture as Before

The garden scene behind the Iron Curtain remains a mystery to the gardener in western Europe. No books on the subject are available, and extensive visiting is difficult. Snippets such as the fact that many Russians had never seen a tulip until after World War II seem to suggest that gardening must have a completely different face in eastern Europe, but this is not so. The present picture behind the Iron Curtain is made up of several dominant features which are associated with other European countries. It is the mixture as before.

First of all, there are sumptuous grand gardens of the Baroque period, similar to those found in France and W. Germany. It is perhaps strange that these ornate reminders of a bygone age of privilege should be preserved; the gilded statues and elaborate fountains of *Petrodvorets* (Peterhof) in Leningrad make many of Europe's well-known facades seem quite homely.

As in Austria, Spain and Italy it is the public park which is the "garden" for most of the urban population. Both quality and numbers are high—in Sofia there are 900 parks and public gardens for a population of less than one million. Botanical Gardens are also extremely important as they are generally open to the public. The size of these experimental and display grounds in European Russia is sometimes immense; the three sections of the State Nikita Botanical Garden at Yalta cover more than 2,300 acres.

These public gardens are essential in countries where the urban population mainly resides in large blocks of flats, but it seems that they are not enough—there is a need to have flowers close at hand. The Russians claim that their love of flowers matches that of the British, and a considerable amount of evidence has been amassed over the years to support this claim. During the Russian Revolution every shop in St. Petersburg closed—except the flower shops. A familiar sight each spring in Moscow is the long queues of people outside the flower kiosks waiting to buy sprays of mimosa.

The Russians therefore are extremely fond of cut flowers and pot plants in home, office and factory. Another phenomenon, which is shared with the Scandinavians, is the desire of working class as well as other families to have a second home away from the noise and bustle of town. These *dachas* (weekend cottages) are extremely popular and are found in the woods and on the river banks on the outskirts of the cities. The garden of the *dacha* is used for flowers, fruit and perhaps a few vegetables.

GRAND GARDENS

In many parts of Europe the rulers and the aristocracy of the 18th century insisted on a garden in Grand French style around their palaces and castles. Examples are still to be found in eastern Europe; each *schlosspark* in East Germany is a reminder of the days when there was no boundary between the two halves of the country. At Potsdam Frederick the Great personally supervised the creation of the great gardens at *Sans Souci* in 1745. Dresden has its *Grosser Garten* and *Moritzburg*, but undoubtedly the best known of all of the great gardens of eastern Europe is the *Petrodvorets* in Leningrad.

Peter the Great brought the distinguished French architect Le Blond to Russia in order to build a Versailles for him near to the new capital of St. Petersburg. All the features of the *jardin français* are there – the long canal, pavilions, parterres, statuary and fountains. Many of the 40,000 planted trees are still flourishing. During the war the palace and gardens were badly damaged but have now been completely restored, and once again the gold-plated statues, the Samson Fountain and the green-and-gold bas reliefs make this a unique European garden.

After *Petrodvorets* the principles laid down by Le Blond were applied in several other grand gardens in Eastern Europe, but some were transformed when Catherine the Great decided that the style of the day should be the informal English landscape, and some of these parks are to be seen today.

PUBLIC PARKS

PARK OF LIBERTY (Sofia, Bulgaria) A 900-acre public park begun in 1882, considerably modified over the years. It now has a large water-lily pond, sports area, woodland, and extensive flower beds.

The public parks of the Communist countries are horticulturally indistinguishable from those in other countries — plantings are governed by climate rather than politics. In the northern regions hardy forest trees and bedding plants predominate, in the Crimea, Bulgaria, Rumania and other southern areas there are fan palms, cycads and semi-tropical shrubs. Everywhere roses are firm favourites. As in many Continental countries both playgrounds for children and sports facilities for adults are of prime importance. The major distinguishing feature of these East European parks is the predominance of large heroic monuments and busts of revolutionary leaders.

THE DACHAS

An estate of *dachas* built in the village of Dubki for workers at the Moscow Electric Lamp factory. Here the families spend their weekends and summer holidays away from the heat and noise of Moscow.

In Russia and several of the Communist countries industrialisation is a relatively new phenomenon. Father or grandfather was a farm labourer, and the *dacha* allows the flat-dwelling factory worker to remember his heritage.

The *dacha* is half way between the chalet garden found in Denmark, Holland or W. Germany and the summer home of the Scandinavian. It has to be more than just an overnight chalet, for it is designed to accommodate the whole family for weekends or the summer vacation. The exodus of hundreds of thousands of Muscovites every weekend to their gardens in the country is a feature of life in Moscow from May until October.

BOTANICAL GARDENS

BRATISLAVA BOTANIC GARDEN (Czechoslovakia) Most extensive collection in Czechoslovakia, noted for roses, orchids and cacti.

PRUHONICE BOTANICAL GARDEN (Czechoslovakia) Largest Botanical Garden in Czechoslovakia — 650 acres. Comprehensive collections of flowering shrubs and alpines.

SLEPCANY ARBORETUM (Czechoslovakia) Main Czech collection of evergreen trees and shrubs. 135 acres.

HALLE-SALLE BOTANICAL GARDEN (East Germany) Large display of cacti, orchids and Mediterranean plants. 12 acres.

ROSTOCK BOTANICAL GARDEN (East Germany) Specialises in Arctic and other alpine plants. 25 acres.

SANGERHAUSEN ROSARIUM (East Germany) The most comprehensive collection of roses in Europe. 30 acres.

BUDAPEST BOTANICAL GARDEN (Hungary) 10 display houses open to the public. Succulent and bulbous plant collections on view. 8 acres.

VACRATOT BOTANICAL RESEARCH INSTITUTE (Hungary) Extensive display of horticultural plants and trees. 75 acres.

KORNIK ARBORETUM (Poland) The main collection of garden shrubs and trees in Poland. 125 acres.

WARSAW BOTANICAL GARDEN (Poland) Contains many collections — orchids, palms, dahlias and wildflowers of Poland. 13 acres.

IASI BOTANICAL GARDEN (Rumania) A large garden — 156 acres with the most comprehensive display of garden plants in Rumania.

KIEV BOTANICAL GARDEN (U.S.S.R.) One of Russia's most important Botanical Gardens for the home gardener, as there are extensive displays of ornamental plants and fruit. 400 acres.

LENINGRAD BOTANICAL GARDEN (U.S.S.R.) 27 glasshouses filled with sub-tropical and tropical plants. 5 acres.

MOSCOW BOTANICAL GARDEN (U.S.S.R.) The main Moscow Botanical Garden covers 1,000 acres and provides a vast display of the whole of the plant kingdom. There are 4 other Botanical Gardens in the Russian capital.

SOCHY ARBORETUM (U.S.S.R.) A famous collection of subtropical shrubs and trees. 150 acres.

Acknowledgments

In order to break new ground in this field of European gardens and gardening we have had to draw on the help and advice of hundreds of people and organisations. To all of them we owe a profound debt of gratitude.

Our special thanks go to Mrs. Margaret Izzard-Brown for her secretarial skills and to John Woodbridge for his artistry and design work; to Louis Penez and John Adkins for their painstaking research in many countries and to Michael Corner and Norman Barber for their artwork. John Pawsey provided helpful suggestions and Miss Pauline Day provided helpful reminders about deadlines. Mr. C. S. Stappard (General Export Services Branch, Dept. of Trade and Industry) organised many useful enquiries throughout Europe. Mr. P. F. Stageman (Royal Horticultural Society) provided library services *par excellence*.

We gratefully acknowledge the specific help we received from the following people and organisations – all are British unless otherwise noted:
A.I.P.H. (Holland), *Amateur Gardening,* Mrs O. Bagot, R. A. Bee, J. Bernhard, B.I.E. (France), Bord Fáilte (Republic of Ireland), Prof. R. Bossard (France), British Tourist Authority, D. Brown, Dr. O. Bünemann (W. Germany), British Pelargonium & Geranium Society, T. Burr, M. Cammaerts (Belgium), Cactus and Succulent Society of Gt. Britain, Cement & Concrete Association, M. Chakarova (Bulgaria), G. M. Chavels (Belgium), Anne Childs, C.N.I.H. (France), Dr. S. Coggiatti (Italy), S. Cohen, M. Constantinidi, D. E. Coult, H. M. McKinley, Pamela Currie (France), P. Damp, Det Jydske Haveselskab (Denmark), Det KGL Danske Haveselskab (Denmark), D.G.G. (W. Germany), F. Doerflinger (Holland), Francisco Domingo (Spain), A. Dupont (France), B. P. Emmett (for information on BBC audience figures), English Tourist Authority, J. R. B. Evison, J. M. Fisher, Flowers & Plants Council, Sylvia Forde, Nicolette Franck, *Garden News, Gardeners Chronicle,* Geological Museum, J. Goffin (Belgium), Mrs. D. B. Gomez, Elizabeth Göring (W. Germany), Föreningen Svenska Trädgårds och Landskaparkitektur (Sweden), S. G. Gosling, Mrs. M. D. Graves, J. Greenwood, *Grün* (Germany), J. P. Hage (Holland), J. Hamer, K. J. Halifax, H. Hammler (W. Germany), J. M. Harzic (France), W. J. Hazeldine, Dr. D. M. Henderson, Horticultural Trades Association, Vivien Igoe, C. Innes, B. Kittlass (W. Germany), R. Klemm (Austria), Prof. A. Klougart (Denmark), B. Lamb, Dr. J. G. D. Lamb (Republic of Ireland), J. C. Lamontagne (France), Landbrukets Emballageforretning Og Gartnernes Felleskjøp (Norway), J. Leyder (Luxembourg), London Tourist Board, N. Luitse (Holland), P. F. McCormack, F. J. Martin, H. Mathys (Switzerland), *Mein Schöner Garten,* W. A. Milligan, Mrs. J. B. Mullard, Miss E. Napier, National Association of Flower Arrangement Societies of Gt. Britain, National Allotments & Gardens Society, National Cactus & Succulent Society, National Chrysanthemum Society, National Dahlia Society, National Trust, Gunnel Nyblom-Holmberg (Sweden), O.G.G. (Austria), S. A. J. Oldham, Østifternes Haveselskab (Denmark), D. Paul, Dr. Piras (Italy), *Popular Gardening, Practical Gardening,* P. Pulby (France), R. H. I. Read, Royal Horticultural Society, Royal National Rose Society, L. Rich, Riksförbundet Svensk Trädgård (Sweden), Dr. D. W. Robinson (Republic of Ireland), T. Rochford, S. Russell, Saintpaulia & Houseplant Society, J. Sander Nielson (Denmark), J. Schmid, L. de Schryver (Belgium), P. Seabrook, T. F. Simpson, M. O. Slocock, S.N.H.F. (France), Miss N. Tanburn, L. Trivier (Belgium), L. Turner, D. Tveito (Norway), M. Van Genabet (Belgium), Mrs. Van Rose, B. Van Zuylen (Holland), C. Verboom (Holland), F. Ward, G. Windsor, J. Wood, Worshipful Company of Gardeners.

The photographs in this book were reproduced by courtesy of the Austrian National Tourist Office, A–Z Botanical Collection Ltd., Bord Fáilte (Republic of Ireland), British Tourist Authority, Cement & Concrete Association, S. Coggiatti (Italy), R. J. Corbin, D. E. Coult, Department of the Environment, Sr. Francisco Domingo (Spain), J. R. B. Evison, Fely Haine (Belgium), Filmbureau Niestadt (Holland), Foto-Archiv Fritz Lachmund (W. Germany), Foto Fürstenberg (W. Germany), French Government Tourist Office, *Garden News, Grün* (W. Germany), Italian State Tourist Office, Professor A. Klougart (Denmark), H. Mathys (Switzerland), *Mein Schöner Garten* (W. Germany), National Travel Association of Denmark, National Trust, Netherlands National Tourist Office, Paisajes Españoles (Spain), Portuguese National Tourist Office, Royal Horticultural Society, Royal National Rose Society, H. C. W. Shaw – Floracolour, Wolfram Stehling (Germany), Springfields, *Soviet Weekly,* Swedish Tourist Traffic Association, Syon Park, Tourism Publicity Centre (Bulgaria).